Pr se for *The Intelligence of Dogs*

"Fascinating . . . What makes *The Intelligence of Dogs* such a great book, however, isn't just the abstract discussions of canine intelligence. Throughout, Coren relates his findings to the concrete, discussing the strengths and weaknesses of various breeds and including specific advice on evaluating different breeds for various purposes. It's the kind of book would-be dog owners should be required to read before even contemplating buying a dog."

—*The Washington Post Book World*

"Excellent book . . . Many of us want to think our dog's persona is characterized by an austere veneer, a streak of intelligence, and a fearless-go-for-broke posture. No matter what your breed, *The Intelligence of Dogs* . . . will tweak your fierce, partisan spirit . . . Coren doesn't stop at intelligence and obedience rankings, he also explores breeds best suited as watchdogs and guard dogs . . . [and] does a masterful job of exploring his subject's origins, various forms of intelligence gleaned from genetics and owner/trainer conditioning, and painting an inner portrait of the species."

—*The Seattle Times*

"This book offers more than its well-publicized ranking of pure-bred dogs by obedience and working intelligence. The author, a psychologist, has cleverly combined scholarship, opinion and anecdotes to 'promote understanding of the behavior and intelligence of domestic dogs' . . . Read this book with your best friend."

—*The Dallas Morning News*

"Everyone thinks that their own dog is brilliant. Coren has written an intriguing study that will help dog owners to gauge realistically their own dog's intelligence. After discussing the evolution of the dog from its wolf ancestry, Coren looks at the canine and what it has meant in history, its influence on religion, and even its image as harbinger of death. But the meat of the book lies in the author's evaluation of intelligence . . . An interesting, at times stimulating, manual for the intelligent dog owner."

—*Kirkus Reviews*

"This highly informative book is packed with new data as well as confirming present knowledge of canine sensibilities. It contributes to greater understanding of how dogs think and is also a useful reference work in selecting and training dogs."

—*The Ottawa Citizen*

"Let's assume you like dogs. Let's further assume that a friend has taken you to a bookstore, and offered to buy you any new dog book that you care to get. I'd say, go for Stanley Coren's *The Intelligence of Dogs.*"

—*Chicago Sun-Times*

"Coren . . . firmly lays out the three aspects of a dog's intelligence that matter to us: instinctive intelligence, the innate skills for retrieving, fighting, guarding, pointing, hunting, herding and hauling that vary wildly from breed to breed; adaptive intelligence, a dog's ability to cope with its environment; and working intelligence, or trainability."

—*The New York Times Book Review*

£8.99

Moreton Morrell Site

**POCKET
BOOKS**

ALSO BY STANLEY COREN IN POCKET BOOKS

How to Speak Dog

How Dogs Think

The Intelligence of Dogs

A Guide to the Thoughts, Emotions, and Inner Lives of Our Canine Companions

STANLEY COREN

POCKET
BOOKS

LONDON • SYDNEY • NEW YORK • TORONTO

This edition first published by Pocket Books, 2006
An imprint of Simon & Schuster UK Ltd
A CBS COMPANY

1 3 5 7 9 10 8 6 4 2

Simon & Schuster UK Ltd
Africa House
64–78 Kingsway
London WC2B 6AH

www.simonsays.co.uk

Simon & Schuster Australia
Sydney

A CIP catalogue record for this book is available from the British Library

ISBN 1-4165-0287-4
EAN 9781416502876

Printed and bound in Great Britain by
Cox & Wyman Ltd, Reading, Berks

This book is dedicated to the instructors of the Vancouver Dog Obedience Club. It is especially dedicated to Barbara Baker, Barbara Merkley, Emma Jilg, and Shirley Welch, who were my first instructors. It is also dedicated to their wonderful working dogs, April, Mori, Meg, Wylie, and Noel, who were the role models I wanted my puppies to emulate as they grew up. Since the first writing of this book some new instructors—Ward Falkner, Christie Ulmer, and Doug Field—joined us, along with their wonderful dogs, Slater, Trooper, and Elvis, among others. Each has brought me additional insights and made my life brighter. This revised edition is a tribute to them as well.

Contents

Preface to the Revised Edition

When the first edition of this book came out in 1994, I was trying to address a problem that most of the books that were being published about dogs at the time did not. There were only veterinary guides, obedience-training books, and breed books that were not concerned about how dogs think. These books had other purposes and thus did not try to describe dogs' intelligence or mental capacity. It was my hope that *The Intelligence of Dogs* would help to fill that gap in the literature by giving readers a picture of how a dog's mind works.

As a psychologist, dog trainer, and avowed dog lover, I set out to describe the mental abilities that are present in every dog. I also went one step further—namely, to explore how various breeds differ in their capacities and behaviours. Before I could do this, though, a bit of groundwork was in order. I began by looking at the origins of dogs, because any animal's mental ability is shaped and limited by its biological makeup and the forces of evolution that have worked on it. Then I briefly examined how scientists have viewed dogs' minds and detailed some of the controversy about the nature of the canine mind and consciousness. Finally, I looked at the various types of dog intelligence and described how dog owners could actually measure their own dog's abilities. While I hoped to make it clear that no breed of dog is without merit or purpose, I also pointed out that not all dog breeds are created equal in terms of their cleverness and mental skills.

The enthusiastic reception of the first edition of this book indicated that many people wanted and needed this kind of information, and since then some other competent dog experts, researchers, and writers have followed in my footsteps by trying to provide information about the thought processes and abilities of dogs. Each has added to our knowledge of the canine mind in his or her own way.

Since *The Intelligence of Dogs* was first published, a lot of new research has been completed, and it has helped us to better understand the behaviour and origins of our dogs. This revised edition therefore became necessary in order to update the original material with some of these new insights. Included in this revision is new material about the wild ancestors of dogs, how dogs came to be domesticated, their communication, thinking, and problem-solving abilities, and their personalities. I have even included some new techniques for expanding your dog's mental capacity—in effect, how to make your dog smarter. Finally, the ranking of working and obedience intelligence has been expanded, and now includes 140 dog breeds.

This book would not have been possible without the assistance of many people. Most particularly, I must acknowledge the help of 208 dog obedience judges. This is more than half the total number of these specialists in all of North America. Each of the 208 took the time to fill in a very complex, involved survey. The completed surveys provided me with much of the information I give in the book. Many of these busy experts also took it upon themselves to independently provide me with extensive written insights into the minds of dogs. More than two dozen of these trained observers of dog behaviour also allowed me to interview them in depth, and most of these interviews lasted several hours. All this helped create a picture of the working intelligence of dogs. In addition to the dog obedience judges, sixty-three small animal veterinarians answered my questions about the personalities of dogs and some of the quirks of individual breeds. Next, fourteen specialists in guard and protection dogs provided data and observations about dogs that have or lack the qualities of interest to their area of expertise. Since the first edition of this book, I have also had numerous discussions and interviews with additional scientists who study animal behaviour and they have helped to bring me up to date with new information from research done in their laboratories. An added bonus is that countless dog obedience competitors and just plain family dog owners have spoken with me or written letters and e-mails to tell me about their special stories and experiences with their own pet and companion dogs.

A very personal acknowledgment goes to the Vancouver Dog Obedience Club, to both its instructors and members, who have served not only as valuable resources but also as good friends over our long period of association. Finally, I would like to thank my wife, Joan, who read and commented on this manuscript but, more important, has put up with me and a house full of dogs, with only occasional lapses into hysteria. Her love and support are a constant comfort to me.

—Stanley Coren

The Intelligence
of Dogs

Chapter One

Do Dogs Think?

> We are alone, absolutely alone on this chance planet; and
> amid all the forms of life that surround us, not one, except-
> ing the dog, has made an alliance with us.
>
> —MAURICE MAETERLINCK

It is remarkable to think that if you were living in the Stone Age, some fourteen thousand years ago, and you glanced across the flickering campfire, you might well have seen a dog that looked much like any dog that you might see in the streets of our cities or even resting at your feet today. For one hundred and forty centuries, humans and dogs have shared their food, dwellings, and lives. Throughout these years, dogs have helped humans in their hunting and herding. At various times, they have served as guides, protectors of the household, garbage collectors, power for transportation, comrades in war, and even as food. Dogs have functioned as comforting companions; they have been trained as actors or athletes to amuse us; they have even served as aids to psychotherapy.

Despite our long association with dogs, humankind has maintained many conflicting attitudes toward these ever-present animals. In some times and places, people have viewed dogs as loyal, faithful, noble, intelligent, courageous, and sociable; in other eras and locations, humans have thought dogs cowardly, unclean, disease-ridden, danger-ous, and unreliable. In some cultures and during certain historical epochs, people have considered dogs to be holy: companions of gods, guides for souls, angels, or even gods themselves. Other cultures view dogs as demons, harbingers of death, and the embodiment of the devil. In certain regions, history records that to be licked or touched by a dog was to be defiled or soiled, while at other times and places, such attentions were believed to play a part in the healing process and signaled that a person was clean, virtuous, and without fault.

Given all the eons humankind has been closely associated with dogs, one might think that we would know the answers to all the major questions about their nature and behaviour. Yet, in reality, humanity's conception of dogs remains complex and contradictory. We may live, work, or play with dogs, but there are still many questions that average dog owners cannot answer about their pets. The most important of these have to do with the nature of the dog's mind. As a psychologist, dog trainer, and dog obedience competitor, I have heard many questions and opinions on basic topics such as:

- Do dogs think, or are they simply biological machines that respond to what goes on around them?
- If dogs do think, are they conscious in the same way that humans are?
- Do dogs have memories of things past and images or anticipations of things to come?
- Do dogs understand human language?
- Do dogs have a system or means of communicating with us (or with other dogs, for that matter)?
- Do dogs have feelings such as guilt, loyalty, and protectiveness or even simple emotions such as joy and sorrow?
- Do different breeds of dogs differ in what we might call intelligence?

Often, when someone asks me questions about the intelligence, problem-solving ability, or consciousness of dogs, I find myself involuntarily recalling an incident from my distant past.

It was one of those sultry, late spring days in Philadelphia. The combination of heat and humidity made one feel very relaxed and languid. My final exams (the last I would be taking at the University of

Pennsylvania) were still three or four weeks away. Overall, I was feeling confident and comfortable: I had already been admitted to Stanford University for graduate work in psychology, and all was right with the world. As I was leisurely coming down the stairs of my parents' house, my reverie was disturbed by my mother's angry voice: "Penny, what did you do?"

Penny was the family dog of my high school and college years. She was a boxer of sorts, although she was a bit too small for the breed and had a face that wasn't quite as jowly as one might expect. She also had a slight limp from a bad accident that had nearly taken her life when she was a puppy. Throughout her life, she favoured one hind leg a bit, which made her walk in a sort of rolling waddle. Penny had many charms, but she also had several behavioural quirks. One of the oddest was her fondness for bourbon, although she would settle for rye or scotch in a pinch. At parties or social gatherings in our house, guests had to be warned not to put their drinks on the floor and to keep an eye out for the dog when they left their drinks on the low coffee table. The sight of a boxer slightly drunk from stealing drinks is not soon to be forgotten.

I walked into the kitchen, where the current drama was being enacted. Penny was standing (perhaps cringing would be a more accurate description) at the back of the narrow kitchen, facing my mother, who was in full fury in the centre. My mother was one of the gentlest souls in the world 99.9 percent of the time. That missing one-tenth of a percent, however, expressed itself with an explosive temper that could be triggered by major calamities, social slights, gaffes, or transgressions by family or acquaintances. The outcome of her short-lived bursts of fury depended on chance factors. If the surrounding environment was relatively bare, she would shout a bit, but her anger would subside fairly uneventfully, and she would turn to the business of remedying the situation. However, if she happened to have something in her hand or close at hand, she would pick it up and throw it at the offender (or anyone unfortunate enough to be around at the moment). Missiles thrown by her had included dishpans full of water, melons, gobbets of ice cream, and a variety of other strange but nonlethal items. That day, she happened to have a leather key case in her hand, which she was just letting fly at Penny as I entered the room.

"Bad dog!" she shouted, and, with the unerring accuracy gained by practising on her offspring, she loosed the key case at the canine sinner. As the missile ricocheted off her rump, Penny let out a yelp. My mother stormed out of the room, presumably to sort out the results of the dog's misbehaviour, all the while muttering something about Penny's ancestry and predictions about how short her future was likely to be.

I have difficulty being harsh with dogs, and since I had no knowledge of what Penny's crime actually was, I walked over to the unhappy dog and stroked her head. She shoved her muzzle against me and looked up with her deep brown eyes.

"Let's go into my room for a while, and we'll get you out of the line of fire," I suggested to the dog, slapping my leg so she would follow me.

As we crossed the kitchen floor, I noticed that Penny made a wide detour around the key case that had been my mother's instrument of retribution. Then, as we neared the kitchen door, Penny stopped, gazed back at the offending key case, and seemed momentarily lost in thought. Then she dashed to the centre of the floor, grabbed the leather case, and shot past me and out of the room. As I watched with some puzzlement, she entered the living room and headed for the sofa. She glanced over her shoulder and then squiggled down behind the couch. Depositing the object that had been her tormenter, she carefully pushed it out of sight with her nose and, satisfied, backed out from behind the large piece of furniture. Then, with an infinitely more relaxed body carriage, she joined me at the base of the stairs to continue the journey to my room.

While this series of events may not be remarkable, it does have certain implications. If a young child had engaged in Penny's behaviour, we would say the child understood that the key case had somehow been instrumental in causing it pain. Furthermore, we might hypothesize that the child anticipated that this "weapon" might be used again and hoped that hiding it would avert that possibility. The mental processes that we would then ascribe to the child include anticipation of the future, planning, some mental imagery, some reasoning, some concept of consequence for the self, and perhaps even the ability to imagine how another individual might view or fail to see a situation.

Although I laughed to myself at what appeared to be a childish attempt at planning for the future, I also recognized that this should not be happening. As I was finishing my undergraduate studies in psychology, I knew that most of my professors would not be easily persuaded that Penny's behavior demonstrated conscious reasoning and intelligence. They would argue that dogs simply do not have such reasoning ability. They would suggest that self-awareness and anticipation of future events (which they would certainly grant to a child in the same situation) could not be involved here. They would suggest that I was *anthropomorphizing*, meaning that I was attributing to the dog the motivations and consciousness that humans have but animals do not. According to the scientific consensus of the time, animals simply lacked the intelligence to engage in such reasoning. Were they correct?

In contemporary society, there is no doubt that dogs occupy an important place and play important parts in the lives of many people. At the time of this writing there are nearly nine million dogs in the British Isles, and more than sixty-two million in North America. Surveys have shown that around one out of every two families in the United Kingdom owns a pet of some kind, and for half of these, that pet is a dog. In North America, even in the cities, 36 percent of all people share their lives with dogs. Given their widespread presence, it is really surprising that we receive no formal education about dogs.

Most school systems today, in addition to teaching reading, writing, arithmetic, geography, and history in the primary grades, also teach other life skills, such as good citizenship, good nutritional habits, personal hygiene, politeness and social graces, and so forth. But in nature or science courses, children are more likely to learn about whales, owls, or frogs rather than about dogs. This is true even though the average city-dwelling child may never see a live whale and may only encounter owls and frogs during the few visits to zoos or aquariums that they might make during their lifetimes. The presumption seems to be that everybody already knows all that there is to know about dogs from their daily association with their own pets or those of others and that, therefore, no formal teaching about the subject is needed.

Yet for most of us, our real knowledge of dogs is quite limited. When we were very young our parents taught us to stroke dogs rather than pound on their heads. As older children, we may have been given bowls and told to "feed the dog". Later on, we might have cleaned up after dogs or taken them out for walks. Then we grew up, moved away from home, and perhaps got a dog of our own. We may go to dog obedience class and learn how to teach our dogs to come, sit, lie down, and stay. Yet, through all of this, no one mentions anything about how dogs think or communicate, other than to note that a wagging tail reflects a positive emotion and a snarl reflects a negative one.

Even so, we all feel that we understand dogs and know what they are thinking. Much of this feeling comes simply from watching dogs and noting their behaviour as presented in literature and entertainment. For instance, many great humorists—among them, James Thurber, Will Rogers, and Ogden Nash—have written about dogs. In such pieces, it is extremely common for authors to take on the persona of their dog heroes and present all the action from the dog's point of view. Thus Mark Twain has a dog narrate in *Aileen Mavourneen:* "My father was a St. Bernard, my mother was a Collie, but I am a Presbyterian. This is what my mother told me; I do not know these nice distinctions myself."

Other, more serious writers, including E. B. White, Louis Untermeyer, Eugene O'Neill, John Galsworthy, and even Lord Byron, also have authored pieces concerning dogs. For many of us, our youthful reading was filled with Jack London and his wolflike sled dogs or perhaps with Albert Payson Terhune and his fabulous collies. In all these writings, the dog had feelings, reasoning ability, and intelligence. A generic passage might read:

Shep recognized that his master was in danger. The blood soaking through Dan's torn jacket where the bear had slashed him told him that. He must get help, and fast. But where?

Now he remembered—the old trapper who had the shack in the valley had been kind to him once before. Perhaps Shep could make him understand that his help was needed.

He paused to lick his master's face in reassurance that he was not abandoning him. When a weak smile returned his affection, he gave the same quick bark that he always used to tell Dan that he was ready to work. With one glance of reassurance over his shoulder the shaggy brown dog started across the snow, heading for the closest possibility of help.

Writers of such prose do not strain our credibility by claiming that dogs can talk. Still, they send readers the clear message that dogs have consciousness and can reason, analyse problems, plan, and communicate.

Even if we were not readers, we could learn about how intelligent dogs are by seeing clever dogs in action in the movies and on television. It all started with Rin Tin Tin, a truly handsome German shepherd. Rinty (as he was affectionately called by his human associates) was born in Germany in 1916. He was rescued from a German trench by Captain Lee Duncan. After the war Rinty moved to Los Angeles with his new master and there, Duncan trained Rinty for a film career. During the 1920s, Rin Tin Tin was a favourite silent film star in sagas such as *Find Your Man, Clash of the Wolves, Jaws of Steel,* and *When London Sleeps.* He even starred in some serials, such as *The Lone Defender,* where his master, a prospector, is ambushed and murdered on the way back from a secret gold mine. Over the next twelve instalments of this early sound serial, Rinty is out for revenge, chasing and then being chased by the Cactus Kid and his sleazy gang of outlaw cronies.

For several years during this era, Rin Tin Tin was actually Warner Brothers' major source of revenue. For this reason, Rinty was given top billing, above that of his human fellow stars. Scripts for the films, which typically contained a mix of drama and comedy, as well as a large dose of adventure and action, were often written by quality people, such as Darryl F. Zanuck. While the advent of talkies meant the end of many film careers, Rinty's vigorous barking worked quite well in the new medium, and he continued in starring roles until his death in 1932. Several other dogs have carried on the tradition. The first was Rin Tin Tin, Jr., but all the subsequent stars who filled Rin Tin Tin's place were simply billed under the original star's name. This included several dogs who played in a weekly television series in which viewers got to watch the dashing German shepherd and his master Rusty battle a variety of western villains. Rinty was also probably the only dog star important enough to rate a biographical film, even though it was a fictionalized satire. The film, released in 1976, was called *Won Ton Ton—The Dog Who Saved Hollywood.* This was the one time when the star did not carry Rinty's name: The title role was played by a dog named Augustus von Shumacher.

The many screenings of Rin Tin Tin's adventures effectively told the casual viewer and dog fancier that dogs are almost as intelligent as humans. Rinty solved problems, surmounted obstacles, and carried out ingenious actions. He carefully brought rope to his stranded master, disarmed dangerous outlaws, carried blankets and food to starving children, untied the captured marshal's hands, and more. We could almost see him think, and the fact that there were handlers offscreen signaling and directing the dog or that several film editors were going crazy trying to make the action appear coordinated, natural, and spontaneous never entered our minds. We knew that Rinty was smart. At some level, we believed that the director merely had to hand the dog a script, and he would do everything required with intelligence, awareness, and full consciousness. At least that was how it seemed.

And then there was Lassie. . . .

The dog that may have done the most to shape the popular conception of dogs and their intelligence was a character born in a short story written by Eric Knight in 1938. This story was later expanded into a best-selling book, and, in 1943, it was translated into a heart-warming tearjerker of a film called *Lassie Come Home*. Lassie, the world's best-known collie, was not only affectionate and courageous but clearly nearly human in her intelligence and understanding.

Actually, Lassie, as portrayed on the screen, is not a lovely female dog at all, but rather a deception perpetrated by a long line of female impersonators. For nine generations, the dogs that have played Lassie have all been male descendants of the first Lassie, actually a dog named Pal. Male collies were preferred for the part, since they are larger and less timid than females. The viewing audience seems never to have noticed the relevant anatomical differences. In fact, all we seemed to notice was that the dog we were watching was a collie with a white blaze on its face. Changes in markings as one dog was substituted for another for different stunts and tricks seem to have passed us by, just as easily as the telltale signs that should have told us Lassie was a lad.

Pal almost didn't get his big break. Fred M. Wilcox, the director, who interviewed over three hundred collies for the role in *Lassie Come Home*, passed over Pal because of reservations about his looks. Pal's trainer, Rudd Weatherwax, argued that the dog was particularly well trained and might be good for some of the specialty tricks and stunts in the picture. Since Wilcox was under a bit of time pressure, he decided to do some filming before he had actually chosen his star. One sequence involved Lassie swimming desperately for her life in floodwaters. Reasoning that all wet collies look alike, Wilcox thought he could edit scenes of Pal swimming with shots of the dog who would later be chosen for the Lassie role. It was at this moment that Pal showed the sensitivity that was to mark Lassie in our minds. The swimming sequence was athletic and effective, but the finale to the performance brought down the house. Pal emerged from the water apparently totally exhausted, without even the stamina left to shake the water off of his fur. He staggered forward a few steps and then dropped down squarely in front of the camera with his dripping head between his paws and his eyes closed. The performance was so convincing and so filled with pathos that Pal got the role and began a dynasty.

Lassie had quite an effect on our beliefs about dogs and their intelligence simply because of the volume of material about her to which we were exposed. First there were the nine feature films. Next came the radio show that ran nearly six years. (It is interesting to note that, although Pal did the barking on the radio show, the whining, panting, snarling, and growling were all done by human actors.) Then came the TV show, which ran for eighteen years, using six different settings and rotations of cast. Many of these episodes are still appearing on television in syndicated reruns today. There was even a Lassie cartoon series that played on Saturday mornings.

Throughout all this, the clear star was Lassie. One reviewer of the first picture described the dog as "Greer Garson in furs". Lassie managed to upstage some of the greatest stars in Hollywood, including Roddy McDowell, Elizabeth Taylor, Nigel Bruce, Elsa Lanchester, James Stewart, Mickey Rooney, and many others of similar stature. The audience always thought more of Lassie than of the costars. Cloris Leachman, who played the mother in one of Lassie's TV families, noted that to make the dog seem extremely clever the script writers had to play down the intelligence of the humans on screen. She observed that "they had to find reasons for us to be morons so the dog could outsmart us."

Those of us who doted on Lassie didn't recognize, or didn't allow ourselves to believe, that most of the stunts, acts of courage, and reasoning were not as spectacular as they seemed. When Lassie crawled under gunfire, sneaked through a tortuous maze of fallen electrical wires, jumped out windows, or leapt through the air to knock a criminal down, the actual actions were not very complex, and the final scenes were greatly assisted by clever film editing. When Lassie seemed to be looking around carefully to study a situation, Pal was actually watching his trainer wave a rag from a catwalk. Those looks of devotion and intense concentration were usually elicited by his trainer patting the pocket in which he always kept a few dog biscuits.

Nevertheless, at the psychological level, Lassie's impact was great. We believed that this dog (thus, by extrapolation, all dogs) could think, plan, sympathize, feel pain, have emotions of sorrow and joy, remember complex facts, and even plan acts of retribution. Hadn't we actually seen Lassie do it?

In the absence of formal training about the nature of dogs, motion pictures and TV programmes depicting the fictional exploits of Lassie, Rin Tin Tin, King of the Yukon, Roy Rogers' dog Bullet, Beethoven, Wishbone, Benji and others, as well as books describing the fantastic exploits of Lad, Bob, Treve, Buck, and one hundred and one Dalmatian pups, among others, served as our education and indoctrination into the nature of dog's mind. In comparison to these brilliant canines, it was clear that our own dear pet dogs and companions did not show the full range of intellectual ability of which dogs were capable, but we knew that it was latent within them. Somewhere in our own dogs was hidden the mental potential that could emerge as an act of heroism or brilliant reasoning.

Many of you are probably thinking that I am being a bit simplistic here. Certainly, we do not learn everything that we know about dogs from movies and works of fiction. After all, there are dozens of nonfiction books dealing with dogs on the shelves of every bookstore and library, and these must certainly contain information about the intelligence and thought processes of dogs. However, a look at the titles shows that they fall into three general categories: veterinary books, books on dog training and obedience, and photograph-filled books describing the various dog breeds.

The veterinary books sport titles like *Dog Care*, *The Healthy Dog*, and *The Home Veterinary Guide for Dogs*, and deal with nutrition, growth, and specific health problems of dogs. While they might include some discussion of how neutering may affect a dog's personality and even a section addressing psychological problems in dogs (usually those that result in biting, chewing furniture, or soiling the house), they cover little about dogs' thought processes or mental capabilities. This is understandable, since most of these books are written by veterinarians who are experts in animal physiology but not formally trained in many aspects of dog behaviour.

The next large group of books deals with dog obedience and training. Common titles are *Dog Training Step by Step, Playtraining Your Dog*, or more specialized titles such as *Guard Dog Training, Search and Rescue Dogs, Training for Tracking*, or *Training Your Hunting Dog*. Some simply attempt to mop up the problems left when obedience training fails, such as *Solving Your Dog Problems, Dogs Behaving Badly*, or *Help! This Animal Is Driving Me Crazy*. Many of these books are extremely insightful and helpful and describe techniques for teaching dogs basic or even advanced obedience exercises. Unfortunately, some are quite glib and attempt to reassure readers with statements such as "All dogs, regardless of breed, are easily trained if we use the natural method", "The trainability of dogs depends on the patience and consistency of the handler rather than on any inherent differences among breeds", "Any dog should be able to reach the highest levels of obedience competition", or "The dog is like a computer waiting to be programmed by the clever trainer." I suppose that if you have bought one of these books because you have a Jack Russell terrier that has chewed through your antique oak furniture, killed the cat, and doesn't even look at you when you shout its name through a megaphone, this is the kind of statement you want to read. But such statements are at the minimum incomplete and possibly entirely inaccurate. They do not take into account the differences in the nature of intelligence among the various breeds of dogs or breed differences in temperament and willingness to work—both factors that are important in determining just how well a particular dog will respond to obedience training.

I suppose that the attitudes reflected in most dog obedience books are understandable. The authors are experts in animal training, not usually trained specialists in animal behaviour. Many of them, such as Diane Bauman, Carol Lea Benjamin, Patricia Gail Burnham, Terri Arnold, Karen Pryor, Michael Tucker, or Joachim Volhard (to name but a few), are brilliant at training dogs. Many have a long list of accomplishments to stand in evidence of their ability. I envy their skills. While their books often do not address breed differences, they are willing to offer comments in their seminars and conversations that seem to recognize that not all dog breeds are mentally equivalent. Thus in one seminar, a trainer whose videos showed only border collies, golden retrievers, and German shepherds at work confided, "I would avoid any kind of terrier if you are seriously considering dog obedience competition."

Most dog obedience trainers do have an implicit theory of dog intelligence and it often determines their training techniques. Some feel that dogs have limited thinking ability and simply learn patterns of responses that they perform at appropriate times. Others believe that dogs are rational and capable of using logic to solve problems, but most stop short of attributing real consciousness and reason to them. A few dog obedience experts feel that dogs are fully conscious and that their thought processes are much like those of a young child, differing only in efficiency and range from those of a human. However, most of these writers limit their comments about dog intelligence and the dog's mind to a few passing pages or paragraphs and then immediately return to their major task, which is to teach people techniques they can use to train their dogs or solve particular behaviour problems.

The final class that you are apt to encounter is the breed book, which varies from a paperback with small drawings of selected breeds to an oversized, comprehensive coffee-table book with beautiful colour photographs. Breed books have titles such as *The Encyclopedia of Dogs, The Complete Book of Dogs, The [fill in your favorite kennel club] Book of Dogs,* and *The All-Breed Dog Book.* The ostensible purpose of these books is to describe the various types of dogs, their history, size, temperament, and behavioural characteristics. Many of these books are really quite wonderful to read, especially for the historical information about the various breeds, and the pictures of magnificent and beautiful dogs are marvellous. Unfortunately, these books are mostly written by dog breeders or representatives of the specialty club for each breed. Most do a fine job describing the standards of their breed, but it is not in their best interests to say anything negative about their dogs. Thus the breed books will not point out that many bulldogs have chronic respiratory problems, that many lines of Dalmatians have a tendency toward congenital deafness, that dachshunds are inclined to develop spinal lesions, or that many of the highly prized smaller Chihuahuas have knee or hip problems. Furthermore, when it comes to describing either the temperaments or the mental characteristics of the various breeds of dogs, these books have a universal tendency to distort the facts to produce a more favourable impression. Thus the breed books do not tell you that many basenjis bite without notice or visible provocation, that many Akitas can be downright dangerous around children unless reared with them, or that many greyhounds, while wonderful and gentle around people, can turn into killing machines around cats or small dogs.

The most important place where the breed books fail is in describing the mental capacities of various breeds of dogs. I believe that at least 90 percent of the dogs mentioned in most of the breed books are described as "intelligent". In some breeds, it is even written into the standards by which the dogs are judged. Yet often, unless one has an odd conception of the true nature of intelligence, the breed descriptions are overly flattering.

Consider, for instance, the Dandie Dinmont terrier. This is a very distinctive little dog with deep soulful eyes. It stands about ten inches (twenty-five centimetres) at the shoulder and weighs in at about twenty-two pounds (ten kilograms). It is one of the older breeds of terrier, and we have clear records that Dandies were being used in the early 1700s to hunt badger, fox, and otter in the Cheviot Hills near the border between England and Scotland.

The popularity of the Dandie Dinmont terrier was assured by a work of fiction written by Sir Walter Scott. It is said that in his travels Scott encountered James Davidson of Hawick, who kept a pack of these dogs. Scott was so impressed by the man and his tough little dogs that he made him the hero of his story *Guy Mannering*, which was published in 1814 (see Plate 1). The fictional character that he created was named Dandie Dinmont, a farmer who kept the "immortal six": Auld Pepper, Auld Mustard, Young Pepper, Young Mustard, Little Pepper, and Little Mustard (where Pepper and Mustard referred to the colours of the dogs). The public was charmed by Dandie Dinmont and his dogs, which were described as gritty, plucky animals (and, indeed, when roused, the Dandie Dinmont is one of the fiercest of all the terriers). Scott has his character say of his terriers, "They fear naething that ever cam' wi' a hairy skin on't." The feisty little dogs were soon universally called Dandie Dinmonts after this literary character, and their fame spread well beyond the original area in which they were bred.

The problem with Dandies might be anticipated on a theoretical level, even before considering the dog itself. Imagine a dog that is willing to go to ground (that is, enter a burrow) to take on a fox or an otter in its lair. A fox will generally be much the same weight and size as this terrier, while an otter can be three times as heavy. While one might be impressed by the courage shown, one might also feel that a more intelligent dog would simply say (figuratively), "This is too dangerous. I'm going to pass this up. This otter has done me no harm." Yet the American Kennel Club standard for Dandie Dinmonts describes them as "independent, determined, reserved and intelligent." While few would quarrel with the first three adjectives, the last is more of a question.

I spoke with one dog obedience trainer who described his interactions with Dandies as follows:

This couple in their fifties brought a pair of these dogs into my beginner's class. It became clear that they would have been more successful if they had been trying to train sacks of potatoes to heel. [At the beginner's level of obedience, heeling requires the dog merely to walk in a controlled manner at its handler's left side while on leash.] If the female was in the mood, she might walk along for a few steps, but the male would sometimes just stop and, after having been dragged a step or two on the lead, would simply roll on its side so that it could slide along the training mat with less friction. Neither of the dogs looked at their handlers when they spoke, and after seven weeks of class, the only command they would reliably respond to was "sit."

The woman in this couple insisted that these were intelligent dogs. She assured me that they had bought them because they had read an article that described them as the "clowns of dogdom." She went on to tell me the strange and funny things that they sometimes did around the house. Since the dogs appeared to have pleasant enough personalities, I didn't want to tell her that I thought the reason they so frequently got involved in unexpected and unusual behaviours (which we interpret as funny or clownish) was that they simply did not have a clue as to what was expected of them.

When I hear stories like this, I always wonder whether the fault is in the dog or in the handler. As someone who trains beginners' classes, I often find that looking at the dog's owner gives a better indication of how the dog will do in obedience training than does looking at the dog. So, as a brief check, I browsed through three randomly selected issues of the *Gazette*, which is the official magazine of the American Kennel Club. Each year, the magazine includes a feature on the number of obedience titles earned by dogs of each breed. For the three years I checked, in all of the United States, not one Dandie Dinmont terrier won a single obedience title. The poor showing of the dogs in the anecdote thus began to seem more like evidence of an intellectual limitation in the breed rather than testimony to the inept performance of a couple of dog handlers.

Chapter Two

The Natural History of Dogs

Animals are not brethren, they are not underlings; they are other nations, caught with ourselves in the net of life and time.

—HENRY BESTON

Ultimately, we are all prisoners of our physiology. Considerations of muscle and bone strength determine the fact that a dog is stronger than a mouse and weaker than a gorilla. The physiology of the dog's eye causes its visual acuity to be poorer than that of humans, while the physiology of the dog's nose makes its sense of smell better. Similarly, the dog's mental abilities and many of its behavioural predispositions are determined by the physiology of its brain. Its brain, like ours, is the result of a particular evolutionary history. To understand the mind of the domestic dog, then, we must first know the animal's biological origins, evolution, and history.

THE FIRST DOGS

There are many folk tales about the first dog. According to the Kato Indians of California, the god Nagaicho created the world. First he erected four great pillars at the corners of the sky to hold it up and to expose the earth. Then he began a casual stroll around this new world and proceeded to create the things to fill it. The myth specifies how men and women were made of earth, how the creeks and rivers were made by Nagaicho's dragging feet, how each animal was made and placed in its proper spot in the world—each animal, that is, except the dog. Nowhere in the story is there any mention of Nagaicho, the creator, creating the dog. Nonetheless, when Nagaicho first started on his walk, he took a dog with him—God already had a dog. It seems likely that to the Katos the idea of a human going around without a dog was both unthinkable and unheard of. The dog always was here. After the world was created, the dog simply tagged along behind the creator, sniffing and exploring and listening to Nagaicho's casual comments about his creations: "See how pure the water is in this creek. Would you like to take a drink, my dog, before all the other animals find it?" After a while, the two wandered north together, God and his dog.

A charm of this myth is that there is an element of truth in it, in the sense that humanity's association with dogs predates the earliest vestiges of civilization. As far as we can tell, the first domesticated animals were dogs, and this domestication was thousands of years before the appearance of the next domesticated species (cattle and/or reindeer).

The trail of the early dog is faint. Following analysis of DNA samples, some scientists have suggested that the first domestication of wolves may have taken place more than a hundred thousand years ago, but newer studies and more sophisticated analyses of DNA in dogs put the date at the end of the Pleistocene era, or around fifteen thousand years ago. Because of the kind of DNA evidence used in these studies, the analysis is somewhat indirect and based on a number of assumptions and speculations. I am much more comfortable with fossil evidence provided by archaeologists and paleontologists simply because it uses the actual remains of ancient dogs. Because the first domesticated dogs appear so similar to contemporary dogs, archaeologists have often overlooked their bones, mistakenly assuming that such bones must have come from modern dogs that wandered into the ancient cave site and died there. Recently more attention has been paid to these canine bones, and items that were recovered in the 1930s through the 1950s have been reanalysed. In this way we have learned a lot about the early ancestors of our dogs.

What may be the earliest unambiguous fossil evidence of domesticated dogs was uncovered from the Bryansk Region, in the central Russian Plain, which is roughly four hundred miles southeast of

Moscow. Radiocarbon dating was used to determine the age of these bones. This method was developed by J. R. Arnold and W. F. Libby in 1949, and has become an indispensable part of the archaeologist's tool kit since then. It depends on the fact that cosmic radiation breaks down molecules of air, which results in the formation of a radioactive form of carbon (carbon 14). This is carried down in rain or snow and is ultimately absorbed by plants, becoming part of their makeup. Animals eating those plants, or eating animals that ate those plants, absorb this radioactive carbon and continue to absorb it from their food as long as they remain alive. When they die, the radioactive carbon begins to decay, and by measuring the remaining radioactivity in their bones we can get an accurate measure of how long ago that animal lived. Such measures suggest that these fossils of a domesticated dog are at least thirteen thousand years old, and may be as old as seventeen thousand years. Careful study of the skulls of these "first dogs" suggest that they looked much like our modern Siberian huskies, only with a broader, heavier head and muzzle.

At first glance, seventeen thousand years may not seem like a long time—after all, dinosaurs roamed the earth one hundred fifty million years ago. Yet our own species, *Homo sapiens,* did not appear until three hundred thousand years ago. Neanderthal man was still predominant in Europe until forty thousand years ago, and the first types of humans physically indistinguishable from modern humans appeared between thirty and thirty-five thousand years ago. Asian tribes first crossed the Bering Strait to begin human occupation of the Americas twenty-five thousand years ago. It is interesting to note that the first evidence of organized agriculture is only ten thousand years old—which is three to seven thousand years after the earliest proof that dogs had established their companionship with humans. Falling within the same general time frame as these Russian fossils is a finding in Iraq of domesticated dog remains that are dated at around fourteen thousand years ago.

Another archaeological finding suggests that even at this early date, dogs were already serving as guards and also as companions. An excavation in southern Europe yielded the skeleton of a Stone Age girl. She had been lovingly folded into the traditional, almost fetal, burial position that is found in excavations of Cro-Magnon dwelling sites. (Cro-Magnon was an earlier version of *Homo sapiens* that looked quite similar to contemporary humans.) This particular burial site was a bit different, however, for around the girl, facing in four different directions, were four dogs. It is hard to avoid thinking that the dogs were placed there as guards for the loved one who had had to travel to the nether regions at such a young age.

Evidence for an early association between humans and dogs comes from many places. In America, a set of bones found at a site called Jaguar Cave indicates that dogs were sharing lodgings with humans eleven thousand years ago. And some ten thousand years ago, there were already two distinct breeds of domestic dogs differing in size in Denmark. Evidence for an alliance between people and dogs also has been dated back to this period in China. It thus appears that a hundred centuries ago dogs had already dispersed throughout the entire globe, and in every region of the world they associated with humans (see Plate 2).

THE ANCESTRY OF THE DOG

There are a lot of theories about the biological source of the modern domestic dog, and in recent years the arguments have become more heated as new paleontological and DNA evidence has been collected. The first evidence for the dog family, Canidae, goes back about thirty-eight million years. The family of canids, which is part of the larger grouping Carnivora (the meat eaters), includes a large variety of different dog-like creatures. Most familiar are the wolves, foxes, jackals, coyotes, dingoes, and wild dogs. Biologists and others are continually speculating about which of the canids was domesticated to produce the domestic dog, with wolf and jackal named as the most likely candidates.

The complete ancestry of the dog may never be known, but there is enough evidence to fill in some of the steps. Paleontologists have generally decided that the precursor to dogs was a strange, little tree-dwelling animal called *miacis*. The animal lived about forty million years ago, which would place it not too long after the earliest modern mammals but well before the earliest of the big apes. *Miacis* was about the size of a mink, with short legs, a long tail, a long body, a moderately long neck, and prick ears (see Figure 2.1). In addition to being

Figure 2.1
Miacis, the tree-dwelling ancestor of all dogs and cats, which lived forty million years ago.

the ancestor of all the Canidae, *miacis* is also the ancestor of all bears and, strangely, all cats as well.

The evolutionary branch that was to lead to dogs continues with an animal called *cynodictis* (see Figure 2.2). This species appeared in the Pliocene era, about twelve million years ago. It had partially retractable claws and may, therefore, have lived in trees or climbed them for protection or while hunting. *Cynodictis* spent more time on the ground than did *miacis* and was better fitted for running. It gave rise to two different evolutionary lines. The first was *cynodesmus*, a line of large animals much resembling the hyena, with some catlike features. Although most of these animals became extinct, wild African and Cape hunting dogs seem to have developed from them, as may have the modern African hyena. The second branch was *tomarctus*, from which all the canids derived. *Tomarctus* would have looked like some form of generic modern dog to a casual observer (see Figure 2.3). Some evidence, however, suggests that *tomarctus*, in addition to differing in

Figure 2.2
Cynodictis, the first on the evolutionary branch where dogs separated from cats, twelve million years ago.

Figure 2.3
Tomarctus, the common ancestor of all canids, would have easily passed for a dog physically but was considerably less intelligent.

some anatomical details from modern dogs, was also somewhat less intelligent. The point to remember is that, through *tomarctus*, the domestic dog shares a common ancestor with all other canids, including wolves, jackals, foxes, and the wild dogs.

Today, there are at least thirty-nine different canid species. All domestic dogs are members of the species *Canis familiaris*, which encompasses a vast degree of diversity. More than four hundred breeds of domestic dogs are registered with various kennel clubs, and, while the current number of breeds of dogs is still a matter of debate, some estimates say that worldwide there are over eight hundred different breeds. Despite this diversity in the species, enough similarities with all other canids remain to raise questions. Is the domestic dog simply a tamed version of one of the wild canids? If not, did the domestic dog evolve from one of the other canid species through some biological process? A look at the characteristics of some wild canids may not provide a definitive answer, but it does offer some interesting information.

Wolves

If you canvassed the majority of dog authorities, most would say that dogs evolved directly from wolves. British dog authority and veterinarian Bruce Fogle is quite explicit when he says, "Dogs are wolves, although they sometimes look like they are in sheep's clothing." If this were true, then in order to discover the nature of the dog's mind, behaviour, and intelligence, we would need only to study the mind of the wolf.

This approach sounds plausible. Wolves certainly do appear to be dog-like in general shape—indeed, some northern wolves are indistinguishable from German shepherds at first glance (see Plate 3). Other wolves, however, are larger and appear to be more like Alaskan malamutes or huskies. At another extreme are some wolves that resemble foxes in their size, shape, and colouration. With all these variations, it can be hard to decide if certain animals are true wolves or not. Thus the coyote (Plate 4), while clearly in the family Canidae, is often called a prairie wolf, though some authorities treat it as a separate group, quite distinct from wolves. Even more difficult is the classification of one of the smaller wolves, which wears one of the larger scientific names—*Canis niger seu rufus*—but is better known as the red wolf of Texas. In some catalogues, this canid is classified as a fox, elsewhere as a jackal, and in other places as a coyote.

The real breakthrough in our knowledge about the origins of dogs comes from genetic studies based on DNA, but not the DNA that we think of as genes and is found in the chromosomes in the nucleus of cells. For each individual, half of this nuclear DNA comes from the mother and half from the father. Rather, these new genetic studies look at the DNA found in the mitochondria, little oval organs in each cell that float around outside the nucleus and are responsible for metabolizing nutrients and turning them into energy. Nuclear DNA changes from one individual to another because the components received from the father and mother are different on each mating, and obviously different for different parents. The DNA found in the mitochondria, however, comes only from the mother.

For people interested in evolution, this is exciting because, in theory, we could use this mitochondrial DNA to get a genetic picture of the "first mother" for any species. Biologists love to study mitochondrial DNA because it can trace a simple line of descent from female-to-female-to-female back to the beginning. However, the DNA many generations down the line is not an exact copy of that of the original mother. Over time, changes, called mutations, occur due to copying mistakes or DNA damage. This means that if at some point in time two species, races, or breeds separated, the mitochondrial DNA of the two diverging lines would become more and more different. Ancestors can be clearly identified when you are studying mitochondrial DNA, because clusters of mutations are not shuffled into new combinations as are the genes on chromosomes. They remain together as a particular sequence and, in effect, become a signature of that line of descent.

When mitochondrial DNA from dogs and wolves are compared, they are found to differ by only around 1 to 2 percent. To give you an idea of how close this similarity is, this is in the same range as the differences found between different races of humans. Scientists consider this to be clear evidence that the closest ancestor of dogs, and the species that was probably domesticated first, was the wolf. Please note that I said the "closest" and not necessarily the "only" ancestor of dogs was the wolf.

Authorities who maintain that dogs were domesticated from wolves suggest that the great variety of sizes and shapes found in dogs is due to the fact that at various times different local strains of wolf were domesticated. This is supported by the DNA evidence. It's possible that the domestication of wolves occurred in at least five different places at different times, starting in Asia and moving toward Europe. There were also at least three different times and places in the Americas when the wolf was domesticated. The evidence also suggests that when early humans crossed from Asia to America over the Bering Strait some twelve thousand years ago, they brought with them some of their domesticated dogs, since many lines of dogs in the Americas have DNA that is very close to that of the Asian grey wolf.

Northern wolves may be the source not only of German shepherds (which they so closely resemble) but also of malamutes, Samoyeds, and the other huskies, as well as chow chows, elkhounds, collies, and some smaller breeds such as Pomeranians, schipperkes, and corgis. The defining characteristics of this group include a sharp pointed face, large prick ears, and a full flowing tail (when the tail is not docked, of course). The mountain wolves (such as the Tibetan wolf) have a somewhat shorter muzzle and are said to be the ancestors of true hounds, mastiffs, and bulldogs. A shorter, square muzzle and jowly appearance are two of the defining characteristics of this line.

Wolves have unique and quite fascinating eyes. One look into the eyes of a wolf will remind you that the domestic dog is not simply a tame wolf. The dog, *Canis familiaris*, has circular pupils in its eyes. Many varieties of wolves, however, have oval, slightly oblique pupils, which give them disturbingly undoglike countenances when viewed closely.

Popular beliefs about the behaviour and personality of the wolf have had some effect on whether scientists and popular writers felt that it was acceptable to suggest that the wolf might be the ancestor of the domestic dog. The lore of the wolf accounts for the comfort most people seem to derive from the thought that their domestic dog might really be a tamed wolf. The evolution of that lore is an interesting story in itself.

To most people, the wolf seems to possess a certain power and nobility. In our fantasy, the wolf is the great hunter, coursing across the snowy plains, under the control of the great wolf king or pack leader. We imagine wolves working precisely as a team to cut out an older reindeer from its herd and then run it down. We can picture how the tall reindeer turns on the pursuing pack. Its antlers savagely slash the nearest wolf. Yet, under the urging and coordination of the pack leader, the others have circled the beast, hemming it in until one leaps on its back and quickly dispatches it with a neck-breaking bite. The final scene, as we run this movie in our minds, shows the pack returning slowly to its camp. The wounded wolf is being gently nursed and urged on by the one of the pack members, while the others carry haunches of reindeer meat for the whelping females and young cubs, who rush forward to greet them with tails wagging, eager to learn of their great exploits.

Actually, this idealized, positive picture of the wolf is quite new. Traditionally, the wolf was seen as a fierce and dangerous predator. We grew up with the story of the "big bad wolf" and understand that when people refer to the wolf at the door, they are not alluding to the arrival of a good friend. Throughout most of human history, wolves had a reputation for being savage and terrifying. They were credited with stealing children, pulling riders off their horses, and spontaneously using their organized pack formation to attack humans. Wolves were known to engage in wanton killing, in the mass slaughter of sheep and cattle. For a poor shepherd or farmer, the destruction of farm animals could mean economic disaster and even starvation. Hence the wolf was feared and loathed. It was viewed as evil and often regarded as an agent of the devil.

Perhaps the clearest expression of the dread that wolves could inspire is found in some of the legends surrounding them. The bloodsucking vampire, for example, could turn itself into a wolf. In Bram Stoker's classic book *Dracula* (published in 1897), Count Dracula refers to the howling of the wolves as "the singing of my children". Other stories link the wolf to the devil, especially in tales of werewolves, where evil men would adopt the shape of a wolf to carry out the devil's dark designs.

This view of the wolf as dangerous and perhaps evil, coupled with the demand for fur, resulted in community and even national campaigns against the animals. Often dogs, such as the Irish wolfhound, Scottish deerhound, and borzoi played vital roles in the attack on wolves. The United States predator control programme began in 1915 with the grey, or timber, wolf as its initial target. The programme was tremendously successful, and the wolf was completely gone in many regions by 1930. The grey wolf, which once roamed over most of the North American continent, is now found only in Alaska and in small numbers in a portion of Minnesota. The wolf has met a similar fate in many other places in the world, such as the British Isles. The results have been that several species, such as the Falkland Islands wolves, are now extinct.

The popular view of the wolf began to change because of the dramatic fictional writing of various authors. For example, Jack London, the American novelist, presented a more sympathetic, noble view of the wolf. He even suggested that wolf and dog were brothers. He used his knowledge of the Klondike and of dog behaviour to write two highly successful books. The first was *Call of the Wild* (published in 1903), in which a dog is lured into the wilderness and joins the society of wolves. The companion piece to this is *White Fang* (published in 1907), which is the story of a wolf gradually drawn into human society. In this second book, the author affectionately describes an instinctive bond between a wolf and a human.

The current compassionate view of the wolf held by many people can also trace its origin to a 1963 book by the Canadian writer Farley Mowat. Entitled *Never Cry Wolf*, the book was phenomenally successful and led to a movie of the same name. His descriptions of the wolf he called George and its mate, whom he called Angeline, are typical of the entire book. Mowat describes George as being "regal" and as having "presence" and "dignity". He notes that the wolf George was "conscientious to a fault, thoughtful of others, and affectionate within reasonable bounds, . . . the kind of father whose idealized image appears in many wistful books of human family reminiscences, but whose real prototype has seldom paced the earth upon two legs."

Mowat continues to anthropomorphize when he refers to Angeline as George's "wife" and describes her as "beautiful", "ebullient", "passionate", and "devilish when the mood was on her". In summary, he comments, "I became deeply fond of Angeline, and still live in hopes that I can somewhere find a human female who embodies all her virtues."

Descriptions such as these made it easy to empathize with the wolf, to see its human characteristics, and to identify with it and feel concern for its welfare. In fact, Mowat's book is credited with launching much of the public criticism of wolf control programmes in North America and even an attempt to reintroduce the grey wolf into a region in northern Michigan in 1974. In the northern regions of the province of British Columbia in Canada, the Forestry and Conservation Services has a wolf control programme that seeks to save the elk and caribou herds from predation by wolves. Because of the modern, positive attitude toward wolves, this programme has been targeted for demonstrations and protests almost annually. While watching a videotape of the television news coverage of such a protest, I heard a speaker extolling the virtues of the wolf, attributing to it courage, loyalty, compassion, love, sensitivity, honour, intelligence, forethought, altruism, and a sense of humour. Despite my own fondness for wolves, I still found it necessary to rewind the tape and listen to the speech one more time to make sure that the speaker was talking about the wolf, rather than giving a campaign speech for some politician. In any event, it is views such as these that make the idea that domestic dogs were derived from the wolf quite popular and readily accepted. Certainly such a noble animal is deserving of our love and companionship. Fortunately, given this bias, the DNA evidence does suggest that the first dog was probably a wolf.

Jackals

Although some very eminent scientists, such as the Nobel Prize–winning zoologist and ethologist Konrad Lorenz, believed that dogs descended from jackals (see Plate 5) rather than wolves, this idea has never quite caught on with other dog authorities. My feeling is that the rejection of this theory is based less on scientific considerations than on more fanciful considerations and biases. Unfortunately, no great jackal literature has arisen to offset the initial bad press. There has also been considerably less study of the behaviour and mental abilities of jackals, compared to that devoted to wolves.

Predominantly found in North Africa and Southern Asia, jackals have a reputation for being scavengers and carrion eaters. The public image of the jackal has them lurking near the body of an animal who was killed by a "noble" hunter, such as a lion, or skulking about village streets, devouring refuse, offal, and filth of every kind. They are believed to follow true predators, picking over the rotting bits of dead prey that have been left behind. They are supposed to be found scurrying around garbage heaps or haunting burial grounds, where they take the opportunity to disinter any bodies buried in shallow graves in order to consume the remaining flesh. They are accused of many base and unpleasant characteristics, from having an offensive smell to being lazy and too cowardly to hunt live game for themselves.

Given these negative views of the jackal, it is not surprising that few people have rallied to the defence of the theory that the jackal was the immediate ancestor of the dog. Who wants to believe that his pet, his best friend, the animal that shares his home and perhaps his bed, is genetically a garbage-eating, grave-robbing, smelly coward? It is much easier (psychologically) to associate our dog with the noble wolf.

These feelings, however, are based on some erroneous views. Jackals are somewhat smaller and lighter boned than the average wolf and lack its savage defensive powers (because of this, in fact, jackals are treated as prey animals by some of the large cats, particularly leopards). Anatomically, however, they have virtually no distinctive features that separate them from wolves or domestic dogs, and any accurate description of the physiology and behaviour of the jackal could apply equally well to any of the small wolves, the coyote, or some domestic dogs.

Physically, jackals do share one peculiar trait with dogs. Many assert that if you see even the tiniest speck of white fur in a dog's coat, no matter where, you will likely see some white at the end of the dog's tail. It seems that jackals, too, often have white spots on the ends of their tails. It is likely that the evolutionary purpose behind this white spot was to make the tail movements more visible to other members of the jackal's group. This helps in communication by serving as something like an easily seen signal flag. In any event, the existence of such markings has been used to support the theory that the origin of the dog may have included genes from jackals. The same characteristic white tail tip is also found in foxes but virtually never in wolves or coyotes.

In their food gathering, jackals have the reputation for being scavengers, but their foraging patterns differ little from wolves. Like jackals, wolves will often scavenge, and in human communities in the extreme north their raiding of garbage dumps is often a problem. Generally speaking, jackals spend most of their time hunting for small animals, such as rodents, in much the same way that wolves do. In many regions, jackals form small packs that hunt with the same coordination as do wolf packs and, like wolves and foxes, jackals breed in burrows.

The DNA evidence shows about a 6 percent difference between dogs and jackals. This is still a remarkably high degree of similarity. We know, for instance, that back in the days of the pharaohs, Egyptians had domesticated jackals and interbred them with dogs.

What impresses me the most, however, is that a glance into the eyes of a jackal reveals pupils that are round, not oval like that of many wolves, and these give it the familiar countenance that we are used to seeing in the domestic dog.

Foxes

Among all of canids, foxes are least likely to be seriously viewed as possible ancestors of the dog (see Plate 6). Foxes are characterized by pointed faces, short legs, long, thick fur, and tails that can be one-half to two-thirds as long as the head and body length combined. Foxes are generally much smaller than dogs. While their body length may average around twenty-three inches (fifty-eight centimetres) and the larger varieties may stand about sixteen inches (forty centimetres) at the shoulder, they are quite slightly built and some weigh only five to ten pounds (two to five kilograms). The behaviour patterns of foxes also seem quite different from those of dogs in many details.

Foxes are omnivorous and will eat insects, earthworms, small birds, other mammals, eggs, carrion, and vegetable matter (they actually show a fondness for certain fruits). Unlike most of the other members of the dog family, foxes do not hunt by running down their prey. Instead, they silently stalk and then pounce on their quarry, much the way cats do. Foxes tend to be skittish beasts, probably because they are routinely preyed upon by wolves, bobcats, and other larger carnivores. The baby foxes (or *kits*) are often taken by hunting birds, such as falcons or eagles.

Other differences between foxes and the rest of the canids include the fact that they are generally solitary during most of the year, gathering together only during the breeding season. Although they breed in earths, foxes do not live in dens, except during mating season, and sleep concealed in grasses or thickets. Here we find the purpose behind their magnificent tails. The fox actually curls its tail around its body for warmth, much like a great fur shawl.

The relationship between foxes and dogs is ambiguous. The skull configuration of most foxes is very different from that of most dogs (even for those dogs who have a foxlike look). Looking into their eyes, we find that most foxes have linear or slit-shaped pupils, which give them an almost catlike appearance. Nothing approaching this pupillary configuration is found in any modern domestic dog. Perhaps the most important fact is that most of the species of fox that are distributed throughout Europe, North America, and North Africa have a different number of chromosomes than the dog. There are infrequent reports, however, from sources reliable in other respects, which suggest that foxes and dogs have occasionally interbred and produced fertile offspring. These accounts may be due to the difficulties of classifying some species of fox, a task that can be as challenging as classifying wolves. Interbreeding may be possible with varieties of fox that are more jackal- or wolf-like in their genetic structure, such as the Niger fox, arctic fox, or blue fox.

An interesting report of some Russian research on foxes directly bears on the issue of the domestication of dogs. The experiment was started in the 1940s by the Russian geneticist Dmitri Belyaev, who worked in a Siberian laboratory with other biologists who were trying to domesticate silver foxes. Their aim was practical as well as scientific, since they wanted to breed these animals for their beautiful fur, which brings a high price on the world market. Since the wild fox can be quite snappish and churlish, the scientists were also trying to create a more docile strain of silver foxes that would allow themselves to be handled and more easily managed. For this reason, only the most gentle of the foxes were allowed to breed. Over a span of only twenty generations, the scientists managed to develop tame, domesticated foxes.

Several surprises resulted from these breeding experiments. In their behaviour, these tame foxes became very doglike. They began to look for human company rather than running from it. They began to wag their tails in response to the same types of situations that cause domestic dogs to wag their tails. They also developed a tendency to lick people's faces. These domesticated foxes also began to vocalize with yips and barks much like dogs and quite unlike adult wild foxes and wolves, which seldom vocalize. There were even important physical changes. Females began to come into heat twice a year, just as domestic dogs do. The ears of some of the foxes became floppy and more doglike. Unfortunately for the experimenters, also following the pattern for domestic dogs, these tamed foxes were often born with fur that was multicolored with patches of different shades, which greatly lowered their market value!

The exciting aspect of this study is that, without being crossbred with dogs, these tamed foxes developed both behavioural and physical characteristics of dogs. This suggests that the genes that produce docility (which the foxes were being selected for) are linked with certain other genetic predispositions. Such genetic cross-linkages are quite common. For example, there is evidence that white dogs are more likely to be deaf, suggesting that the genes associated with coat colour are also associated with genes that control aspects of the sensory system. If this is true across all canids, then the very act of domesticating wolves, jackals, or wild dogs by breeding them for tameness should begin to produce dog-like physical and psychological characteristics in them.

Dingoes, Wild Dogs, and Pariahs

The last set of canids to consider as possible ancestors of domestic dogs are the so-called wild dogs. These are characterized by triangular faces, pricked ears that stand well forward on the head, and a flat brow, with a sharp vertical drop to the muzzle (called a "head stop"). This group of dogs is spread throughout the Near and Middle East, and large populations of these dogs exist throughout Africa, Australia, and South Asia (including Malaysia and India). Unfortunately, we know even less about the minds of these canids than we do about those of wolves, jackals, or foxes.

The species known as the dingo (Plate 7), which physically is very similar to the Asian wolf, seems to have been introduced to the Australian continent by the nomads who later became the Australian aboriginals. They appear to have reached Australia around the end of the last Ice Age, when the sea level was low. The DNA of the dingo is virtually identical with that of Asian dogs, which has led scientists to suggest that the dingo started out as a domesticated dog that accompanied its master on his journey to the Australian continent and later reverted to the wild.

When the first Europeans arrived in Australia, they found that many of the aboriginal families kept dogs, which were generally well cared for, clearly valued, and actively used in hunting. Several early explorers noted that these dogs were virtually indistinguishable from wild dingoes. This is not surprising, since many aboriginals acquire their dogs by stealing wild dingo puppies. When reared by humans, dingoes become loyal and faithful housedogs, and are usually as trustworthy as other domesticated breeds of dogs.

The dingo is the only large mammalian carnivore found in Australia. Dingoes form packs, much the same way wolves do. Extremely large groups of seventy-five or more animals have been seen; however, the typical hunting party size is around five or six. Like the rest of the canids, dingoes prefer some form of burrow for breeding purposes, and they are often found nesting in holes in hollow trees. And, in common with the rest of the canids, they have a strong territorial sense, will defend their own territory, and will respect the territory of other packs of dingoes.

The wild dogs of Africa and Asia are quite similar to dingoes, differing only in that they are somewhat heavier boned and have stockier builds. While the dingo carries its tail down and over its anus, like wolves, most of the other wild dogs have short, curled tails that they hold high against their backs. Among domestic breeds, the basenji is the closest to this original wild dog stock in that it is physically indistinguishable from the wild dogs in the regions of Africa formerly known as the Congo and the Sudan. The basenji also resembles the wild dog in that the female comes into season only once a year, rather than twice a year like most other domestic dogs.

Some dog specialists, such as Michael Fox, have suggested that domestic dogs may have developed from some form of wild dog. The argument is that a missing link in the form of a basenji-like wild dog served as the intermediary between wolf and domestic dogs. Paleontologists, however, have found no fossil evidence for such a missing link. On the other hand, there is evidence of wild dogs interbreeding with domestic dogs to produce currently recognized breeds. The DNA evidence suggests more marked differences between the African wild dogs and our domestic dogs, with about a 7.5 percent difference between them, which suggests that their genetic contribution to our modern dog's genetic heritage is somewhat less than that of other canids.

In addition to the basenji, another breed that appears to have a good deal of wild dog blood is the Rhodesian ridgeback. These are large dogs, with a height of twenty-five to twenty-seven inches (sixty to seventy centimetres) at the shoulder and weighing around seventy-five pounds (thirty-five kilograms). The stock that went into their development was a domesticated wild dog originally tamed by the Hottentot tribe, or Khoikhoi. This tribe is closely related to the African Bushmen and lived in the Cape of Good Hope region in South Africa. A few of these so-called Hottentot ridged dogs were obtained in the late 1800s by Cornelius van Rooyen, a South African who hunted big game for a living. He crossed the dogs with some imported European breeds to obtain what was first known as the lion dog, or van Rooyen dog. The distinguishing characteristic of the Rhodesian ridgeback is a ridge of hair on the back that is formed by hair growing in the opposite direction to the hair on the rest of the coat. This ridge starts immediately behind the shoulders and tapers down to a point over the dog's hips. This ridge also links the breed to dingoes and other wild dogs, which have a similar ridge that is not as pronounced but usually becomes visible when the animal is angry, frightened, or aroused.

When away from human influence, wild dogs follow the typical pattern of most canids. They tend to hunt small game in organized packs and will also coordinate to hunt antelope and gazelles, usually singling out the young or infirm. However, even wild dogs have had a long association with humans and many packs have given up hunting and now are fully dependent on scavenging the refuse of city dwellers. Such dogs are usually called *pariahs*, which name does not specify a particular breed or species but rather refers to dogs that depend for their survival on the waste and garbage generated by urban humans. Such pariah dogs are well known throughout India and Egypt and the rest of the Middle East. In biblical times, they were known in Palestine and mentioned in scriptural writings.

COMMON FEATURES OF THE DOG AND ITS COUSINS

Since the ultimate aim of this book is to promote understanding of the behaviour and intelligence of domestic dogs, it makes sense to consider some of the characteristics all the canid species share. Physically, all canids have large chests and narrow waists, which makes them very fast runners. All have very strong scent discrimination abilities and good hearing. Regarding their minds, zoologist Fredrick Zeuner concluded that canids' "intelligence is far superior to that of other carnivores, including the large cats." Behaviourally, all dog-related species use similar methods of communication: All use the same body and facial signals to signal anger, fear, pleasure, dominance, and submission. All howl, and, though barking is a rare event in the wild, all wild canines are capable of barking and most will learn to do so if they are reared with domestic dogs. And all bury bones and surplus food, returning to such caches during times of need.

All canids also enjoy an occasional roll in carrion and other foul-smelling filth. It is likely that this behaviour began as a hunting strategy. Many prey animals, such as antelopes or gazelles, have a good sense of smell and can detect an approaching canine predator. However, by rolling in antelope or gazelle droppings, which of course give off a safe, familiar smell, the hunter masks its scent and so can get much closer before he is detected.

In domestic dogs this behaviour is no longer functional, but seems to have persisted because dogs have an aesthetic appreciation of odours, which some experts have compared to our own fondness for music; it has no real purpose but seems to give the dog pleasure. Some owners find the practice offensive and have tried to eliminate it by punishing their dogs, but this generally is to no avail. Occasionally, one can find a perfume or other scent that the dog likes (usually one with a musk base), which, when dabbed on either side of the dog's throat and behind its ears, may cause the dog to pass up opportunities to roll in the nearest pile of dung or other smelly refuse. This sometimes backfires, however.

My daughter by marriage, Kari, had a marvellous mixed-breed dog named Tessa, whom we often took along when we went to our little hideaway farm. At the rear of the farm is a large drainage canal, which, at various times of the year, takes on a rather pungent odour if stirred up. When the canal reached this pitch of smelliness, Tessa always took the very first opportunity to plunge into the canal and coat herself in the muck. This always resulted in our hosing her down and then leaving her outside for several hours until the essence wore off. Once, prior to a morning walk, I decided to see if I could avoid the inevitable wallow in the smelly canal by pretreating her with some aftershave lotion that smelled quite fine to me. She seemed a bit puzzled by all of this, and when I opened the gate, instead of the usual chase-the-stick romp that starts our walks, she made a direct beeline for the scum-filled canal. She returned afterward, soaking wet and odoriferous, ready to start our play. Apparently she felt a need to mask

her uncharacteristically perfumed aura with something more aestheti-
cally pleasing to her canine mind.

All members of the dog family, except the fox, are highly social.
Most band together in packs for hunting or simply for company. All
show well-developed social habits. They establish and maintain a dominance hierarchy focused on a pack leader and seem to show loyalty to
the pack and all its members. All act protectively toward young puppies and will often guard and nurture another's young pups when the
mother is away from the litter.

All canids use urine, mixed with the secretions from the preputial
glands (near the sex organs), to mark the limits of their territories. In
males, this marking behaviour is usually accompanied by leg lifting to
direct the urine against large objects (trees, rocks, bushes) to place the
scent at nose height for other dogs and to allow the scent to radiate
over a larger area. Some African wild dogs have been seen to use their
hind legs to scrabble as high up the trunk of a tree as possible before
squirting their message.

Some specialists think that members of the canid family can gather
a lot of information from these scent signals. It is believed that the smell
identifies the urinater, its sex, age, health, and even what it has been
eating. Certain hormones dissolved in the urine may also inform others
of the psychological state of the originator at the time of the marking—
whether it was angry, frightened, or content, or had recently engaged in
sexual behaviour. (The scratching that most canids perform in the soil
near their excreta seems to serve a similar, albeit less informative, function, using the sweat secretions from the pads of their feet.) Thus a
prominent tree or rock in the wild, or a corner fire hydrant or gate post
in the city, becomes the newspaper and gossip column for all the canids
in the neighborhood. After sniffing their way through the latest news
report, most dogs (particularly males) will add their own bit of information by topping the previous signal with their own marks.

Perhaps the most important commonality among the canids is their
ability to interbreed. The wolf, coyote, jackal, dingo, wild dog, and
domestic dog can all breed with each other and produce live, fertile
offspring. This ability is often taken as evidence that individuals are the
same species. The ability of dog and fox to interbreed is less clear, as I
noted above: Most dogs will ignore a vixen in heat, and, at least for the
common red fox and dogs, there may be genetic incompatibilities.

Much of the interbreeding across the canid species has been deliberately encouraged or arranged by human beings. Eskimos and natives of the high north are known to cross their working dogs regularly with wolves to try to get sled dogs with greater stamina and larger size. Usually this process involves tying a bitch in season to a stake in a region that wolves are known to frequent. An interested male wolf will often stop and partake of such an opportunity, and the bitches seem to accept the attention willingly. Of course, when times are harder and food is scarce, the bitch may be viewed as a candidate for lunch, rather than love, by the wolf pack.

In Germany and in the Netherlands, several experiments have resulted in the crossing of German shepherds and the European timber wolf. The results of these crosses have been dubbed "wolf-dogs," and have proven to be popular pets. At first glance, these wolf-dogs are not readily distinguishable from the purebred German shepherd dog, and their behaviour is remarkably doglike as well. One problem with wolf-dogs is that these crossbred dogs seem to be at a much greater risk of being involved in serious biting incidents. Remember that by back breeding to a wolf you are essentially undoing much of what has been accomplished by many generations of breeding dogs for their tameness and nonaggressive behaviour.

There have been many intentional and unintentional crossbreedings between jackals and dogs. The ancient Egyptians provided detailed descriptions of such crossbreeding endeavours. It was considered good luck to have a jackal-dog, which was supposed to honour the jackal-headed god Anubis, the god of the dead who helped to lead the worthy to eternal happiness in the afterlife. Biologists believe that a cross between dog and jackal was responsible for the development of the dog breed that we now call the pharaoh hound. Carved reliefs, hieroglyphs, and paintings of such dogs may go back as far as 3000 B.C. (see Figure 2.4).

King Tutankhamen, ruler of upper and lower Egypt, who lived around 1350 B.C., owned an early version of the pharaoh hound named Abuwitiyuw. Tutankhamen loved to watch this graceful hound leaping with joy at the sight of a gazelle and enjoyed having him as his companion on the hunt. When the dog died, the king ordered it to be buried in a manner that would befit a nobleman. Abuwitiyuw was wrapped in fine linen and laid to rest in a coffin. He was perfumed and

Figure 2.4
An example of the dogs produced by ancient Egyptian experiments with crossbreeding dogs and jackals, possibly the direct ancestors of contemporary breeds, such as the pharaoh hound.

anointed with preservative ointments so that he might be honoured before the god Anubis. A model of the dog was even placed near the entrance to Tutankhamen's own burial place, a tomb found almost intact by Howard Carter and Lord Carnarvon in 1922 in the Valley of the Tombs in Luxor.

THE TRUE ORIGIN OF THE DOMESTIC DOG

With so many potential ancestors and progenitors for the domestic dog and so many commonalities in physiology, DNA, and behaviour among the various canid species, can we draw any firm conclusions about the actual origin of dogs? Some biologists doubt that we can ever know for sure, but the likeliest theory is that the domestic dog contains, to various degrees, the genes of all the wild canids. The DNA evidence suggests that the domestication of the dog was not a single event, but may have occurred many times in different locations and during different historical eras. The evidence seems to indicate strongly that the first dog was a tame wolf, and while the wolf is the wild canine species that was most often domesticated, it also appears clear that at later dates jackals, wild dogs, and coyotes were also tamed and their genes allowed to enter the mix. In other words, wolves seemed to be the easiest to tame (perhaps because they were less fearful around humans) so they came first, but other members of the dog family that happened to be around also became candidates for domestication.

Since wolves would often stay near human camps to get an easy meal from tossed-out garbage, rather than going through the exertion and danger of the hunt, it is likely that pups would be whelped near where people lived. Perhaps one group of Paleolithic hunters found some wolf cubs and tamed them. In another location, a different group of hunters may have found some jackal cubs and tamed them. In still another place, a coyote or wild dog may have mothered cubs that some human later kidnapped and raised by the fire. Over several generations, the more tractable, useful animals were kept, each forming a breed: a tamed Northern wolf-dog here, an Asian wolf-dog there, a jackal-dog, a dingo-dog, and an African wild dog-dog or coyote-dog in other places and at other times. As people migrated from place to place, they doubtless brought their dogs with them. When the owners of the wolf-dogs and the jackal-dogs met, while the humans exchanged goods, stories, food, or hostilities, the dogs (being dogs) exchanged genes.

This suggests that commerce and travel over the globe created the numerous varieties of the domestic dog. The DNA evidence makes it likely that each variety of what we call our modern dogs has the genetic complement to earn it the name wolf-jackal-coyote-dingo-fox-dog hybrid. One breed might be 30 percent wolf, 30 percent jackal, and 40 percent dingo, while another is 60 percent wolf, 10 percent coyote, 20 percent wild dog, and 10 percent jackal. Lacking specific knowledge of their diverse genealogies, we call them all dogs, adding the additional distinctions of "spaniel", "hound", "collie", and the like to define visible characteristics of the various mixtures and outcomes.

The rich mixture of available genes from all the canid family that is built into the domestic dog stock has allowed humans to create hundreds of different breeds through controlled matings. Somewhere in that genetic mixture, people isolated the separate genes for retrieving, pointing, tracking, herding, guarding, and many other physical and behavioural qualities. The history of dogs suggests that if we look hard enough, we usually can find some specific genetic mix that fits whatever requirements we have; we simply have to find dogs that show the desired characteristics and then breed them selectively to create a new kind of domestic dog.

THE EFFECTS OF DOMESTICATION ON THE DOG

Suppose we knew that one particular member of the canid family (call it canid X) was the sole ancestor of domestic dogs. You might think that this would allow us to say that if canid X has a certain behaviour or shows a specific mental ability, the same behaviour and mental ability must exist in dogs. Sadly, this would not be true. Even if domestic dogs contained the genes of only one of the wild canids, they would not be simply tamed versions of the wild variety. The process of domestication itself has made dogs different, not only physically but also psychologically, from their wild cousins.

In breeding dogs, people have systematically selected for puppylike characteristics. The technical term for this is *neoteny*, meaning that the adult maintains many of the characteristics of the immature animal. This neoteny involves both physiology and behaviour in the animals.

Physically, one of the principal differences between dogs and wild canids is that dogs have shorter, more juvenile-looking muzzles. The nose is a bit flattened, and the teeth become crowded together in some breeds. The extreme examples of this are bulldogs, pugs, Pekingese, English toy spaniels, boxers, and the like, which have what might be called "push-faces". Less extreme are the retrievers and spaniels. Even in the so-called "long-faced" dogs, such as greyhounds, Doberman pinschers, Afghan hounds, borzois, or the pharaoh hounds, the muzzle is proportionally shortened relative to their wild ancestors.

A second difference is size. On the whole, canids are smaller than wolves and jackals. There are, of course, exceptions. The Great Dane, mastiff, Saint Bernard, Great Pyrenees, Newfoundland, Irish wolfhound, and Scottish deerhound are exceptions, but, I will show later, these are designer dogs that have been selectively bred for their large size and are really rarities. The vast majority of domestic dogs remain smaller than wild dogs.

Colours have also changed. Most wolves, jackals, and wild dogs are relatively uniform in colour, with only an occasional light blaze on the face, underside, or tips of the feet or tail. Domestic dogs, on the other hand, vary tremendously in colour. There are many more whites than we find in the wild. Then there are the spectacular reds of the Irish setter, the purple sheen of the Kerry blue terrier, the magnificent spots on the Dalmatian and harlequin Great Danes, or the fascinating complexity of the merle coats seen on some rough collies and Shetland sheepdogs. Humankind likes striking, interesting patterns and has selectively bred dogs that show them.

While wolves, jackals, and wild dogs have pretty much the same kinds of coats, differing only in length and density to adapt to the relative cold or warmth of their native climates, dogs have a variety of different coats that have been selectively cultivated. You can get a dachshund with a smooth, hard, short coat or with a long, soft coat or with dense, wiry hair. The large herding dogs, pulis and komondors, have a bizarre coat that twirls into curly cords; the mass of the coat is so great that if an adult dog were completely shorn, it might weigh ten pounds less. Some terriers, such as the cairn and the West Highland white, have double coats that consist of an outer hard, protective coat and an inner soft, insulating coat. Some dogs, such as the Mexican hairless or Chinese crested, have virtually no coat. Some dogs, like poodles or Portuguese water dogs, have hair that grows continuously and hence theoretically has no maximum length, as opposed to typical dog fur, which grows to a particular length and is then shed.

Some of these coat variations were chosen for artistic reasons. Still others were chosen for functionality. A hard-coated or wire-haired terrier was better protected from the sharp rocks lining burrows and also from the teeth of its prey. The malamute needs a very dense, insulating coat to protect it from the arctic weather. In the poodle, however, the continuously growing hair simply seems to provide us with endless opportunities to reshape and restyle it to fit our changing fancies and sense of fashion.

When it comes to ears, no adult canids in the wild have hanging or lop ears: All wild canids have upright, prick ears. The puppies of many wild dogs, however, often do have ears that flop over, but these straighten up as the dogs mature. Of course, many juvenilized domestic dogs, such as spaniels and many hounds, retain the lop ears of the puppy throughout their lives.

Behaviourally, our domestic dogs are also more puppylike. When dogs lick people's faces, as most domestic dogs will, they are actually mimicking the behaviour of puppies, who will lick their mother's face to get her to regurgitate food for them. Hence your dog's kisses really mean that it is treating you as its parent and, of course, asking for a snack.

Another behavioural characteristic of the domestic dog is its relative docility. One effect of neoteny is to have the dog act like a puppy, and puppies simply do not challenge the adult members of the group for leadership or dominance over the rest of the pack. In the wild, the growing canid first challenges the smallest and weakest members of the pack and then moves up in dominance. Since humans don't want a dog that would be a threat to their children (the smallest members of our human pack), we have fostered submissiveness, tractability, and puppylike dependency in the domestic dog. In larger breeds, we often have cultivated activity levels that are lower than those usual of wild canids. Dogs like Great Danes, Saint Bernards, and Newfoundlands are often referred to as "mat dogs" because, given a choice, they would simply curl up on a mat in front of the hearth and lie quietly for most of the day.

In addition, domestic dogs have been bred to reduce their *neophobia*, or fear of new and unfamiliar things and people. Such fear is quite common in wild canids, and it is not easy to eliminate. In domestic dogs, it is considered an undesirable trait. We refer to neophobic animals as anxious, fearful, or apprehensive and describe them with terms such as "touch-shy" or "spooky". Breeders actively screen these traits out of the genes of domestic dogs. Thus we have managed to create animals that have a high tolerance for strangers and for handling new situations.

I believe that we have also selected dogs so that, like puppies, they love to play. Most of us have been moved to laughter or silliness by the antics of our dogs, and, though it is sometimes difficult to admit it to anyone, we do spend significant amounts of time in aimless play with them. Even the stodgy clergyman Henry Ward Beecher, best known for his advocacy of reconciliation between the North and South after the American Civil War, could see this, noting that "the dog was created especially for children. He is the god of frolic." The literary critic and scholar Samuel Butler took this observation one step further, recognizing that dogs were also here for adults to frolic with when he said,

"The greatest pleasure of a dog is that you may make a fool of yourself with him, and not only will he not scold you, but he will make a fool of himself too."

People have consciously designed some breeds for particular functions and specific jobs and other breeds for specific temperaments (for example, some dogs are sharp and aggressive, to serve as guards, while others are soft and gentle, to be playthings or merely companions). How primitive humans discovered that they could manipulate the genes in various lines of dogs is a mystery. A lot of it was clearly accidental, followed by trial-and-error experimentation. Probably, the first deliberate experiments were matings set up after it was discovered that the offspring of two dogs with desirable characteristics often shared their parents' good qualities. Later, only those offspring that turned out "right" were kept and interbred further.

Jasper Rine of the Department of Molecular and Cell Biology at the University of California at Berkeley demonstrated how we might go about creating a new dog breed after he noticed some behaviours of border collies and Newfoundlands that were quite contradictory. For example, Newfoundlands love water and seek it out, but border collies are quite indifferent to it. Newfoundlands bark somewhat frequently and carry their tails high, while border collies are relatively quiet and carry their tails low. Finally, of course, border collies show the various components of herding, such as crouching, staring, and making hard eye contact, all of which are absent in Newfoundlands.

Rine crossbred a border collie and a Newfoundland. In that first generation the puppies clearly had a mixture or blend of the parents' characteristics. If we consider the frequency of barking, the first generation was noisier than border collies usually are, but were quieter than Newfoundlands normally are. The pups all had some dominant characteristics, such as the crouching and glaring behaviours of the border collie and the water-loving behaviour of the Newfoundland. When a second generation was created by mating these crossbred dogs to each other, however, strange mixtures of behaviours began to emerge. For example, one might crouch and carry its tail low (collie traits) but love water and bark a lot (Newfoundland traits). Its littermate might be exactly the opposite, never crouching, holding its tail high, hating water, and seldom barking. This shows that theoretically you can produce a dog with any combination of behavioural traits that you want through selective breeding. But it also shows that, for these traits to sort themselves out and reach some stable pattern, you might need several generations of controlled breeding. Obviously, creating a new breed of dog is not a task for someone in a great hurry.

Selective breeding is a dynamic process. Many dog breeds that have been described historically are no longer in existence, either because their particular characteristics were no longer desirable as times and conditions changed or because they did not breed true. In a way, we could say that while the genes clinging to our pet's chromosomes may have had their origin in one, many, or all of the wild canids, the living examples of dogs were designed and selected by humans to fulfil the needs and desires of our own species. No wonder dogs seem so perfectly matched to humanity's requirements and so perfectly adapted to our lives: We created them to be so. However, as this book will soon show, our creation of the many dog breeds has also created identifiable groups of animals that differ in their intelligence and in many specific mental abilities and behaviour patterns.

Chapter Three

Early Views of the Dog's Mind

A dog is not "almost human" and I know of no greater insult to the canine race than to describe it as such.

—JOHN HOLMES

A colleague of mine has pointed out that a book with the title *The Intelligence of Dogs* could be very short. He noted that, as a psychologist, I could simply choose to define *intelligence,* or at least *thought,* as something that occurs only in humans, and this would spare me a lot of work and research time. Many psychologists, biologists, and ethologists (particularly those who like to call themselves "behaviourists") do exactly this. For instance, in a recent research book entitled *Cognitive Psychology and Information Processing,* three research psychologists (R. Lachman, J. L. Lachman, and E. R. Butterfield) conclude that "whenever higher mental processes are involved, we heartily disagree that human and animal behaviour are necessarily governed by the same principles."

The situation is not simple, however, and many eminent scientists have disagreed with this rather negative conclusion. Charles Darwin, for example, wrote in *The Descent of Man* that the only difference between the intelligence of humans and that of most of their lower mammalian cousins "is one of degree and not of kind." He went on to say that "the senses and intuitions, the various emotions and faculties, such as love, memory, attention, curiosity, imitation, reason, etc., of which man boasts, may be found in an incipient or even sometimes in a well-developed condition, in the lower animals."

Obviously, neither Darwin nor any sensible person will try to say that the intelligence of dogs is the same as that of humans in all ways. There are clear limits to a dog's intelligence. A dog has never written an opera or novel nor ever designed bridges or explored cybernetic theory. No dog has ever been elected as a president or premier of a country (except in an uncomplimentary metaphoric sense, as defined by the opposition parties).

As I write this, it dawns on me that I might be wise to stay away from the subject of dogs occupying political posts, since there are stories of dog-kings. Probably the best known of these comes from an Icelandic saga that tells of an upland king known as Eystein the Bad. Eystein conquered the people of Drontheim and then made his son Onund their king. The people of Drontheim were not at all happy with this arrangement and ended Onund's reign abruptly and violently. To show his displeasure at this turn of events, Eystein returned to Drontheim, ravaged the land, and reduced the people to total subjugation. Then, to cap his vengeance, he offered the survivors a truly dishonourable choice: They would be ruled either by one of Eystein's slaves or by one of his dogs. The people of Drontheim apparently felt that they could more easily manipulate the decisions of the dog. As kings go, the dog (whose name was Saur) was apparently not a bad ruler. The saga claims that the dog "had the wisdom of three men". It also reports that the dog "spoke one word for every two that it barked", presumably meaning that it had different whimpers, growls, and other sounds that were interpreted as signifying different ideas and moods. The people responded by according the dog all the expected pomp and ceremony that are due to a ruler. They furnished him with a throne, so that he "sat upon a high place as kings are wont to sit." They also provided him with regal apparel, such as a gold collar. His attendants or courtiers, whose duty it was to carry their canine king on their shoulders whenever the weather turned bad, wore silver chains to signify their office.

Unfortunately, the story ends rather badly, with what has always appeared to me to be the culmination of some form of plot or a secret revolt against the dog-king. Obviously, such a revolt could not simply involve assassination, since this might make Eystein suspicious and cause him to return to mete out further vengeance and perhaps even to appoint a still less desirable king. Instead, the plotters capitalized on a chance occurrence. One day, wolves broke into the royal cattle pens. Instead of calling for help from the men-at-arms, the courtiers (traitors?) rallied the dog-king to defend his livestock. With all of the bravery that the sagas accord to one born into royalty, he immediately mounted an attack, but, being badly outnumbered, he was killed in battle. Thus ended the reign of Saur, the canine king.

Great literature and poetry might be written *about* dogs, but certainly never *by* them. Where, then, on the scale of animal intelligence, or in comparison to human intelligence, do dogs stand?

Scientists, like everyone else in any society, grow up with a set of attitudes that have been shaped by the cultures in which we live. Although we try to distance our theoretical or research-related thinking from the cultural, religious, and philosophical attitudes that surround us, they still influence us, sometimes in very subtle ways. The influential early American psychologist William James warned that "a great many people think they are thinking when they are merely rearranging their prejudices." We must understand that, since dogs are present nearly everywhere in our society we have developed certain attitudes toward them. These attitudes may be enshrined by religious, educational, and governmental institutions, or simply embedded in the opinions of the general public. These attitudes subtly but inevitably influence the way in which the society's scientists approach even apparently objective issues, such as the nature of dog intelligence and behaviour. For this reason, it is worthwhile to pause a moment and consider how humans have regarded dogs through history.

When I first did my training in psychology the belief was quite strong that dogs (and all other nonhuman animals) did not have consciousness. We were assured, for instance, that a beagle is not a conscious, thinking creature with self-awareness and emotional feelings but rather a beagle-shaped bag of reflexes, automatic responses, and genetic programming. We were encouraged to view dogs as simply biological machines. Dogs' learning was considered to be more like the reprogramming of reflexes, which doesn't involve consciousness any more than the reprogramming of a computer requires that the computer be consciously aware. It was not thought to credit dogs with the sorts of cognitive modifications observed in humans.

This viewpoint is due, primarily, to René Descartes, the seventeenth-century French philosopher known for his contributions to mathematics, physiology, and psychology. Descartes proposed that all animals were without consciousness, intelligence, or thoughts analogous to those found in a human mind. According to this theory, a dog is merely an animate machine. Many psychologists and physiologists subscribed to this view, and it still shows up in many scientific writings today.

Primitive people, however, had no problem allowing dogs to have intelligence and even suggested they had speech. For example, when Europeans began to colonize the African Congo, they encountered many indigenous stories about the dog as the bringer of fire, the great hunter, and even as a teacher. A typical example comes from the Nyanga people, whose folk hero Nkhango supposedly negotiated for fire with the dog Rukuba: The dog would steal some fire from the high god Nyamurairi in exchange for eternal friendship from humans. After keeping his part of the bargain, Rukuba joined with Nkhango on the hunt, and together they achieved great success, even against dangerous prey, such as the wild boar. As the dog's cleverness became more and more obvious, Nkhango learned to trust him with even more tasks. Finally, Nkhango made a decision to use the dog as a messenger. Rukuba, however, did not want to be a messenger; he wanted to lie by the fire in comfort, and, since he was the one who had supplied the fire in the first place, he felt that it was his right to do so. Musing that people would always be sending him to this place or that on errands, because he was clever and trustworthy and could speak, the dog Rukuba concluded, "If I could not speak, then I could not be a messenger. So I will simply never speak again!" From that day on, the dog of the Nyanga ceased speaking; he still has the intelligence and capacity to do so but simply chooses not to.

In the same way that primitive folk beliefs took a high level of intelligence in dogs as a given, so did the early scientists who studied animal behaviour. Prior to Descartes, scientists shared the conclusions of the Greek philosopher Aristotle, whose real interest was in life itself, not just intelligence. He felt that there were several different qualities of life and that different creatures displayed more or less of each of these qualities. The basic components of animal life involved the abilities to absorb food, to produce offspring, and to move around the environment. The remaining aspects of life, however, all had to do with mental ability, or what we loosely call the mind. These capacities included the ability to perceive the world through sense organs, the capacity to have emotions and motivations, and, finally, the intellectual capacities that include the ability to learn, to reason, and to analyse. Aristotle anticipated Darwin's view of dog intelligence which would come some fifteen hundred years later, when he argued that dogs and humans differ only in the degree to which they possess certain mental abilities. Humans and dogs both have emotions, but human emotions are more complex. Humans and dogs both learn, remember, solve problems, and benefit from experience, but humans do better at each of these things.

Aristotle's reasoning was influential, and many great thinkers accepted his views, among them Saint Thomas Aquinas, one of the most influential Roman Catholic philosophers. In the thirteenth century, Aquinas established as formal church doctrine the idea that humans and animals differ only quantitatively (in the degree to which their mental abilities express themselves), rather than qualitatively (in the specific nature of those mental processes). This led to some complications, because philosophers from this era tended to view intelligence and consciousness simply as aspects of the spiritual entity we call the soul. Thus for some scholars, particularly those in the Christian church, accepting that dogs (or other animals) had intelligence was tantamount to conceding that they also have souls. Such a conclusion was simply unacceptable to many theologians and intellectuals of the time.

The insertion of religion into the issue of animal intelligence was unfortunate. It subtly biased some of the scientific thinking about dog psychology and particularly thinking about dog intelligence.

DOGS AND RELIGION

Many religions have something to say about dogs. When most religions speak about dogs, they tend to use them as symbols of good or evil or in the roles of helpers, companions, or guards. Few comment about dogs' intelligence or mental abilities, although some beliefs about this issue are implicit in various tales.

Judaism and the Dog

The ancient Hebrews considered all dogs to be utterly unclean, because the most commonly encountered dogs—namely, the pariah dogs—were scavengers. Living outside the walls of the cities, pariah dogs subsisted on refuse, garbage, and even human corpses. An example of this appears in the story of Jezebel. According to the Bible, the wife of King Ahab reintroduced idolatry in the form of the worship of the god Baal. Queen Jezebel, who later came to epitomize the ultimate wicked woman, counted among her sins defiance of the great prophets Elijah and Elisha and rejection of God's commands. As punishment, she was thrown off the city wall and left for the dogs to devour. While this appears to have been a bizarre, unique event, there was nothing unusual about throwing dead bodies to the pariah dogs—especially if the bodies were those of criminals or the poor that had been unclaimed by friends or relatives.

Any contact with a corpse was ritually defiling for the Israelites, partially because of religious beliefs but also because of health reasons—contact with a body whose death had been due to disease could pass on infection. Thus the Hebrews concluded that any animal that fed on such unclean sources must itself be unclean. It is likely that an additional point against the dog was that they were worshipped and otherwise held in high esteem in Egypt. The gods of your enemies easily become the devils of your own religion.

Despite all this, Judaism does hold some positive opinions about dogs. The Talmud, the accepted authority for Orthodox Jews everywhere, says that the dog, despite its uncleanness, should be tolerated. It is claimed that dogs' access to ritually unclean food was the reward God granted them in return for their silence (which kept Pharaoh's guards from being alerted) on the night the Israelites began their exodus from Egypt. Perhaps the most positive statement about dogs in the Talmud is the suggestion that the sign of protection that God gave to Cain was a dog.

The Talmud Yerushalmi (a commentary on biblical scriptures that was compiled around A.D. 5) is one of the few Hebrew texts that discussed the intelligence of dogs. It notes that dogs differ from cats in that they recognize and acknowledge their owners while cats do not. The dog is recognized for its fidelity to people and commitment to their welfare. For instance, one of Rabbi Meir's fables in the Talmud tells the story of a shepherd's dog who had observed a snake dripping venomous poison from its mouth into a bowl of curdled milk that was about to be served to its master and a group of other shepherds. When the man prepared to serve the meal, the dog circled the bowl, barking frantically, but the shepherd did not understand the warnings. As he reached for the poisoned food, the dog made a desperate dash for it, gulping it down in one or two great swallows. The result was that the dog died in agony but saved its master and the other men. In grateful acknowledgment of this heroism, the shepherds buried the faithful dog with honours and prayers.

Christianity and the Dog

Christianity inherited some of Judaism's negative attitudes toward the dog, but they have been much diluted by many positive tales of the dog in popular versions of religious lore. For instance, since the Christian account of the birth of Jesus is associated with shepherds, and shepherds require dogs, dogs are often shown in nativity scenes, where they impart no hint of uncleanness. One tale from Granada claims that three dogs followed the three shepherds into Bethlehem. There, they found the infant Jesus and had the chance to gaze on him. The dogs' names were Cubilon, Lubina, and Melampo. My informant told me that many people in Granada still give their dogs these names as a sort of good luck charm.

The most common view of the dog in Christianity is as a faithful companion. In the Old Testament apocryphal Book of Tobit, Tobias sets off on a trek to collect a debt to help his blind father, accompanied by the angel Raphael and a small dog. After all the adventures have finished, he returns home, the dog running ahead to announce his arrival. Tradition maintains that this dog even preceded Tobias into heaven. This story accounts for the sustained popularity of the name Toby for dogs.

The stories of a number of Christian saints also are bound up with dogs. In some cases, the references are significant but not focal to the saint's life. The legend of Saint Margaret of Cortona tells of a beautiful peasant girl living in central Italy who, at the age of seventeen, was seduced by a young nobleman. Devoted Margaret lived with her lover for nine years, during which she bore him a son, but her idyll ended when the nobleman apparently disappeared. The nobleman's dog, however, never stopped searching for its master. Eventually, he found the body of the murdered man. Seeking to inform Margaret, the dog grabbed the hem of her skirt and pulled until she followed it to the place where her lover lay dead. Devastated, Margaret returned to her family home, there to meet with rejection because of her sinful and immoral relationship with the nobleman. In penitence, she took the veil and led a life of extreme piety, which eventually led to her sanctification. The dog remained with her throughout its life, serving as a comfort and companion. Traditional artistic representations of Saint Margaret usually include the dog pulling at her hem or on a leash by her side (see Figure 3.1).

Figure 3.1
Margaret of Cortona, one of the many Christian saints whose lives were affected by the devotion and fidelity of dogs.

In other instances, the dog is shown to be extremely sensitive to the holiness of some particular saint or sage. Consider Patrick MacAlpern, later Saint Patrick, whose life was strangely entwined with dogs. Around A.D. 400, at age sixteen, Patrick was abducted from a Scottish coastal village by Irish marauders. He was enslaved and kept as a shepherd for six years, his sole companion being a dog. In response to a dream, he made his way some two hundred miles to the coast, where he found the ship that the dream foretold would return him to his own land.

The ship was from Gaul, and the master had put into Irish waters in order to get a cargo of hunting hounds, which were bringing fabulous prices on European markets. Not surprisingly, as a penniless runaway slave, Patrick was received rather unsympathetically when he tried to gain passage. However, just as he was leaving, he was suddenly called back. It seems that, to maximize his profit, the captain had opted for stealing, rather than purchasing, his cargo of dogs. Over one hundred great Irish wolfhounds now packed the holds and filled the deck of the ship. Taken from their masters and their familiar surroundings, the giant dogs were frantic and furious, ready to savage anyone who came near. Some of the sailors had noticed that during Patrick's brief visit to the ship, he had spoken with some of the dogs and seemed to have a calming effect on them. Therefore, in exchange for his services—which would involve feeding, cleaning up after, and otherwise caring for the dogs—Patrick received passage to the continent (see Figure 3.2).

The ship was badly underprovisioned and reached a ruined and deserted section of Gaul with its stores exhausted and nothing left to feed dogs or men. Because the dogs were worth more than the ship, the crew took the animals, abandoned the ship, and set off on foot, heading inland. Finding no inhabitants or food in the area, the dogs and men were soon all in jeopardy of dying of starvation. The shipmaster, who had learned that Patrick was a Christian, turned to him and in a taunting manner said, "If your god is so great, then pray to him to send us food." Patrick did so, and, the story goes, a miracle occurred. A herd of wild pigs appeared, seemingly from nowhere. Instead of bolting and running, as one might have expected, the swine stayed within reach long enough for the starving men, with the assistance of the dogs, to kill a number of them, providing meat for all. Predictably, Patrick's reputation rose considerably, and, after the dogs were marketed, the crew made a gift to him of some food and a bit of money to help him on his way.

St. Patrick's association with dogs did not end in Gaul. Many years later, after a number of adventures, he returned to Ireland. This time it was of his own free will, and his goal was to preach Christianity. On his return, his rapport with dogs came to the fore again. It seems the news that a strange ship had just landed, from which had emerged white-robed men with clean-shaven heads who chanted in a strange tongue, prompted an Irish prince named Dichu to go to the coast to investigate the situation, accompanied by his favorite large hunting hound. Observing St. Patrick's missionary group, Dichu decided that the best course was to kill these odd clerics and be done with it. With a wave and a shout, he set his dog at Patrick. The dog leapt forward in full fury, but when Patrick uttered a short, one-sentence prayer, the dog halted, grew quiet, and then approached Patrick and nuzzled his

Figure 3.2
A fanciful rendition of the ship filled with dogs that took St. Patrick to freedom.

hand. Dichu was touched by this scene and, in the end, aided Patrick's mission in Ireland in many ways.

The point of these stories seems to be that the dogs could somehow sense and respond to Patrick's piety. According to Irish folklore, Saint Patrick repaid dogs for their deference to him by allowing the legendary character Oissain (the son of the hero Finn MacCumhail) to take his hounds to heaven with him when died, where we can suppose that they are keeping Tobias's little dog company.

Other stories of saints place the dog more squarely in the spotlight as examples to be admired. There is, for instance, the well-known history of Saint Roche, whose life was saved by the faithful dog who brought him loaves of bread and tended to him when he was sick with plague. Less well known, but much more contemporary, is the story of Saint John Bosco, who lived almost to the twentieth century, dying in 1888. Bosco's life revolved around his efforts to shelter, rehabilitate, and educate homeless youths. To continue this effort, he created the Salesian order. The dog who plays a role in all this was a huge, hulking grey mongrel by the name of Grigio. Grigio's pedigree, parentage, and origin were as obscure as those of the many homeless children whom the man who came to be known as Don John tended to gather around him. Grigio simply appeared from nowhere and appointed himself Don John's bodyguard. One day, John was walking through one of the narrow streets in the Vadocco section of Turin, near the spot where he had opened his first hospice. Suddenly, a thug leapt out of nowhere, grabbed the saint, and demanded money. Don John virtually never had any money of his own, because all he obtained went immediately to the waifs he was trying to help, but when he denied having anything to give his attacker, the thief began to get very nasty, brandishing a knife and threatening John with mortal consequences if he didn't produce some money quickly. Suddenly, Grigio appeared—a savage grey blur that hurled itself at the thief, knocking him down and away from John. Then, snarling, he reeled to interpose himself between John and his attacker. The thug thought better of pursuing his original course and rapidly disappeared down the street.

After this first encounter, Grigio adopted Don John. From that moment on, he was always at hand when John was in danger, which apparently was quite often. Several times Grigio defended John from attack, always placing himself between the saint and the threat, and once he warned him of an ambush that had been set to assassinate him. Grigio would materialize at times of need, stay awhile to ensure that all was well, and then disappear for days. He was a guard and companion when Don John needed him most.

Ultimately, the Salesian order began to succeed. At long last, Don John convinced the Garibaldi government that he could be trusted to run his schools. His educational and other projects were safe from interference and functioning well. Now the general public, the government, the local residents, the homeless children, and even the criminal element no longer treated Don John as a threat. Rather, they recognized his altruistic motives and protected him from harm. Obviously, Grigio's heroic services were no longer needed. As the saint sat in the refectory one evening at dinner time, Grigio came to him once more. He rubbed his head against Don John's habit, licked his hand quietly, and then lifted up one tentative paw and placed it on John's knee. Then, without a sound, the great grey dog turned and wandered out into the night. Grigio was never seen again after that.

Islam and the Dog

Islamic tradition also begins with a negative view of the dog, but here the situation is complex, mixed with many positive elements. As in Judaism and Christianity, dogs are generally considered to be unclean, with the stigma arising from the scavenging pariah dogs. For Islamic fundamentalists, to be touched by a dog is to be defiled and requires an act of purification. A bowl from which a dog has eaten or drunk must be washed seven times and scrubbed in earth before it is again fit for human use.

Packs of pariah dogs were a major problem in many Islamic centers. They carried rabies and various other diseases, but it was recognized that their scavenging filled an important function. Thus Xavier Marmier wrote in the mid-nineteenth century that "disagreeable as these animals may be, in the state of Constantinople they are practically a necessary evil. Rectifying the lack of foresight of the city police, they cleanse the streets of a great quantity of matter which otherwise would putrefy and fill the air with pestilential germs."

The prophet Mohammed was once confronted with the problem of stray dogs overrunning the city of Medina. At first, Mohammed took the uncompromising position that all the dogs should be exterminated. On reflection, however, he mitigated his decree, for two major reasons. The first was religious: Canines constituted a race of Allah's creatures, and He who created the race should be the only one to dictate that it should be removed from the earth. The second, more pragmatic, was that some categories of dogs, particularly guard dogs, hunting dogs, and shepherd dogs, were useful to humans and had hence earned their right to exist. (Some legends say that the Prophet himself actually owned a saluki that he used for hunting.) In the end the Prophet concluded that only black stray dogs, particularly those with light patches near the eyebrows (a clear mark of the devil to Arabs), would be exterminated.

Perhaps the greatest acknowledgment to a dog in Islam comes from the story of the Seven Sleepers, which is told in the Koran (although Christian versions of it exist as well). During the short reign of the Roman emperor Decius around A.D. 250, Christians and other nonbelievers were systematically persecuted, in an effort to strengthen the state-supported religion. In the city of Ephesus (now in western Turkey), seven faithful young men fled to a cave on Mount Coelius. The pet dog of one followed them in their flight. Once in the cave, some of the men feared that the dog—Kitmir by name—might bark and reveal their hiding place, and they tried to drive it away. At this point, God granted the dog the gift of speech, and he said, "I love those who are dear unto God. Go to sleep, therefore, and I will guard you." After the men had settled down to sleep, leaning on the back wall of the cave, the dog stretched out with his forelegs facing the entrance and began his watch.

When Decius learned that religious refugees were hiding in some of the local caves, he ordered that all the entrances be sealed with stone. Kitmir maintained his vigil, even while the cave was being sealed, and made sure that no one disturbed the sleepers. The men were forgotten, and they slept for 309 years. When they were finally awakened by workers excavating a section of the mountain, the dog finally stirred and allowed his charges to return to the world, which was now safe for their faith. According to Muslim tradition, the dog Kitmir was admitted to paradise upon his death.

Folk Religion and the Dog

Some common beliefs about dogs are so widespread that they defy classification in a specific religion. Judaism, Christianity, Islam, and Hinduism, for example, all hold that dogs are sensitive to the onset of death. The howling of a dog is often taken as a death omen. When I was training with the army in Kentucky, an old woman whom I only knew as Aunt Lila told me that if a dog gives two howls close together, it signifies that death is coming for a man; three howls mean that a woman is going to die. "Dogs look in the direction of the person about to die," she said. "My daddy said it was good luck to have a dog howl with his back to you."

Many other tales link dogs with death. A family dog in Mexico is believed to howl as it sees the devil fighting with the guardian angel of a dying person for possession of his soul. In the Wild Hunt in Wales, a ghostly rider and his pack of spirit hounds come to claim the soul of some poor unfortunate. Rather than cataloguing any more of these folk beliefs, I would like to recount a tale told to me by my Eastern European grandparents. The story contains elements common to many folk conceptions of dogs and provides a typical example of how we acquire some of our attitudes toward dogs.

One early evening when I was about six or seven years of age, my dog Skipper (whom I remember as a beagle) began to whimper unaccountably. He was looking with great discomfort at one end of the room where nothing seemed out of place. I was at home with only my maternal grandparents at the time. My grandmother, Lena, looked up from her knitting and watched Skipper for a few moments. Then she turned to me and said, "He sees the Angel of Death. The angel's name is Azrael. When Azrael comes or goes, dogs can see him. They say that dogs have spirit sight and can see devils and angels and ghosts. You can see them, too, at least sometimes, if you look where the dog is looking. In order to see clearly, you have to look right over the top of the dog's head and through the space between his ears."

My grandfather, Jacob, who had been listening, lit one of the cigars that were his passion in life and took up the story from there.

"If he is a brave dog and if he really loves a person, he will bark. When a dog barks, it calls the prophet Elijah. Elijah will sometimes step in to save a good person from the Angel of Death. Sometimes the barking wakes the ghosts of family members who have died, and they come to fight Azrael and to try to protect their loved ones. Other times the noise convinces the Black Angel that he'll have a strong fight on his hands, and he simply goes away to try to sneak back some other time when he can get the job done without any trouble.

"No matter what, though, you should never stop a dog from barking, since he may be trying to save the life of someone in the family— maybe even yours. When you hear your dog bark, you should make sure that a door or a window is open a crack so Elijah and the good ghosts can get in and so that if Azrael wants to make a quick run out of the house he can do it."

My grandfather took a long puff of his cigar and studied the ember at the end of it as if there were writing in it. Then, adjusting himself a little, he went on.

"They say that the reason dogs have such a short life is that sometimes Azrael won't give up and decides to take the soul anyway. When that happens, good dogs will try to stop the Angel of Death from touching someone they love. When dogs do this, they look like they are growling and snarling and barking at nothing, but what they are really doing is putting themselves between their master and the angel. If he keeps coming, some dogs will actually try to jump up and bite him, while others will just block the way. Unfortunately, one touch from Azrael kills them either fast or slow. You know, it's a really brave thing that dogs do, and what's more, it usually works. You see, the Angel of Death can only carry one life with him at a time. So when his hands are filled with the dog's soul, he has to run back and drop it off. Of course, this means that he is going home without his real victim. Anyway—and here is the good part—because old Azrael has taken a life (remember, that's his real job in the first place), he gets to cross a name off his list. I don't know whether that angel likes dogs to begin with or maybe just appreciates how brave they are, but it seems that he often just crosses off the name of the fellow that owned the dog. That means that unless God draws up a new list soon, Azrael won't be coming back for that person for quite a while. So even though it sometimes goes bad for the dog, it means that the one the dog loved and tried to protect is usually saved."

I remember a great surge of panic as I dived across the room to grab my dog, shouting in my tiny voice, "No! Skippy, don't touch him! It's OK—we'll just run away!" while my grandparents looked on with somewhat bemused expressions.

Obviously, although religious views of the dog may be both positive and negative, and frequently the same faith will mix attitudes, the original consensus was that dogs had intelligence, reason, and consciousness; otherwise, there would have been no point to the many tales of devotion and bravery told about them. It was also agreed that animals' qualities of mind were similar to those of human beings, just not as sharp or powerful. In other words, the mental difference between humans and beasts was assumed to be quantitative rather than qualitative.

A while ago Bruce Fogle, a veterinarian who has written extensively about dog behaviour, conducted a survey among a group of British veterinarians to determine some of their religious ideas and beliefs and how these related to their views of dogs. First, he asked the veterinarians about their attitudes toward life and the afterlife. He found that veterinarians constituted a very sceptical group of scientifically minded professionals. In fact, only two out of every five believed that human beings have an immortal soul and that this soul lives on in an afterlife. Among this group of believing veterinarians, fully half also subscribed to the notion that dogs have immortal souls and are entitled to reside in an afterlife. A year later, Fogle had the opportunity to give the same survey to a group of practicing Japanese veterinarians. Japanese culture has been much influenced by the traditions of Buddhism and Shintoism, which are much more liberal in their views of the soul than are Western religions and tend to grant some form of consciousness and sanctity to almost every living thing. In this Japanese survey sample, every single veterinarian granted the existence of a soul and an afterlife to the dog!

This argument over whether the dog has a soul generates the controversy that ultimately divides psychologists, biologists, and others interested in the behaviour of dogs into two warring camps over apparently objective scientific questions of the nature and extent of the dog's intelligence, consciousness, and ability to reason.

Chapter Four

Modern Views of the Dog's Mind

Dogs are not people dressed up in fur coats, and to deny
them their nature is to do them great harm.

—JEANNE SCHINTO

By the time René Descartes turned his mind to the issue of animal
intelligence, the Christian ecclesiastical establishment had reconsid-
ered its views about animals' intelligence and consciousness. Although
they had previously accepted Aristotle's viewpoint and maintained it
through the time of St. Augustine, it now seemed to raise certain problems; it now seemed that if the Church conceded that animals possessed *any* aspects of mind, it might have to acknowledge that they
possessed *all* aspects, including a spiritual life and a soul. And if animals have souls, then they are candidates for an afterlife, including
heaven.

This prospect of animals with souls caused many problems. While
one might accept the presence of a favourite dog (or even a cat) in
heaven, the idea that cattle, pigs, flies, and spiders would all be present on the Day of Judgment was too much for Church doctrine to
accommodate. A heaven occupied by such a collection of souls would
fill to overflowing, and such an afterlife would not hold out adequate
promise of a blissful existence to keep congregations on the straight
and narrow path of virtue during their earthly years. In addition, the

existence of the animal soul would raise a whole series of ethical problems pertaining to the practice of killing animals for food, denying them free will by forcing them into servitude, granting them access to the church and baptism, and this would lead to philosophical and theological chaos.

During Descartes's era, the Church controlled most research and scholarship. It had great power, including the ability to suppress ideas that it did not like and to bring very strong sanctions against anyone who disagreed with church doctrine. The scholars of the time yielded to this pressure and thus denied the possibility that animals had souls. For the sake of consistency, withholding one aspect of mind from animals meant they had to withhold them all; rejecting the possibility that animals had souls, in order to prevent a population crisis in heaven and a philosophical problem on earth, they also had to reject the possibility that animals had intelligence, emotions, consciousness, and all the other aspects of mind.

THE MECHANICAL DOG

Descartes, always sensitive to the requirements and beliefs of the Church, adopted its position wholeheartedly in his *Discourse on Method*. Having accepted the basic premise of the soulless beast, he turned his powerful mind to justifying the position on scientific, philosophical, and theological grounds. He began by belittling those who might reach the opposite conclusion, noting that, as errors go, "there is none more powerful in leading feeble minds astray from the straight path of virtue than the supposition that the soul of brutes is of the same nature with our own."

Descartes's goal was to prove the hypothesis that animals were simply machines, with no consciousness and no intelligence. He was convinced that this was a reasonable position after observing the automated life-size statues in the royal gardens of Saint-Germain-en-Laye, the birthplace and home of Louis XIV. Constructed by the Italian engineer Thomas Francini, each statue was a clever piece of machinery powered by hydraulics and carefully geared to perform a complex sequence of actions. In one grotto, a figure of the mythological Greek musician Orpheus made beautiful music on his lyre. As he played, birds sang and animals capered and danced around him. In another grotto, the hero Perseus fought with a dragon; when he struck the dragon's head, it was forced to sink into the water. The action of the figures was triggered when visitors stepped on particular tiles on the pathway. The pressure of their steps tripped valves that then permitted water to rush through networks of pipes in the statues and cause them to move.

In the *Treatise on Man*, published in 1664, Descartes draws a parallel between the human body and the animated statues, or *automata*, in the royal gardens. He reasons that the nerves of the human body and the motive power provided by them are equivalent to the pipes and water contained in the statues. He compares the heart to the source of the water, the various cavities of the brain with the storage tanks, and the muscles with the gears, springs, and pulleys that moved the various parts of the statues.

Descartes reasons that in some ways the human body is like one of these statues, moving in predictable ways and governed by mechanical principles. However, no matter how complex the movements of any machine might be and no matter how variable and intricate the engineers have made its behaviour, a machine will always differ from a human being: Human beings not only have bodies (controlled by mechanics) but also souls (controlled by the spirit). To have a soul or a mind is to have the capacity to think and to be conscious. According to Descartes, then, the difference between humans and machines is that humans think and machines do not.

Now Descartes makes the final leap, arguing that animals are really only biological machines. He asserts that everything in animal behaviour could be reproduced mechanically. No matter how complex, animal activity goes on without any consciousness or thought. After all, we don't need consciousness to control our heartbeat; it is an activity of the machine part of our existence, as is digestion or breathing or many other functions of the body. Even some activities that seem to require reason and intelligence do not really require or use consciousness (when you quickly withdraw your hand from a hot surface, for example, it is without any voluntary or conscious command to your muscles to do so; indeed, the sensation of pain generally occurs *after* its cause has already been removed). According to Descartes, this is the only level at which animals work. Their basic bodily functions and apparent responsiveness to their environment have nothing to do with consciousness, intelligence, self-awareness, or a soul.

Descartes offered many so-called proofs that animals are simply soulless machines. An example is when the Marchioness of Newcastle raised an argument that Darwin would offer two centuries later. She asked Descartes to consider the possibility that animals with organs similar to humans' might have thoughts similar to humans' "but of a very much less perfect kind." Rather than addressing the issue on the basis of evidence, he simply found a way to restate his basic conclusion. In a letter written to the marchioness on November 23, 1646, he said, "I have nothing to reply except that if they [animals] thought as we do, they would have an immortal soul like us. This is unlikely because there is no reason to believe it of some animals without believing it of all, and many of them, such as oysters and sponges, are too imperfect for this to be credible."

This is an odd argument: It says, if an oyster can't think, then a dog can't either, because both are animals. Wouldn't a reasonable extension of this argument be, if a dog can't think, then neither can a human, for they, too, are both animals? Furthermore, the marchioness's question related to animals that have organs like ours—as dogs do and oysters do not. If similarity is the issue, couldn't Descartes as easily have reversed his argument to say, if a human can think, then so must a dog, because both animals have similar types of organs? For that matter, if physiological resemblance is proof of spiritual similarity, then a human's ability to think can have no implications for the oyster, since they are physically so different. Descartes chose not to consider those alternate arguments.

Descartes's other arguments are based on two tests that can be used to distinguish thinking beings from simple machines. The first is based on the argument that only a conscious rational being can use language creatively. Descartes argues that no animal is capable of "arranging various words together and forming an utterance from them." Contrasted to animals, even the dumbest people can at least use language to express their thoughts. He concludes that "this shows not merely that the beasts have less reason than men, but that they have no reason at all." Chapter 6 of this book delves into the question of dog language and communication, with results that might have startled Descartes.

The second test concerns creative action. Animals and machines can do only what they are designed to do. In the royal gardens, the statue of Orpheus will never spontaneously turn and wave at the visitor; it can only follow the fixed pattern of strumming on the lyre. Conscious beings, however, can vary their actions through reasoning processes. Descartes says that "although many animals show more skill than we do in some of their actions, yet the same animals show none at all in many others," suggesting a lack of flexible response to the situations around them. He continues that animals "have no intelligence at all, and that it is nature which acts in them according to the disposition of their organs" in the same way that the gears and pulleys fix the action of the moving statues.

Descartes clearly didn't do the sort of systematic observation of animal behaviour necessary to test his hypothesis adequately. There are many examples of situations where dogs show creative action. One account comes from a friend of mine who had a fox terrier named Charger. While making some café au lait for breakfast, my friend found that he had heated too much milk and decided to offer the excess to Charger (who was then just a puppy) as a treat. He poured some in a saucer and placed it on the floor. Unfortunately, he had forgotten just how hot the milk was, and when the dog began to lap at it, he scalded his tongue. From that day onward, whenever he was presented with a dish of milk, Charger would first approach it and very gingerly put his paw into the saucer, apparently to see if the liquid was too hot. Only when he was satisfied that it was not, would he touch it with his tongue. Certainly such behaviour is not part of the fixed-action patterns of most dogs but rather shows memory, anticipation of possible consequences, and an adaptive response to a situation.

Another tale told to me involves a great black Newfoundland dog named Peggy who was living alone with a young woman. One day, a friend of theirs came to visit and brought along her own dog, a tiny white Maltese (whose name I never learned). The Maltese was clearly in a frisky mood and nipped around the Newfoundland several times, offering to play by making hyperactive dashes between the larger dog's paws. At one point, the little white beast dashed toward the big dog, and Peggy, apparently getting annoyed, simply dropped one large paw over the Maltese's back. With the small dog pinned to the floor, quiet reigned in the room for a few minutes. The little dog would not, however, stay put and eventually wriggled free. Loosed from her confinement, she became even more dynamic and active in her play. Finally, Peggy could take the pestering no longer. She stood up, and, as the

Maltese went streaking in front of her, she reached down and grabbed the small dog by the scruff of her neck in much the same way a bitch will carry her pups. The white dog instantly went limp, probably from fear, and while the two women watched in amazement, the Newfoundland strode out of the room with her burden. Peggy walked deliberately to the bathroom, which contained one of those old-fashioned bathtubs that stand on lion's paws and have very high sides. She dropped the little dog in the tub and watched for a few moments while the Maltese tried, without success, to jump out. Then she turned, walked back to her resting place in the center of the living room, settled back into a comfortable position, and fell asleep, while the two watching women convulsed with laughter. Certainly, of all the myriad actions that one might imagine the dog using to solve the problem of her annoying guest, this was one of the most creative, and nonviolent, that the dog could have hit upon.

ETHICAL CONSEQUENCES

Unfortunately, when Descartes threw out intellect, reason, and consciousness for animals, it had more than scientific and intellectual consequences. In denying animals these higher mental abilities, Descartes also denied them feeling and emotion. According to him, the cry an animal releases when struck does not indicate pain but is rather the equivalent of the clanging of springs or chimes you might hear after you drop a mechanical clock or some wind-up toy. Nicolas de Malebranche, a French philosopher who extended Descartes's work, picked up on this idea when he claimed that animals "eat without pleasure, cry without pain, act without knowing it; they desire nothing, fear nothing, know nothing."

The upshot was that Descartes's analysis was subsequently used to justify massive cruelty to animals. Bernard le Bovier de Fontenelle once visited Malebranche at the Oratory on the rue Saint-Honoré. While they were conversing, he saw Malebranche kick a pregnant dog who had been rolling at his feet. The dog let out a cry of pain, and Fontenelle sprang forward to defend it. Malebranche passed the incident off, saying "Don't you know that it does not feel?" In due time, such reasoning led to experiments where animals were nailed to boards by their four paws in order to do surgery on them to see the circulatory system working in a live being. People who pitied the poor creatures for their pain were laughed at as unknowing fools. After all, these were not to be considered sentient and feeling creatures; they were only machines being disassembled for study. Accordingly, moral concern was inappropriate, since the pain and suffering of animals were not real.

One might be tempted to dismiss these attitudes as the unenlightened thinking of the past. However, viewpoints just this extreme are still found today, nearly three hundred fifty years after Descartes's theorizing. For instance, P. Carruthers, in the prestigious *Journal of Philosophy*, recently wrote of animals that, "since their experiences, including their pains, are nonconscious ones, their pains are of no immediate moral concern. Indeed, since all of the mental states of brutes are nonconscious, their injuries are lacking even in indirect moral concern."

It is interesting to note that scientists and philosophers with these views often act and believe quite differently in their personal lives. The extreme notion that only humans have consciousness and intelligence and that only human pain and suffering is of any significance is apparently much more difficult to hold in private life, especially if one is living with a pet animal. For example, history tells us that Descartes had a dog named Monsieur Grat—quite a pampered pet, to whom Descartes spoke in the same manner that we speak to our own dogs. He worried about the dog's health and referred to things that the dog liked or did not like and sometimes privately speculated on what the dog might be thinking. So much concern for an unconscious machine? Would one talk to a machine such as a wristwatch and speculate on its health and its likes? Obviously, in Descartes's everyday interactions, the presumption of consciousness for his dog was not only convenient, but perhaps unavoidable.

THE BEHAVIORIST POSITION

Having been an experimental psychologist for all my professional life, I have interacted with many ardently committed researchers who call themselves behaviourists—the heirs to the philosophical legacy of Descartes. They have a basically mechanistic viewpoint of behaviour, though in modern science the machinery is controlled by neurons, muscles, and hormones. The very term *behaviourist* indicates an approach to animal actions that focuses on externally observable movement patterns rather than on internal states. Words like *desire, intention, reason,* and others that might suggest conscious thought are excluded from the professional vocabulary of the behaviourist.

Some historians of science argue that behaviourism is not just a positive response to the philosophical position held by Descartes but also a response to a scientific embarrassment that did a lot to discredit a number of psychologists in the eyes of other scientists. The incident occurred early in the twentieth century and centred on a performing horse. Clever Hans, as he was often referred to, was advertised as the ultimate thinking horse, one that could actually do mathematics. To demonstrate the animal's intelligence, his handler would first present the horse with a mathematical problem—simple addition, subtraction, multiplication, or division—usually by writing it on a card. The horse would then do the computation and indicate the answer by tapping the ground. Many famous psychologists of the day were convinced that the horse was indeed doing some sort of mental arithmetic, and they used Hans's performance as a prime example of animal consciousness and reasoning.

There were some sceptics, of course, and some problems. For instance, Hans took just about the same amount of time to solve difficult problems that he took to solve simple ones, which seemed odd. At first, some thought that the handler was engaging in some sort of trickery. However, when someone whom Hans had never seen before gave him a problem, he could solve it just as easily and as accurately, even if the handler was out of sight. For many scientists, this seemed to confirm the horse's intelligence. Several world-renowned psychologists wrote papers indicating their belief in the higher mental abilities of Hans. But in 1911, Oskar Pfungst, a less-renowned psychologist, collected some data that burst the bubble. In a series of carefully conducted experiments, Pfungst was able to show that Hans was not actually looking at the written numbers. What then was he doing? It appears that Hans was actually watching the people who presented him with problems and responding to the inconspicuous signals that they would make unconsciously as they were watching him and waiting to see if he stopped after the correct number of taps. Even when people deliberately tried to hide their responses by standing still or attempting to control their facial expressions, Hans still seemed capable of picking up subtle clues from their reactions, and he used these to respond correctly. If no person was visible to the horse or if the person presenting the problem didn't know the answer, Hans simply tapped his foot a random number of times.

The whole sequence of events, especially the part where famous scientists were apparently hoodwinked by a horse into thinking that the animal had special intelligence, became an embarrassment to the field of psychology. When I was a student, the case of Clever Hans would always be brought up by my professors as the definitive example of how any conclusion that suggested higher mental abilities in animals was apt to lead only to humiliation and disgrace. It was not until many years later that it dawned on me that this application of scientific caution had been blown up beyond what was warranted and had now become the basis for denying that animals have even the slightest conscious thought. The fact that a horse could not do mental arithmetic had been expanded into the conclusion that animals had no ability to think or reason at all. I remember an incident in the classroom when one student asked, after hearing the Clever Hans story, "Couldn't the horse still have consciousness? We know that he can't do arithmetic, but couldn't he be thinking something like 'I'll keep tapping my foot until that man smiles and then I'll stop and it will please him.' Wouldn't that kind of conscious thinking still be consistent with the results?" The professor dismissed the question with the response, "That doesn't require consciousness; that's just responding to stimulus cues."

In retrospect, it seems to me that one major unstated motivation for the mechanistic nature of behaviourist reasoning ever since this incident has been to avoid getting duped by another Clever Hans. The possibility that psychologists might be making the opposite error—or, to use the old cliché, throwing out the baby with the bath water—by not recognizing conscious mental activity when they encounter it seemed not to concern behaviouristically oriented psychologists.

The scientific behaviourist's notion that animals are mere machines seems to be confined to the laboratory and the analysis of the scientific studies that emanate from them. As in the case of Descartes and his dog, the view that dogs lack consciousness seems to drop away when the behaviourist leaves the laboratory. Virtually all the dog-owning behaviouristic biologists and psychologists that I have known seem to think of their personal pets much the same way as do nonscientific dog owners. When dealing with their own pets and everyday situations, rather than with laboratory animals and experimental situations, behaviouristic psychologists seem to find it perfectly understandable—and, in fact, probably quite necessary—to attribute conscious mental states to their own dogs. I am not saying this to scoff at the inconsistency of some of my scientific colleagues but rather to point out that the presumption of consciousness in dogs and other animals seems to work even for those who have a stake in denying it publicly.

The simple fact is we seem to understand our animals quite a bit better if we accept the fact that they have simple feelings, fears, desires, and beliefs, make plans, have goals, and the like. How can anyone live with a dog without thinking, "The dog is thirsty and wants some water", when it stands over an empty water dish, barks, and then pushes it toward you with its nose? How can one avoid thinking, "The dog wants to go out", when your dog barks at you and paws at the front door? How many other such phrases crop up? "The dog is in pain." "The dog really likes children." "The dog wants to play." "The dog dislikes my mother-in-law." "The dog is happy." "The dog misses our daughter." "The dog doesn't like that brand of dog food." "The dog is acting like that because he expects dinner soon." The list goes on and on. Terms such as *likes*, *wants*, *misses*, *expects*, and so forth all imply an inner mental life and consciousness.

If such mentalistic descriptions are not scientifically valid according to the psychological theories of behaviourists, why do we find these same brilliant scientists using them to describe their own dogs or even animals in the laboratory when not writing scientific reports? The answer is, because these terms and mentalistic analyses have predictive and explanatory power. They allow us to select actions that will change the behaviour of our dogs in predictable ways. Suppose that we did not use them but instead held to a strict behaviourist viewpoint. This would mean that we could not allow any consideration of conscious experiences or thought but rather would have to speak in terms of simple responses to stimulus inputs and instinctual and genetic programming. Under such circumstances, I doubt that we could make any sense at all of dog behaviour.

Consider the following simple sequence of behaviour described to me by one dog owner. The behaviour begins with her dog (a springer spaniel named Rowdy) going to their hall closet. The closet has a sliding door, which the dog paws open. Next, Rowdy grabs hold of the leash, which is hanging on a hook. Since the hand loop is over the top of the hook, the dog has to jump up and snap its head to the side to dislodge it. The leash in his mouth, he then walks into the living room, where his owner is sitting. If Rowdy's mistress does not appear to notice the dog sitting there, the spaniel drops the leash and barks. As his owner looks up, he picks up the leash and drops it in her lap, prances a few steps toward the door, and barks again. If Rowdy's owner still doesn't move, the spaniel walks back to her, grabs one end of the leash in his mouth, shakes it once or twice, drops it, barks again, and repeats the little dance toward the front door. The simplest description of this behaviour is obvious: The dog wants to go for a walk and knows how to communicate his desires to his owner.

Pity the poor behaviourist, however, who has to describe this string of actions. A pure behavioural description can't allow the use of any form of intention, and the dog can't have a goal held in consciousness that guides the behaviour. The behaviourist, at least in scientific discourse, can't refer to any mental consideration of where the leash is, any conscious plan to get it off the hook, any imagery of where its master might be, any conceptualization of cause and effect that might initiate the sequence of the dog's moving back and forth between master and door to stimulate his master to take him out for a walk. Instead, stimuli that trigger automatic and mechanical responses must be used, along with simple learned sequences with no conscious components. Just what is the stimulus that triggers the "go for a walk" sequence? Perhaps a full bladder? If so, then the dog should simply relieve himself on the spot, shouldn't he? "No," says the behaviourist, "he has learned that that behaviour only brings punishment." Then shouldn't the dog simply paw at the door, which is the only barrier between him and the unpunished place to eliminate? Why should the dog spend all that time working at the closet door if there is no image of a leash inside? He has never been formally taught to open the closet door. If he has learned to open closet doors, and this is triggered automatically by the sight of the door, why does he open only that particular door rather than every closet door he sees? Also, why does he usually pass by this closet door without opening it at other times during the day, if the sight of the door automatically triggers the opening response? And what is the significance of the leash? The dog certainly does not need it for any of his own activities. It serves no function in this string of actions unless there is some conscious connection, perhaps even a symbolic connection, in which it can serve as an intermediary to advance the dog closer to the desired goal of walking. If the leash is a goal object of its own, why drop it in his master's lap instead of doing something else with it? Why the bark, if not to alert the master? Why the prancing toward the door, with glances back to see if this has caused any immediate response? Why . . . ?

The behaviourist must analyse each component of each act without reference to forethought, intelligence, reasoning, or consciousness. A clever behaviourist might be able to do such a theoretical analysis. It would require, however, the isolation of a multitude of specific stimuli and their linked automatic, mechanistic responses. There would have to be myriad individual learned components, each shaped over time with specific rewards (reinforcements) that would need to be described. Then there would have to be some procedure for linking all these responses together so that they formed one integrated, auto-matic, unthinking sequence of muscle movements. Of course, any slight change in the stimuli in the environment would require addi-tional learning and stimulus-response sequences. The behaviourist would have to explain why the behaviour adapts to different condi-tions—say, when his master is in the kitchen rather than in the living room—why he modifies his behaviour in a meaningful and adaptive manner—for example, when his master is standing, he drops the leash at her feet, whereas when she is sitting, he places it in her lap—why he still opens the closet door even after it has been repainted and so looks and smells somewhat different. Each tiny modification should depend on a separate set of stimuli, responses, learned components, and so forth, much the same way that each individual thing a computer pro-gramme does demands additional lines of programming codes and specific means of branching from the previous lines in the programme.

Realistically speaking, whatever the requirements of theoretical ori-entation, is it likely that even the most committed behaviourist breaks down each behaviour involved in complex sequences such as the one described above? I doubt that any behaviouristic psychologist sitting at home observing an action pattern like the one just analysed ever called out to his or her spouse, "Dear, the dog has emitted a behavioural sequence terminating with the placement of the leash in my hands. I believe that the next set of stimuli that it should be exposed to should be from the exterior of the house. If we do not allow this, the dog will not be rewarded for the behaviours thus far elicited from it, and this sequence of responses will soon be extinguished and fail to be produced when later opportunities to do so present itself. In addition, it is likely that the pressure from the full bladder, which I assume initiated the behaviours that have resulted in the present pattern of responding, will soon override the learned restraints on relieving himself in the house, thus causing us to have to clean up after him." Probably not. Rather, I would bet that the behaviourist would call out, "Dear, the dog wants to go for a walk." Such a desire would explain all the behaviours that had happened and predict the dog's future behaviours, such as its excitement and rush to the door when its master stands up with lead in hand. It also predicts the joyful tail wagging that will follow (if we admit that dogs are capable of feeling joy).

PUTTING THE SOUL BACK INTO THE MACHINE

Even without resorting to informal arguments that look at behaviourists outside of their professional environments, simple logic challenges the basis of their argument that animals are nothing more than unconscious biological machines. When directly pressed, as in a scientific setting, behaviourists argue, "Since we cannot directly know the subjective experience or feelings of another living being, it is simplest to assume that they do not have consciousness, feelings, and so forth." Behaviourists have chosen a very specific viewpoint, based on a method of reasoning that begins by doubting virtually everything and then looks at what is left when all the data is accounted for. Thus the starting point of their argument would be that a dog's behaviour must lack consciousness and intelligent planning unless there is proof to the contrary.

It is interesting to note that behaviourists do not push this argument to the obvious extreme, which would be to apply the same line of reasoning to other human beings. If I chose to do so, then I could not assume that you are conscious until you proved it to me! How could you do that? How could I know that you are actually conscious and not responding in some complex mechanical way with automatic or programmed responses? After all, certain computer programmes, and even some of those automated phone-answering systems that we encounter when trying to get service from governments and large corporations, cause one to feel as though one is having a meaningful (even if annoyingly simple) conversation with them. Some make at least as much sense as certain cocktail party conversations that I have had with human beings who, I presumed, were conscious. Behaviourists do not push their doubt that far, however. Instead, they start with at least one assumption that they never subject to any challenging doubt: the belief that, since they are human beings and conscious, it is logical to assume that every other living thing that can be classified as a human being is similarly capable of consciousness. The disbelief and denial of consciousness applies only to nonhuman animals.

Of course, the behaviourist could just as logically have started from the opposite extreme. It is just as defensible to set acceptance of consciousness as the starting position: That is, if humans are conscious, then, logically, all other beings that are alive and responsive must also be assumed to be conscious, unless it can be proven that they are not. This argument makes as much sense as the other, and both should ultimately be capable of revealing the truth, at least in areas where objective data can be obtained.

Now when I say that we should begin with a presumption of consciousness and intelligent forethought, I am not saying that we should do so in every situation. A few cautions should be exercised here. Most important among them is Morgan's Canon, one of those almost religious principles taught in any undergraduate psychology or biology course that treats animal behaviour in any detail. This principle was first proposed by C. Lloyd Morgan, a British psychologist who produced a number of influential books on animal psychology starting in the 1890s and continuing through to the 1930s. In Morgan's own words, the principle is, "In no case may we interpret an action as the outcome of the exercise of a higher psychical faculty, if it can be interpreted as the outcome of the exercise of one which stands lower in the psychological scale." Behaviourists universally adopted this idea as their own, interpreting it as meaning that crediting consciousness to animals can't be justified if the animal's behaviour can be explained in any other way, because consciousness is certainly a "higher psychical faculty." Actually, their interpretation is wrong, since Morgan was perfectly happy with the idea of animal consciousness; he even gives examples of it directly taken from dog behaviour. Thus in *The Limits of Animal Intelligence*, he describes a dog returning from a walk "tired" and "hungry" and going down into the kitchen and "looking up wistfully" at the cook. Says Morgan about this, "I, for one, would not feel disposed to question that he has in his mind's eye a more or less definite idea of a bone."

Morgan's Canon really applies to situations where the level of intelligence credited to an animal's behaviour goes well beyond what is really needed for a simple and sensible explanation. Thus application of Morgan's Canon would prevent us from assuming that, when a dog finds its way home after being lost for a day, it must have the ability to read a map, or that, if a dog always begins to act hungry and pace around the kitchen at 6 P.M. and is always fed at 6:30 P.M., this must indicate that it has learned how to tell time by reading the position of the hands of the clock on the wall. These conclusions involve levels of intelligence that are simply not needed to explain the behaviours.

Proper application of Morgan's Canon could well have prevented the Clever Hans debacle. The problem with the interpretation of Hans's behaviour was that the first set of psychologists concluded that the horse could do mental arithmetic. This is a higher mental capacity that is denied to many animals (including me, as can be seen by the sad mismatches between my computations in my chequebook and the balances on my bank statement). The psychologists could more cautiously have asked, "Does he really need to do arithmetic to provide the right answers? Could he accomplish the same task if he were consciously attending to some other features of the situation?" The answer to this would have denied Hans the ability to do arithmetic reasoning but still granted him consciousness for other behaviours (such as watching people's responses to his foot taps).

With these restrictions in mind, I would like to offer a modest proposal for looking at the minds of dogs and other animals. We could start by saying that since we attribute consciousness and intelligence to other human beings, we have no right, in the absence of other data, to deny the same to animals, certainly higher ones such as dogs. These animals are provided with nervous systems that use the same general building blocks and operate according to the same physiological principles as those in humans. To the physiologist, the similarities in the structure of the nervous systems of all the mammals, from the gross organization of the brain down to the levels of the chemistry of the transmitter substances and electrical responses that carry information to and from the brain, are remarkable. This explains, of course, why animals are used in behavioural studies and why psychologists can use observations made of a lowly rat to predict the behaviours of children in the classroom.

I will certainly admit that it is not always easy to determine whether consciousness and intelligent planning are playing a part in any given behaviour when the only information comes from watching the behaviour being performed. It is probably true that, for most behaviours, one can argue for or against consciousness without coming into direct conflict with the objectively observed facts. Where does that leave us? Well, it is clearly the case that scientific observation and psychological experiments can help to clarify the situation. These sources of information can show us whether the behaviour of dogs and other animals is objectively similar to the behaviours in human beings that we know from our own experience are accompanied by consciousness. If we observe a situation where conscious reasoning takes place in humans and we note that dogs respond in much the same way and are affected by the same factors that affect the behaviours of humans, then I would propose that we should accept consciousness and intelligent reasoning in the dog as a plausible hypothesis. If by placing ourselves (figuratively) in the place of the dog, we can accurately predict its behaviors using our own reasoning and consciousness, I would say that this is further evidence consistent with the view that consciousness and intelligent analysis play a role in the dog's behaviour.

Ultimately, I fear, the question of whether consciousness, forethought, reasoning, imagery, and rational planning exist in species other than our own simply can't be answered conclusively until we have gathered a lot more scientific data. What is more, in animals, where language is not possible, it is difficult even to know what evidence would be sufficient to prove or disprove the existence of consciousness and all its trappings. Clearly, in situations where objective evidence can't settle the issue, conclusions must be based on some form of logical and philosophical evaluation of the situation. It must, then, be left to the philosophical biases of each scientist and each individual until such time that someone cleverer than those in my generation locates or produces the data that will unambiguously resolve the issue. Fortunately, a new generation of scientists is beginning to accept the idea of "animal cognition," which is the technical name given to higher thought processes in animals. New data is emerging from labs studying this issue, and perhaps the data that will prove whether dogs have consciousness or not is in the process of being collected right now.

Surprisingly, some of the answers may come from watching dogs play. Two psychologists, Robert Mitchell from Eastern Kentucky University and Nicholas Thompson of Clark University, studied dogs playing with people. They were particularly interested in the kind of play that seems to involve deception. The reason that deception is important is that it involves a special form of consciousness that goes beyond simple self-awareness and awareness of the world around you. It requires a "theory of mind", which recognizes that other individuals have minds and consciousness as well, and that their perceptions and conclusions might differ from your own. To deceive someone you must go through an internal process that goes something like "If I do this, then he'll think that, and I can do the following. . . ."

Videotapes of dogs and people showed that both use a lot of deception during play. We can call the two types of deceptions "keep-away" and "misdirection". When people are in control, their deceptions might go like this. They show the dog a retrieving object (such as a ball), entice him to come close by seeming to offer it to the dog, but then quickly move it out of reach, hide it behind themselves, or throw it as the dog lunges for it. Alternatively, they might pretend to throw the object, but not let it go.

The dogs played similar games as well. In the canine version of keep-away the dog holds an object in his mouth and moves toward the person, close enough to lure him into going after it, but hopefully not close enough for the person to get it. Sometimes the dog deliberately stops and drops the object. He then stands over it, or even backs up a step or two, as if offering it to the person. If the person is drawn in by this enticement and moves to grab the toy, the dog immediately grabs it, or knocks it away and then grabs it, quickly making a dash to keep out of arm's reach. An alternate game involving more misdirection could be called "self keep-away", which involves the dog running toward the person but dodging his advances once the person has committed himself to moving in order to catch the dog.

Succeeding in deception seems to be part of the fun of playing for both dog and person. This would explain why 78 percent of the people frequently tried to deceive the dogs, and 92 percent of the dogs tried to deceive the people. This also suggests that dogs enjoy deception a bit more than humans do. When a human tries to deceive a dog during play, he succeeds around 47 percent of the time. When a dog tries to deceive a human during the game, he succeeds about 41 percent of the time. If a successful deception depends upon using your theory of mind to accurately determine what your counterpart will see, interpret, and do next, then this means that humans have a more accurate theory of mind than dogs; however, the difference of only 6 percent is much smaller than most people would have predicted. Dogs try deliberately to deceive and seem to do it almost as well as people do, suggesting that they have a theory of mind, with some level of consciousness, forethought, and complex anticipation as well.

I initially wrote this chapter during a very grey and rainy spring. The day I finished it, more than a week had gone by without any noticeable sunshine. That particular afternoon, though, the clouds seemed to part and a burst of afternoon sunshine shone through the window, forming a big golden patch on the hardwood floor. Completing my work, I was moving toward the kitchen to get a cup of coffee when I noticed my Cavalier King Charles spaniel Wiz standing in the circle of light. He looked up at the window and then down at the floor as if he were contemplating something, and then he deliberately turned and ran from the room. Within a matter of moments, however, he reappeared dragging a large terry-cloth towel that he had stolen from the bathroom. He pulled the towel into the centre of the patch of sun, looked at it, and then pushed at one lumpy section with both front paws. Having arranged the towel to his satisfaction, he then circled around and settled down for a nap on his newly created bed in the warm afternoon sun. If one of my young grandchildren had done this, I would have said that she felt the warmth of the sun and thought that it would be nice to take a nap in it. Then, remembering the towel in the bathroom, she went and retrieved it so that she could sunbathe more comfortably.

All this requires consciousness, intelligence, and planning. Does my dog Wiz have it? It is easier for me simply to recognize that my dog's behaviours in this situation were similar to behaviours that are accompanied by consciousness in a human faced with the same situation. In the absence of any evidence to the contrary, I will presume that I am dealing with consciousness and intelligent behaviour in my dog as well.

Chapter Five

The Nature of Dog Intelligence

> My dog can bark like a congressman, fetch like an aide, beg like a press secretary, and play dead like a receptionist when the phone rings.
>
> —CONGRESSMAN GERALD SOLOMON

What, exactly, do we mean by the "intelligence of dogs"? As with many questions, the answer seems obvious until we begin to think carefully about the matter. In our everyday language, we all use the word *intelligent* and its synonyms *smart, clever, brilliant, wise, perceptive, sage,* and so forth. We also use the antonyms *stupid, dumb, dense, witless, slow, moronic,* and others to describe people and particular actions. Yet most people, when asked to be specific about what they mean by *intelligence,* seem to have no precise idea of what the concept actually refers to. What are the limits of intelligence? How does intelligence influence or organize behaviour? How can we recognize the difference between an act that was guided by intelligence and one that was not? When pushed to answer such questions, most people simply resort to statements such as, "It's difficult to define, but you recognize it when you see it," which, of course, translates as "I don't know, so leave me alone."

Psychologists really haven't done much better. In 1926, the *Journal of Educational Psychology* asked a number of leading scholars and psychologists to define intelligence. Although individual psychologists had theoretical definitions and rationales for why their definition was meaningful and useful, the group as a whole was unable to reach any consensus. Fifty-six years later, in 1983, psychologists Robert J. Sternberg of Yale University and Douglas K. Detterman of Case Western Reserve University tried again. They solicited the viewpoints of twenty-three world experts in intelligence as to what intelligence really is and how it should be measured, and published the results in a book called *What Is Intelligence?* There was still a good deal of disagreement over what intelligence is, how it is organized, how it relates to or affects many behaviours; however, some progress had been made in the half century since the first attempt to define the concept. Several of the researchers shared common interpretations of intelligence, suggesting that, though the issue was far from resolved, our knowledge and understanding of the issue had advanced considerably.

GENERAL AND SPECIFIC INTELLIGENCE

When we look at what is known and what is speculated about the nature of human intelligence, we find a number of ideas that will help us to understand the nature of dog intelligence as well. One important concept has to do with the breadth or scope of intelligence. Most people believe that when people are intelligent, they show this intelligence in everything they do. This became very clear to me during an encounter with Nobel Prize winner in physiology and medicine David Hubel, whose area of expertise is in the neurological factors that allow the brain to process visual information from the eye. He is a brilliant researcher, an expert in the physiology of the brain and nervous system, with a vast degree of competence in electrical and chemical measurement of neural activity levels. One evening, a couple of years after he won the award, he was visiting my university. We were having dinner together and just chatting, when he began to describe how his life had been changed by the award. After winning the Nobel Prize (which for most people certifies the winner as definitely "intelligent"), he suddenly found that people came to view him as an expert on virtually everything. "They ask me questions about literature and music, child-rearing, the state of the environment, how to stop the disappearance of the Atlantic fish stock, and the solution to world political problems and religious strife. They expect me to have an instantaneous and authoritative opinion on all such issues. They seem to feel that Nobel Prize winners are 'really smart' and must have intelligent solutions and insights about everything." He sipped his wine, smiled a bit, and then continued, "At least they don't expect me to sing or dance well!"

This everyday view of intelligence as a general skill that can be applied to all areas of behaviour actually does have supporters among psychologists. The most notable of these was Charles E. Spearman, a British psychologist who, in 1904, published a classic paper entitled "General Intelligence Objectively Determined and Measured". In it, he observed that there seemed to be some general factor of intelligence (he called it g) that applied to everything an individual does. His conclusion was based on data that measured the relationship among various tests of specific mental abilities. For instance, suppose that a person takes a dozen or so tests. If each test measures a separate and independent mental ability, then the score that the person gets for any one test will be unrelated to the other scores. Thus one might test well in arithmetic but poorly in vocabulary. If, however, intelligence is a general or global characteristic, then it would mean that it will affect all of a person's abilities. Thus an individual who is smart and does well on an arithmetic test should also do well on a vocabulary or a logical reasoning test, while a less intelligent person would do poorly on all of their tests, regardless of the specific subject matter.

When he actually collected data on this issue, Spearman found that the idea that intelligence was a broad general characteristic was only partly supported. Scores on tests that were designed to measure specific, supposedly unrelated, intellectual abilities were found to be moderately related to one another: That is, a person who scored better than average on an arithmetic test also was likely to score better than average on a reading test, a memory test, a spatial reasoning test, and so forth. Spearman argued that the test scores were related because the general intelligence factor (g) influenced all of them. However, the relationship between the test scores was far from perfect. For instance, one person might score extremely well on some tests but only a bit above average on others. This forced Spearman to modify his original viewpoint somewhat to admit that the idea that intelligence was a general ability was not adequate to explain all of the data. While we can safely say that in general people who are intelligent do well in most things, while less bright people tend to do poorly, each person will also have a set of task specific ability levels. Typically people will have some mental skills where they excel and others where they are considerably less competent.

If specific as well as general abilities are involved in intelligence, that may help to explain the lack of consistency that people often show in their mental prowess. For instance, Napoleon Bonaparte was clearly a brilliant military strategist and showed some evidence for general intelligence in that he had the verbal and reasoning skills to appeal to the masses of the French public. This general intelligence is demonstrated by the fact that many of the judicial, educational, and political reforms that he introduced still stand today. Yet Napoleon also showed specific deficits in some areas. For instance, he demonstrated real stupidity when he began the ill-fated invasion of Russia that ultimately led to the downfall of his regime.

Another similar case is the Nobel Prize–winning physicist Albert Einstein, whose discoveries include the general theory of relativity and the photoelectric effect. Evidence for his general intelligence comes from the fact that Einstein was also verbally brilliant, as his many philosophical writings show, and musically talented in his playing of the cello. His downfall was simple arithmetic. His addition and subtraction skills were so bad that his personal chequebook was always completely out of agreement with the records of the bank.

Brilliant individuals seem to have specific coexisting areas of both high and low intelligence. We all know stories of a champion chess player who barely scraped through school and seems lost in ordinary conversations. We hear stories of the great theoretical physicist who doesn't know how to programme his video recorder, the highly competent research chemist who can't follow a simple recipe to bake a cake, the famous general who does not know how to discipline his own children, or the clinically proficient psychologist who doesn't have a clue about what to do when his or her own marriage begins falling apart. In all these, the tendency to act intelligently and to act stupidly are found in different specific abilities in the same person.

The same situation holds in dogs. While some dogs seem to be generally bright and capable of learning virtually anything (showing us a high g, or general intelligence), others seem to have limited and specific abilities. Hunting breeds, such as the English setter or pointer, will point or mark game with virtually no training yet may be unable to learn to herd animals no matter how much training they receive. On the other hand, Shetland sheepdogs and collies seem to have the ability to herd built into them but are incapable of learning to point or mark game. These high and low points in capacity reflect differences in the specific abilities.

MULTIPLE INTELLIGENCES

The fact that people can be so variable in their abilities eventually led some researchers to suggest that we really ought to look at intelligence as a collection of primary mental abilities, each of which can be considered as a separate skill or a separate dimension of intelligence. Harvard psychologist Howard Gardner terms these abilities "multiple intelligences". According to Gardner, an intelligence is an ability to solve problems, fashion products, or produce behaviours that are of consequence in a particular environmental setting. Environmental settings include cultural and social situations, as well as task requirements and geographical, physical, and climatic conditions. For Gardner, there are seven important intelligences: linguistic intelligence, logical-mathematical intelligence, spatial intelligence, musical intelligence, bodily-kinesthetic intelligence, interpersonal intelligence, and intrapersonal intelligence. Though Gardner's theory was designed to describe human intelligence, it includes some abilities that dogs also seem to possess, as well as others that are more debatable.

Spatial Intelligence

Let's start with the obviously "dog-possible" dimensions of Gardner's intelligences. The first dimension to consider is *spatial intelligence*. This involves the ability to hold in one's head a model of the organization of the surrounding world—where objects are located, the relative distance between places, and so forth. A dog who remembers where a favourite toy is in the house, where you have stored his leash, or where his bed is, is displaying this type of intelligence.

One of my former dogs, a cairn terrier named Feldspar, had good spatial intelligence and a clear means of demonstrating this ability. If I asked him the whereabouts of my children, he would immediately run to where he had last seen them and bark furiously when he got there. When my children were very young, we used to play hide-and-seek, with the role of *it* usually falling to me. As the kids grew a bit older, they became quite proficient at the game, finding increasingly sophisticated hiding places. Surreptitiously, I would tell Feldspar to stay with whichever one of them was proving to be the hardest to find on a given day. For example, I might say, "Watch Ben," and the dog would tag along behind my son. When it came time to find him, I would call him back to me and then ask, "Where's Ben?" The dog would run to his hiding place and bark (usually eliciting screams of "Feldspar, go away!" followed by howls of "Daddy, you're cheating!"). That the dog was basing his responses on spatial memory (rather than simply searching until he found the child) became apparent when my daughter Rebecca learned how to outsmart her father and the dog. She would hide and wait until I called Feldspar back, when she would change hiding places. The dog responded on the basis of where he saw her last. Thus Feldspar might return to the closet where she had first hidden and bark to indicate this, whereas she might have switched to the bathroom across the way. She was still easy to find, though, because her giggling at how well her subterfuge had worked was easy to hear. Although my use of Feldspar as a covert assistant shows I was not above cheating at the game, I would invariably pretend not to know where my daughter was, just to reward her for her cleverness.

A number of recent studies show that dogs learn their map of their environment by memorizing where things are relative to certain prominent landmarks. When there are few landmarks they have greater difficulty making a mental map of the world, and if a landmark is moved or removed they can make major errors in trying to locate things. Humans do much the same thing. For example, I have been traveling the same route to the library for more than twenty-five years. Recently, I went to return some books that I had borrowed two or three weeks earlier, and drove past one corner where I usually make a right-hand turn. I only discovered this many minutes later, when I found myself lost in unfamiliar territory. This all occurred because since my last visit a gasoline station that had always been on the corner where I turned had been torn down and replaced by an excavation for an apartment building. My familiar landmark had been removed and I was lost, and much the same happens with dogs.

Kinesthetic Intelligence

The second dimension of Gardner's multiple intelligences that dogs have is *bodily-kinesthetic intelligence*. This includes the ability to move and coordinate the body skilfully, as is required for touch typing, dancing, and sports. Dogs that have learned to jump high jumps or broad jumps or to balance on a beam or climb a ladder are displaying this form of intelligence. Certain aspects of obedience competitions or agility tests measure this type of intelligence. In North America, there is even a musical freestyle competition, the dog equivalent of the freestyle competition in figure skating, except that it not only is done by single individuals with one dog but also may involve teams of four to six people with a matching number of dogs. The competition involves performing a routine to music. At its best, the dogs and the handlers seem to be dancing together in a coordinated flow. Sometimes the dog is required to dodge in and out between its handler's legs, to jump over an outstretched arm, to circle and return to its partner, and to move in synchrony with its teammates across the large open spaces used for the display. In many ways, these are the same bodily-kinesthetic skills used by dancers.

Intrapersonal and Interpersonal Intelligence

Another set of abilities that dogs seem to have is *intrapersonal intelligence*. This is self-knowledge, such as knowing one's own capacities and limitations. A dog who hesitates or refuses to jump over a barrier or gap that it knows is too high or wide for it is displaying this kind of intelligence. Intrapersonal intelligence is theoretically very important, since the dog probably must use some kind of conscious processing, or perhaps even imagery, to display it. Thus the dog considers the height of the jump, judges it in light of its own capabilities, perhaps imagines how high it can leap, and so forth. Of course, there are also other ways to explain what dogs are doing in these circumstances; I'll return to those in a moment.

The next kind of intelligence dogs have reflects the fact that they are social creatures. This is *interpersonal intelligence*, which includes social skills such as the ability to get along with others or to assume leadership and other roles. Certainly, wild canids, such as wolves, know who is in charge and respond appropriately to the leader of the pack. Dogs also respond with appropriate social signals to humans and other dogs (as when your dog looks up at you and tentatively wags her tail in the hope that you will share some food with her). Such behaviours are evidence of interpersonal intelligence. This kind of intelligence also is evident when a dog initiates playing activities with other dogs or tries to communicate its needs to a person. Interpersonal intelligence, in other words, is the foundation for communication: If one doesn't recognize that other individuals exist and that their behaviour can affect one directly, then there is no need to engage in any communication.

You may be wondering, "Why do social competence and social responsiveness get thrown into the mix of abilities that we call *intelligence*?" Answering this actually brings us back to the question of consciousness. The link is that some psychologists, such as Nicholas Humphrey at the London School of Economics, have argued that consciousness, and perhaps much of higher intelligence, evolved in the first place to allow animals to deal with social situations. Getting on with other individuals of one's own species, predicting their actions, guessing their motives or goals, finding an appropriate mate, controlling the behaviours of offspring are, according to Humphrey, about the most complicated things that an animal will ever have to deal with. It is, therefore, not surprising that brains should evolve a number of capacities to meet these challenges.

Consider an animal that has everything it needs to get on in the world. It has limbs to move around, some ability to grasp and move objects, good sensory systems to receive stimulation and information from the environment, plus some form of information-processing and decision-making centre in the brain. What it lacks, however, is the inner eye of consciousness. Compare this creature to another identical in every way except that it does have consciousness, that inner eye that allows it to look in on the states of its own mind. At a purely behavioural level, the two creatures might appear to be generally indistinguishable. Both might seem to be very intelligent and show emotional behaviours, including those we call "desires", "moods", or "passions". The difference is that, for the unconscious animal, behaviours just appear to happen, achieved through some sort of psychological autopilot, while for the conscious animal, intelligent activities are accompanied by some awareness of the thought processes involved.

Specifically, in the conscious animal, its visual stimulation is accompanied by conscious perception and its emotions by conscious feeling. For this animal, the inner eye of consciousness is looking down on these activities and, in effect, is reading the individual's mind. From this, the conscious animal knows what it is like to be itself. This self-knowledge also makes it easier to make sense of the actions of other individuals. The conscious animal can imagine what others might be feeling or how they might respond in a given situation. It does this by making realistic guesses about the inner life of others based on its own self-knowledge and its picture of how it would respond in a similar situation; in other words, he has that *Theory of Mind* that we referred to in the previous chapter. In essence, consciousness of its own states has given it the ability virtually to read the minds of others. At the positive end, this could open the door to empathic responses, such as sympathy, compassion, and trust, but it also makes possible treachery, double-crossing, and deceit. In other words, it allows the rich diversity of adaptive and meaningful behaviours that we expect of humans, dogs, and other social animals. According to this theory, then, to be an effective social animal requires both intelligence and consciousness. If the theory is true, we can further assert the corollary that the very existence of complex social interactions should serve as evidence that an animal has both consciousness and intelligence.

Musical Intelligence

While the dimensions of intelligence discussed so far are quite obvious in dogs, some other dimensions of intelligence are more debatable. The first of these is *musical intelligence*. This set of abilities could only be considered as "dog-likely" if there was evidence that dogs had an appreciation of musical factors such as harmony, since actual music production is probably out of the question. In observing the musical freestyle competition that I described earlier, where dogs and handlers move or dance to music, I have never seen any evidence that the dogs are actually keeping time with the music itself. They move with their handlers, pacing their movements to those of the humans, rather than developing any rhythmic responses themselves. Thus the illusion of dance derives from the human being's responding to the musical score.

Some stories do suggest that dogs might respond to music. I have been told things such as, "My dog really likes Mozart's chamber music and other similar classical works. He will come into the room and lie down near the speakers whenever this kind of music is on. However, when I put on a tape of rock music, he tends to leave the room." Research confirms that dogs have musical preferences and react differently to different types of music. Psychologist Deborah Wells at Queen's University in Belfast exposed dogs in an animal shelter to different types of music. The dogs' responses were observed as they listened to either a compilation of popular music (including Britney Spears, Robbie Williams, and Bob Marley), classical music (including Grieg's *Morning*, Vivaldi's *Four Seasons*, and Beethoven's *Ode to Joy*), or recordings by heavy-metal rock bands such as Metallica. In order to see if it were really the musical aspects of the sounds that the dogs were responding to, they were also exposed to recordings of human conversation and periods of quiet.

The dogs responded differently to different types of music. When the dogs were played heavy metal music, they became quite agitated and began barking. Popular music or human conversation did not produce behaviours noticeably different from having no sound at all. Classical music, on the other hand, seemed to have a calming effect on the dogs. While listening to it, their level of barking was significantly reduced, and they often lay down and settled in place. In her paper published in the scientific journal *Animal Welfare*, Wells summarized her findings by saying, "It is well established that music can influence our moods. Classical music, for example, can help to reduce levels of stress, whilst grunge music can promote hostility, sadness, tension and fatigue. It is now believed that dogs may be as discerning as humans when it comes to musical preference."

I have often been told of dogs that sing. In one instance, I was told of a basset hound that would howl whenever his family of humans would gather around the piano for Christmas carol sing-alongs. I experienced an extreme version of such a performance in New York's Carnegie Hall in 1980. I was attending the debut performance of *Howl*, a musical work for twenty humans and three canines. The piece was composed and conducted by Kirk Nurock, a pianist and arranger who has worked with the likes of Dizzy Gillespie, Judy Collins, Bette Midler, and Leonard Bernstein. Trained at the Juilliard School of Music, Nurock would go on to compose and perform *Sonata for Piano and Dog* (1983) and *Expedition* (1984), an arrangement for jazz trio and Siberian husky. In each of these pieces, dogs howled to accompany music, with occasional barks and yips as punctuation.

Should we view such howling as music making, and hence musical intelligence, on the part of the dog? I have no real evidence to discount the possibility; however, based on other considerations, it seems unlikely to me. Wild dogs and wolves are known to join in a chorus of howling or yipping in response to the howling of another member of their pack. It is believed that this is a form of communication, the dogs' vocalizations effectively saying "I'm here" or "We're all part of the same pack," rather than serving as attempts at music. On the other hand, when I was in my early teens learning to accompany my singing on a ukulele, Tippy, my fox terrier, used to howl most pitifully when I would start to practice. While this did not necessarily reflect any musical appreciation on my dog's part, the consensus of the other members of my family was that it certainly represented valid musical criticism!

Logical-Mathematical Intelligence

The next aspect of intelligence to consider is *logical-mathematical intelligence*. In people, this shows itself as the ability to solve problems, use mathematical techniques, create scientific solutions, and so forth. This aspect of intelligence, however, must be modified, clarified, and somewhat limited before it makes any sense to talk about it in terms of dogs. Put simply, dogs do not do science. Although finding the fastest route from one place to another, or figuring out just when to jump to catch a Frisbee, may take some kind of internal computation based on solving a problem using calculus, dogs do not consciously set out to solve algebraic problems or engage in the abstraction of complex general principles and rules to explain the functioning of the natural world. This certainly places a ceiling on the dog's intelligence in this area.

We should not, however, dismiss dogs when it comes to this set of abilities. Dogs are certainly capable of solving problems and applying rational strategies to new situations. But when considering relationships involving quantity or size, which are part of the mathematical realm, dogs are usually said to lack the ability to think in these terms. For example, Samuel Johnson, the eighteenth-century English writer, critic, and creator of the first dictionary of the English language, once rejected dog's abilities in this area of intelligence. "Did you never observe," Johnson asked, "that dogs have not the power of comparing? A dog will take a small bit of meat as readily as a large, when both are before them."

Daniel Greenberg, editor of *Science and Government Report*, suggested an easy experiment that you can try at home to disprove Johnson's observation and to show that dogs do compare logically in terms of quantity. First form some large and small balls of ground beef (for a large dog such as a German shepherd or a rottweiler, the small meatballs might be the size of Ping-Pong balls and the large ones the size of tennis balls, while for small dogs such as Yorkshire terriers or miniature schnauzers, the small meatballs might be the size of a marble and the large ones the size of golf balls). While the dog watches, place one large and one small meatball on the kitchen floor. You will find that the dog will generally eat the nearest bit of meat, whether large or small. While this choice might seem to indicate that the dog failed to compare and evaluate size, it turns out to be the result of simple opportunism, reflecting a mentality that honors the maxim "A bird in the hand is worth two in the bush": The closer meatball is simply easier to get and a more certain prize. On the other hand, if you adjust the gap between the dog and the bait so that both balls of meat are the same distance from the dog, it will almost invariably go for the larger one first. This demonstrates an ability to compare quantity and to formulate a plan of action based on a mathematical assessment, however primitive.

In other situations dogs seem to exercise quantitative judgment. I was told a story about two men out hunting ducks with the assistance of a golden retriever named Buck. In the afternoon, when the hunters returned to their van to go home, one of them remembered that they had left their hats next to their blind. Buck's master had taught him to retrieve any object that he pointed to, so rather than go back for the hats, Buck's master simply sent the dog back to collect them. The two hats, one a baseball cap and the other a cowboy-style hat, were lying next to each other. As the men watched, the dog first picked up the cowboy hat and then tried to pick up the cap. When that didn't work, he dropped the larger hat and picked up the baseball cap first but still could not adjust his grip to hold both at once. Dropping the cap, he then studied the two objects for a moment. Eventually, Buck picked up the baseball cap and dropped it into the cowboy hat. He then used his front paw to stuff the smaller hat securely into the larger. Finally, he grabbed the larger hat, now serving as a sort of a basket for the smaller, and, his tail swinging merrily, brought the two back to the waiting men.

Obviously, the dog was engaging in logical problem solving; in addition, however, the solution required quantitative and relational judgment. Remember that the dog placed the smaller hat into the larger, rather than trying to do the reverse, showing that some consideration of size had been made.

Dogs can go even further than these kinds of assessments, to a point where virtually everyone would concede that they are really counting. One spring afternoon, I was participating in a dog obedience trial on Vancouver Island in British Columbia, Canada. One of the other dog competitors and I had finished for the day, and we were out walking in a large nearby field with his lovely female Labrador retriever named Poco. The man had a box of large rubber retrieving lures with him, and he explained to me that he would use these to demonstrate that his dog could count.

"She can count to four quite reliably and to five with only an occasional miss," he said. "I'll show you how it works. Pick a number from one to five."

I picked the number three. While the dog watched, her master tossed three lures out into the high grass of the field. The lures were tossed in different directions and to different distances. After I got down on my hands and knees and verified that the lures were not visible from the dog's eye level at the starting position, my companion simply told the dog, "Poco, fetch," without pointing or other cues. The dog went out to the most recently thrown lure, picked it up, and brought it back. Her master took it from her and then repeated "Poco, fetch," causing the dog to start to cast about and search for the next one. After she brought back the second lure, her master again commanded, "Poco, fetch," and the dog went out after the third and last lure. Removing the last lure from the dog's mouth, he once again ordered, "Poco, fetch." At this, the dog simply looked at him, barked once, and moved to his left side, to the usual *heel* position, and sat down.

He then turned to me and said, "She knows that she's retrieved all three and that that is all there were. She keeps a running count. When there are no more lures to search for, she lets me know with that 'They're all here, stupid' bark and simply gets ready for the next thing that I want her to do."

We repeated the exercise for the better part of a half hour, varying the number of lures up to five, with me and another spectator tossing the lures and sending the dog to fetch as sort of a check to see if something hidden in the way the items were placed or the commands given accounted for her success. Once we even had someone toss out a set of lures in such a way that the dog saw where they landed but the person giving Poco commands didn't know how many lures were thrown and therefore couldn't give any covert clues to the dog like those Clever Hans used in his counting tricks. None of these variations seemed to matter, and even at five, the dog never missed the count once.

Dogs even seem to have a rudimentary ability to add and subtract. Robert Young of the Pontifical Catholic University in Brazil and Rebecca West of the University of Lincoln in the United Kingdom used a modified version of a test designed to determine that young humans have such abilities. First the dog is shown a large treat, then a low screen is put in front of it to block the dog's view. While the dog watches, the experimenter takes another treat, shows it to the dog, and then lowers it down behind the screen. If the dog can count, he should expect that when the screen is raised he should see two treats, and sometimes he does. However, sometimes the experimenter secretly removes one of the treats so that now when the screen is raised there is only one treat visible. Thus instead of the expected $1 + 1 = 2$, the dog is presented with $1 + 1 = 1$. Alternatively the experimenter can secretly add an additional treat, giving the dog the result $1 + 1 = 3$. When any of the wrong answers appear, the dog reacts by staring at the results for a much longer time than he does if the expected $1 + 1 = 2$ appears. This is taken as evidence of surprise and puzzlement on the part of the dog, suggesting that he has done the mental addition and knows what the correct result should be. Such an ability would be useful for mother dogs, which would then know if one or more of their pups has gone missing from the litter, and by inference she would also know how many of them were gone and must be found.

While no one will claim that dogs are mathematicians or logicians, it may be fair to say that dogs do have some mathematical and logical abilities. Specifically, the ability to compare quantities and to count are the basis of mathematics, and the ability to solve novel problems demonstrates logic and reasoning.

Linguistic Intelligence

The last of Gardner's intelligences is *linguistic intelligence*. Here Descartes seems to rear his head again. Obviously, dogs can't speak and produce language and so cannot attain the higher levels of the ability to use language. But even if a dog as a poet laureate must remain a fantasy, to deny that dogs have linguistic abilities is going too far.

The issue of the dog's linguistic intelligence is important to humans because we obviously want to communicate with our animals, and it is clearly important to dogs because they are social animals, and social organization and structure cannot exist without some form of communication. The more complex the social structure and activities, the more complex the language or communication required. In the wild, dogs and wolves coordinate hunting in groups, maintain social positions in the pack, and distribute duties such as the care of pups that are no longer nursing but still too young to hunt. All this suggests that they must have a reasonably rich communication system. Philosophically, of course, the issue of animal language has been the focus of arguments about whether nonhuman animals can think and have consciousness. For all these reasons, it would seem sensible to spend a bit more time on the issue of linguistic intelligence in dogs than I have devoted to the other aspects of dogs' mental abilities covered in this chapter.

Chapter Six

Linguistic Intelligence in Dogs

No one appreciates the very special genius of your conversation as a dog does.

—CHRISTOPHER MORLEY

Language has always been one of the characteristics that we have viewed as exclusively human. By selecting the presence of linguistic capacity as a test of whether intelligence was present in an animal, Descartes thus stacked the deck against all animals other than man. However, the 1970s dealt a blow to Descartes's notion that language is not possible in nonhuman species. Psychologists Beatrix and Allen Gardner made the breakthrough using a chimpanzee. Before then, several attempts had been made to teach chimpanzees to speak by rearing them as one would a human child, with the usual intensive daily exposure to human language. Unfortunately, the most successful of these experiments had resulted in a primitive spoken vocabulary of only four words. The Gardners reasoned that the previous failures in training animals to use language might be due to the fact that many of the trainers were expecting the animals actually to speak. Since most primates (and certainly dogs) lack the control of tongue, lips, palate, and vocal cords that humans have, it seemed possible that primates might not be able to use speech even if they did have the mental capacity to master other aspects of language. In order to bypass the vocal component of language, the Gardners began to teach a chimpanzee the American Sign Language (ASL) used by the deaf. ASL uses hand signals rather than vocal sounds, and chimpanzees are very adept at learning to manipulate their hands and fingers. Their first chimpanzee, Washoe, was able to learn an extensive vocabulary of more than one hundred and fifty signs. She could form simple sentences, follow basic grammatical principles, and put together novel ideas. These and other abilities suggested that the chimpanzee had developed a language competence equivalent to that of a child of two and a half to three years of age.

Other researchers have gone further with nonhuman language. Using plastic symbols for words, David Premack was able to teach his chimpanzee Sarah to effectively read and write. Sue Savage-Rumbaugh and her colleagues now at Georgia State University's Language Research Center in Atlanta taught two chimpanzees (Sherman and Austin) to type using a special keyboard on which each key was imprinted with a symbol (called a *lexigram*) that represented a word or wordlike fragment. After a while, the chimpanzees' language ability had proceeded to the stage where they could type messages to each other. These messages were about matters of distinct relevance to them. For instance, one chimp might indicate in writing to the other chimp that he needed a particular tool to extract food from certain places where the experimenter had placed it. The chimpanzee receiving the message would respond by selecting the appropriate tool and passing it to the closer animal. Both would later share the booty gained from such successful acts of cooperation.

Savage-Rumbaugh then moved on to study bonobos, or pigmy chimpanzees, which actually share 98 to 99 percent of human genes. With these animals she could expand the keyboard to four hundred symbols. Furthermore, she claims, "If you talk to apes and point to little symbols, they learn to understand language just as I'm talking to you." This means that instead of rewarding the apes with food each time they use a word correctly, she is permitting the animals to pick up words in "normal" conversation, much the way that human children do. Savage-Rumbaugh finds that the bonobos use language much like humans do. One day a bonobo named Panbanisha grabbed the keyboard and repeatedly pressed the three symbols "fight", "mad", and "Austin", a combination that she had never used before.

Savage-Rumbaugh then asked Panbanisha, "Was there a fight at Austin's house?" and the chimp replied "Waa, waa, waa," her usual sound indicating affirmation. The researcher checked and found that her chimp, Austin, had indeed had a fight with his mother that morning over a toy and had actually bitten her ear. The interesting aspect of this "conversation" was that the bonobo was not asking for food or any other kind of reward, but rather, like humans, was simply using language to gossip.

Not all psychologists agree that the signs and signals produced by chimpanzees, gorillas, and other primates are actually language. Some have argued that they lack the complexity of true human language. It seems to me that the difference is one of degree, rather than of substance. For most anthropologists, for example, a primitive people's ability to add and subtract would be taken as evidence of basic mathematical knowledge, even though a higher criterion for presuming mathematical ability—say, knowledge of multiplication and division or even the ability to do algebra—would exclude such a culture. Many of the behaviourists who want to deny that apes can use language seem to be demanding that they master the linguistic equivalent of calculus before they can serve as evidence for nonhuman speech.

The best way to assess language in nonhumans is to compare it with the language of young children. We certainly credit children with linguistic ability when they know only a few words and gestures but are already able to communicate their wishes and states of mind. In fact, *Webster's Eleventh New Collegiate Dictionary*, which records the most prevalent usages of terms, gives as part of the definition of the word *language* not just "audible, articulate, meaningful sound as produced by the action of the vocal organs" but also "a systematic means of communicating ideas or feelings by the use of conventionalized signs, sounds, gestures, or marks having understood meanings", which would certainly include most of the material discussed here.

If we use the MacArthur Communicative Development Inventory, used to test the language ability of children at around two years of age, the Gardners' chimpanzee Washoe and Premack's chimpanzee Sarah would certainly score very high. Kanzi, Savage-Rumbaugh's star pupil, would score as high as a human three-year-old. If high scores on such a scale indicate linguistic ability in children, it seems fair to use a similar interpretation when assessing linguistic ability in chimpanzees.

DOG-RECEPTIVE LANGUAGE

It is all well and good to speak of language in nonhuman primates with their high degree of genetic overlap with humans, but what about language in dogs? Here we have to make a distinction that Descartes seemed to forget: The earliest stages of language development involve language comprehension, rather than language production. The ability to produce sounds or signals to communicate with others follows the ability to understand language, and it represents a higher level of linguistic achievement.

The so-called receptive language ability of dogs is quite good, as shown when dogs respond to spoken words appropriately. For example, consider this minidictionary of my own dogs' vocabularies. Each word is presented along with the actions that demonstrate the dog's comprehension. Obviously, some of the words and phrasings are idiosyncratic to me. Moreover, not all my dogs respond to all the words; this depends on their level of training. On the other hand, my partial list includes only words that I deliberately use to get responses from the dogs and omits words that they may understand but aren't formally required to respond to.

Away: The dog moves back from whatever it was investigating or attending to.

Back: Used only in the car, this causes the dog to move from the front to the back seat.

Bad dog: This is a term of displeasure that usually causes the dog to cringe and seek an exit from the room.

Be close: Used when walking, this causes a lagging dog to narrow the distance from me.

Be quick: I use these as trigger words when housebreaking a dog. Once learned, they cause the dog to start searching for a place to urinate or defecate.

By me: This causes a free-ranging dog to return to the general area of my left side, near the *heel* position.

Collar off: The dog lowers its head to allow its collar to be slipped over and off.

Collar on: The dog lifts its head, pointing its muzzle up, to allow its collar to be slipped on.

Come: The dog comes and sits in front of me.

[Dog's name]: Each of my dogs knows its own name and at the sound of it will turn its head toward me and await a further instruction.

Down: The dog lies down.

Downstairs: The dog goes down the set of stairs in front of it.

Do you want to play?: This causes the dog to circle, bark, and bow playfully.

Drop it: The dog spits out anything it is holding in its mouth.

Excuse me: Used when a dog is blocking my path, such as lying across a doorway, this causes the dog to get up and stand aside, at least until I've passed.

Find glove: The dog retrieves a dropped glove, which is out of sight (part of a formal obedience exercise).

Find it: The dog finds an item with my scent among a group of items (part of a formal obedience exercise).

Front: The dog straightens its position in front of me (part of obedience practice).

Give: This causes the dog to release pressure on the object it is holding in its mouth so that I can remove it.

Give me a kiss: The dog licks my face.

Give me a paw: The dog lifts the paw nearest my hand.

Go back: The dog moves away from me in the direction indicated.

Good dog: This is a term of praise that usually causes tail wagging (interchangeable with *good boy* for my all-male collection).

Heel: The dog walks at my left side or returns to sit at my left side (the *heel* position).

Hugs: The dog jumps up in front of me, with its paws on my thighs, to allow me to pet it without bending.

In: The dog passes through an open door or gate in the direction indicated by my hand motion.

Jump: The dog leaps over the indicated object or obstruction.

Kennel: The dog goes into its kennel. (*In your house* is a substitute phrase that dogs also respond to in the same way.)

Lead on: The dog lifts its head to provide access to collar ring. (*Lead off* produces the same response.)

Let's go: The dog follows me, but not necessarily at the *heel* position at my left side.

No: The dog freezes, stopping all action.

Office: The dog goes to my office at home to wait for me.

OK: This indicates that an exercise is finished, and the last command made. It causes the dog to break from position and come for praise. (*Play time* produces the same response.)

Open your mouth: This causes the dog to open its mouth so that I can clean its teeth.

Out: The dog exits the room or kennel.

Protect: This causes the dog to stand between me and any person near and to bark in a threatening manner.

Puppies: I use this in lieu of a single dog's name when I am talking to more than one of my dogs. Each of my dogs reacts to this word as if it were its own name.

Quiet: The dog stops barking.

Relax: The dog slows its walking pace or stops to relieve pressure on the leash.

Roll over: The dog rolls on its back for a belly rub.

Seek: The dog follows the indicated scent (part of a tracking exercise).

Settle: Usually accompanied with a hand signal, this causes the dog to remain quietly in a given area.

Sit: The dog sits.

Sit high: The dog sits on its hind legs with its front legs off the ground in the traditional begging position.

Stand: The dog stands.

Stay: The dog remains in position until released.

Steady: This variant or reinforcement of *stay* is used during grooming when the dematting brush or some other tool is pulling at the dog's hair. It causes the dog to lock and hold its position despite the momentary discomfort.

Straight: The dog adjusts into a straight *heel* position (part of obedience practice).

Swing: The dog goes around me and into a *heel* position.

Take it: The dog retrieves an object on the ground in front of it.

Time to clean your eyes: This is used only for my spaniel. It causes it to place its head in my left hand so that I can perform the ritual of cleaning the tear stains from around its eyes.

Towel time: The dog goes to centre of kitchen floor and waits to be dried off after a walk in the rain.

Up: This causes the dog to jump up on the indicated surface.

Upstairs: The dog goes upstairs.

Wait: The dog temporarily stops current activity but continues to watch me.

Watch me: This alerts the dog to keep its eyes on me.

Where's Joannie?: The dog goes to the room where my wife is or to the stairs if she is upstairs or in the basement.

Where's your ball?: The dog goes to find its ball.

Where's your stick?: The dog goes to find its stick.

Who wants a cookie?: The dog runs to kitchen counter to wait for a dog biscuit.

Who wants a ride?: When outside, the dog runs to the van and waits to get in. (When inside, it goes to the door and waits.)

Who wants some food?: The dog runs to kitchen and faces the place where its food bowl is put out.

Who wants to go for a walk?: The dog goes to front door and waits.

X-pen: This causes the dog to wait near the exercise pen until I open it so that it can go inside.

This list of over sixty words is incomplete, as I've said; I've only listed the frequently used vocabulary items and left out words that produce untrained responses. The word *bath*, for example, always caused my cairn terrier to look for a place to hide, whereas my Cavalier King Charles spaniel simply went to the door of the bathroom to await the inevitable. I am sure that they respond to other words as well, such as to the phrase *dog class*, but the responses are less predictable.

The receptive language ability of my dogs also includes a number of gestures or signals (the equivalent of sign language). Many of these signals can simply substitute for common spoken words, while others provide vital information to clarify a spoken command. Thus there is a hand signal for *come*, two different hand signals for *down* and two for *sit* (depending on whether the dog is at my side or at some distance in front of me), a signal for *heel* (as in walk by my left side), one for *stay*, and another hand signal for *away*. There are two separate hand signals to send the dog to *heel* position, depending on whether I want the dog to circle around my back or pirouette at my left side. There are also two signals for *stand*, depending on whether the dog is moving or sitting at the time. I use numerous directional signals as well: pointing to the right or left, to indicate the direction that a jump is to be taken; pointing left, right, or centre to indicate which item is to be retrieved in response to a *take it* command; pointing to a specific door, gate, or opening for an *in* or *out* command; tapping a specific surface to indicate where I want the dog to go in response to an *up* command;

indicating the direction I want the dog to run in after a *go back* command. Yet another signal indicates where the scent is that I want the dog to track after the *seek* command, and a further signal traces an imaginary line that the dog is not to cross after a *settle* command.

Recently a border collie named Rico was tested by Julia Fischer and other psychologists at the Max Planck Institute for Evolutionary Anthropology in Leipzig, Germany. They found that he could understand over two hundred words, most of which corresponded to the names of objects. Like a young human child, Rico would quickly form a rough hypothesis about the meaning of a new word after a single exposure by inferring that the new word is connected to an object he is seeing for the first time. One example of this is learning by an *exclusionary principle*. Suppose that we put out seven toys and say to Rico "Go get the *framis*." Rico has never heard the word "framis" before. However, he goes out to the pile of objects and finds that he knows the name of six of them. He then takes the next step and assumes that the one he doesn't recognize must be the framis. If we test him later, even weeks later, with a new pile of objects that includes the one that we labelled the framis, he will quickly identify it. This is a complex form of language learning that that up to now we thought was possible only in humans and language-learning apes.

While I have concentrated only on deliberately delivered sounds and signals, dogs also recognize body language. To a psychologist, body language refers to how we move and position ourselves and even to our facial expressions. These change as our emotions change, and they also change in different social situations. Dogs are quite responsive to the nuances of body language. If you are angry, even if you are not angry at the dog, or are trying to suppress your feelings, you may find your dog slinking about with its tail between its legs as though it had done something wrong. The dog is simply responding to your unconscious signals to it. In dog-training classes, we often notice that if a handler or owner is tense, the dog doesn't seem to work very well or learn very much—the dog also seems to be tense and uncomfortable. We have a saying for this: "The tension flows down the lead", which means that the dog is picking up its master's unconscious body language signals and responding to them. Obviously, trying to isolate all the subtle additional signals that dogs receive and respond to would be difficult. In general, though, the dog's ability to interpret body language should probably be credited as an additional factor in its communication ability.

DOG-PRODUCTIVE LANGUAGE

All these signals and words serve as language that conveys information from the human to the dog. However, dogs are also capable of communicating to us, and, like us, they do so using both vocalizations, signals, and gestures. Some of the signals are universal to almost all dogs and perhaps to wolves, jackals, and wild dogs, as well, while others are unique to a particular household (analogous to a local dialect). In my book *How to Speak Dog*, I collected together the universal items associated with emotional expression, which included twenty-seven distinct sound signals, forty-eight body signals, plus sixty additional signs. Notice that there are many more signals and signs that are meant to be seen rather than to be heard. This makes evolutionary sense since the pack hunters that dogs evolved from would not want their potential prey to overhear their communications and thus be forewarned of their approach.

Psychologists have found that dogs use productive language to communicate about three main topics. The first deals with their emotional states. The second pertains to social relations, which include aspects of dominance or social standing and territorial concerns. Lastly, dogs communicate to express wants and desires. It is in this last realm that dogs are most variable and are most apt to show learned language or signalling.

Dog Vocalizations

Humans may be faulted for not listening closely to their dogs and thus failing to discriminate much of the meaning present in dog sounds. The human ear is so insensitive to dogs' voices that there is not even any consensus as to the basic sound that dogs make. To the English or American speaker, dogs say *bow-wow, woof-woof,* or *arf-arf.* To the Spanish, they say *jau-jau;* to the Dutch, *waf-waf;* to the French, *woa-woa;* to the Russian, *gav-gav;* to the Hebrew speaker, *hav-hav;* to the German, *wau-wau;* to the Czech, *haff-haff;* to the Chinese, *wung-wung.* Of course, the dogs may simply be speaking in local dialects.

When scientists pay careful attention to dog sounds, however, they identify a number of different vocalizations with different nuances of meaning. Let me list some of these with their approximate English meanings and some indication of the contexts in which they are used.

There are a couple of important dimensions to attend to in dog vocalizations. The first is the pitch of the sound. For barks and other sounds, low-pitched sounds usually indicate threats, anger, and the possibility of aggression, while higher-pitched sounds can mean fear or pain or, when they are less sharp, pleasure or playfulness. Psychologists have identified these same characteristics in human speech. When humans are angry, the pitch of the voice tends to drop, and, when fearful, the voice becomes shrill, high pitched, and words tend to be clipped in length. Our voices also lilt in a singsong manner to indicate playfulness or when we are talking to babies and young children. Janet Werker, a Canadian psychologist, has been able to demonstrate that people can recognize whether an individual is talking to an adult or a baby, even when the words used are exactly the same, solely by changes in the tone or pitch of the voice.

The second dimension in dog vocalizations is the frequency or repetition rate of the sound. Sounds that are repeated often, at a fast rate, indicate a degree of excitement and urgency. Sounds that are spaced out or not repeated usually indicate a lower level of excitement or a passing state of mind. The duration of the sounds is also important. High-pitched sounds of short duration frequently indicate fear or pain, while the same sounds repeated at a slower rate indicate playfulness or anticipation of pleasure. Generally speaking, more sustained sounds indicate intentionality, that actions have been thought out or behaviour is about to happen, such as the low-pitched, sustained growl that precedes attack.

BARKS

Continuous rapid barking, midrange pitch: "Sound the alarm! Call the pack! There is a potential problem! Someone is coming into our territory!"

Continuous barking but a bit slower and pitched lower: "The intruder [or danger] is very close. Get ready to defend yourself!"

Barking in rapid strings of three or four with pauses in between, midrange pitch: "I suspect that there may be a problem or an intruder near our territory. I think that the leader of the pack should look into it."

Prolonged or incessant barking, with moderate to long intervals between each utterance: "Is there anybody there? I'm lonely and need companionship." This is most often the response to confinement or being left alone for long periods of time.

One or two sharp short barks, midrange pitch: "Hello there!" This is the most typical greeting sound.

Single sharp short bark, lower midrange pitch: "Stop that!" This is often given by a mother dog when disciplining her puppies but may also indicate annoyance in any dog, such as when disturbed from sleep or if hair is pulled during grooming and so forth.

Small nuances or changes in the dog's verbalizations can change the intended meanings quite a bit. This is analogous to the way that changes in voice inflection can change the meaning of statements in English. The simple statement of fact "It's ready" can be interpreted as the question meaning "Is it ready?" if our inflection rises at the end of the phrase, rather than diminishing. Similar changes are evident in the single or short bark sequences:

Single sharp short bark, higher midrange: "What's this?" or "Huh?" This is a startled or surprised sound. If it is repeated two or three times, its meaning changes to "Come look at this!" alerting the pack to a novel event. This same type of bark, but not quite as short and sharp, is used to mean "Come here!" Many dogs will use this kind of bark at the door to indicate that they want to go out. Lowering the pitch to a relaxed midrange means "Terrific!" or some other similar expletive, such as "Oh, great!" My cairn terrier, Flint, for example, who loved to jump, always gave this single bark of joy when sent over the high jump. Other dogs give this same bark when given their food dish.

Single yelp or very short high-pitched bark: "Ouch!" This is in response to a sudden, unexpected pain.

Series of yelps: "I'm hurting!" "I'm really scared!" This is in response to severe fear and pain.

Stutter-bark, midrange pitch: This is really the combination of a breath growl "harrr" and a single short bark "ruff." This stutter-bark "harrr-ruff" means "Let's play!" and is used to initiate playing behaviour.

Rising bark: This is a bit hard to describe, although once you've heard it, it is unmistakable. It is usually a series of barks, each of which starts in the middle range but rises sharply in pitch—almost a bark-yelp, though not quite that high. It is a play bark, used during rough-and-tumble games, that shows excitement and translates as "This is fun!"

GROWLS

Growls can stand alone or be used to modify barking sounds to add a degree of threat.

Soft, low-pitched breath growl: This breath growl sounds like the stereotypical pirates' "Harrr" and it means "Beware!" "Back off!" This is used as a threat and usually causes the listener to move away, giving the dog more space.

Low-pitched growl-bark: This is a clear growl that leads to a bark. It means "I'm upset and I'm ready to fight!" This is a clear warning that pressing the dog will lead to aggression.

Higher midrange-pitched growl-bark: "I'm worried [or frightened], but I will defend myself." This is the threat of a less-confident animal that will, however, most likely fight back if pushed.

Undulating growl: This is a growl that goes from low midrange to high midrange with a kind of a semibark often added as the pitch rises. It means "I'm terrified. If you come at me, I may fight or I may run." This is the fearful-aggressive sound of a very unsure dog.

Noisy growl, with teeth hidden from view: "This is a good game!" "I'm having fun!" It is usually part of the play sequence and may be tucked in between a series of stutter-barks. It usually indicates intense concentration, as in a tug-of-war or play-acting aggression.

OTHER VOCALIZATIONS

Soft whimpering: "I hurt!" "I'm scared." The average person is most likely to hear this at the veterinarian's office, when the dog is suffering, or when a submissive dog is in a strange place that appears threatening. This is really a carryover of the mewing sound that young puppies make when cold, hungry, or distressed.

Louder, more prolonged whining sound: "Please give me . . ." "I want . . ." A dog usually uses this sound when waiting for food, or for the leash to be put on, or when trying to get its master's attention, and so forth.

Sighs: This vocalization, which is invariably accompanied by the dog's lying down with its head on its forepaws, can have two meanings, depending on the context and certain facial expressions. With eyes half-closed, it is a sign of pleasure, meaning "I'm content and am going to settle down here." With eyes fully open, it is a sign of disappointment when something anticipated has not materialized, best interpreted as "I give up!"

Baying: This is the characteristic sound of hounds during a hunt. It is usually interpreted as "Follow me!" "Let's get him!" or "All together now!"

Yip-howl: This is really more of a yip-yip-yip-howl, with the final howl quite prolonged. It usually means "I'm lonely," "I feel abandoned!," or "Is anybody there?"

Howling: "I'm here!" "This is my territory!" "I hear you out there!" A confident animal will often howl simply to announce its presence. Howling also often occurs in response to a yip-howl from another dog. It has a more sonorous sound to the human ear than does the yip-howl, which is often described as mournful.

Moaning: This sounds something like "ar-owl-wowl-wowl . . ." over a short interval of time. It is a sound of spontaneous pleasure and excitement that means "I'm excited!" or "Let's go!" A dog usually moans when something it really likes is about to happen.

Panting: "Let's go!" This is a sign of excitement, but can also indicate stress.

Dogs also can learn specific vocalizations. For instance, the bark that dogs give to the command *speak* sounds qualitatively different from a spontaneous bark. The same can be said for the bark that police and protection dogs learn to give. Some dogs can even be taught specific sounds for specific settings, ranging from simple barks, moans, or play-growls to more complex sounds that may sound like yodels or attempts at speech. For example, psychologist Janet Werker had a poodle that stayed home alone during the day. Each night when the family members returned home, they habitually said hello to the waiting dog in a cheerful and singsong tone of voice. After a while, the dog learned an imitative two-syllable "arl-row", which it gave in greeting spontaneously when family members enter the house. This vocalization, however, was reserved for family and was never given to strangers.

Dog Signals and Gestures

Dogs also use their bodies to communicate about social and emotional matters. A dog's tail, eyes, ears, and mouth all speak to us, and whole body postures add further information, serving to modify the message given.

TAIL

Tail position is an important indicator of social standing and mental state. There will be some variations, of course, depending upon the natural tail position of the dog: a West Highland white terrier will carry its carrot-shaped tail higher than a golden retriever carries its flowing, feathery tail, and a greyhound's relaxed tail position is lower yet.

Almost horizontal, pointing away from the dog but not stiff: This is a sign of attention. It roughly translates as "Something interesting may be happening here."

Straight out horizontally, pointing away from the dog: This is part of an initial challenge when meeting a stranger or an intruder. It roughly translates as "Let's establish who's boss here."

Tail up, between the horizontal and vertical position: This is the sign of a dominant dog, or one who is asserting dominance, and translates as "I'm boss here."

Tail up and slightly curved over the back: "I'm top dog," this says. It is the expression of a confident, dominant dog who feels in control.

Tail held lower than the horizontal but still some distance from the legs: "I'm relaxed." "All is well."

Tail down, near hind legs: This changes its meaning with the posture of the dog. If the legs are still straight and the tail slightly brushes back and forth, it means "I'm not feeling well" or "I'm a bit depressed." If the legs are slightly bent inward, giving a slight downward slope to the back, it means "I'm feeling a bit insecure," especially in an unknown setting or situation.

Tail tucked between the legs: "I'm frightened!" or "Don't hurt me!" This is especially common in the presence of a dominant dog or person, when it can also mean, "I accept my lowly role in the pack, and I'm not trying to challenge you."

The information from the position of the tail is moderated by several factors:

Bristling hair down the tail: The bristle in the dog's tail is a sign of aggression. It may modify any tail position. Thus, with the tail straight out it means "I'm ready to fight if you are!" and with the tail slightly up or over the back it means "I'm not afraid of you and will fight to prove I'm boss."

Crick or sharp bend in the tail when held high: This is more characteristic of the dogs that look like wolves, such as the German shepherds, and means much the same as the tail bristling. It is the precursor to possible aggression.

Tail wagging can come about simply as a sign of excitement, the degree of which is indicated by the vigor or speed of the wag. In judging excitement, you should attend to the speed of wagging independent of the size of the actual movement. A sporting dog with a full, flowing tail might seem to move it much more than a terrier moves its carrot-shaped tail (where a furious wag may seem like nothing more than a tremor). Yet in both cases, high-speed movements simply mean "I'm excited." The relative size of any single dog's tail wag does convey other information, however.

Slight tail wag: This is usually a greeting, best interpreted as "Hello there." To a human master, it is often given with the meaning "I see you looking at me. You like me, don't you?" and is simply a response to social attention.

Broad tail wag: "I like you." This is often shown during play, when one dog seems to be attacking the other, pouncing, growling, and barking. The wagging tail serves as reassurance that this is all in fun. It also means "I'm pleased" in many contexts.

Slow tail wag, with tail at half-mast: During dog training, I interpret this as "I'm trying to understand you. I want to know what you mean, but I just can't quite figure it out." When the dog finally solves the problem, the speed and size of the tail wags will usually markedly increase.

Tail wagging is a completely social gesture. In some ways, it serves the same functions as a human smile. Humans seem to reserve most of their smiles for when somebody is around to see them or when they are thinking about somebody or something special. For dogs, the tail wag seems to have the same properties. A dog will wag its tail for a person or another dog. It may wag its tail for a cat, a horse, a mouse, or a leaf moved by a breeze that might be a living thing. But when a dog is by itself, it will not wag its tail to anything it perceives as lifeless. A dog will wag its tail to express its gratitude to you as you put its food bowl down, but should the dog walk into the room and find the bowl full, it will approach and eat the food just as happily, but with no tail wagging other than, perhaps, a slight excitement tremor. This is one indication that tail wagging is meant as communication or language. Just as we don't talk to walls, dogs do not wag their tails to things that are not apparently alive and socially responsive.

For most breeds of dog, the tail will tend to lighten toward the tip, and on many breeds there is a characteristic white tip to the tail. As I noted earlier, this marking is also quite visible in jackals, foxes, wild dogs, and dingoes. Some evolutionary biologists have suggested that the purpose of this light area is to make tail signals more visible. For some wolves, the tail is marked with a dark tip, which, of course, can serve much the same function of making it easier to see the tail position and motion. Clearly, dogs whose tails have been docked are at a disadvantage. The absence of this vital communication channel may impair their ability to exchange information with other dogs.

At the other end of the dog, lots of evidence suggests that the ways a dog uses eye contact, holds its ears, and moves its mouth are designed to carry information and to modify the behaviours of other dogs and humans who are socially interacting with it.

EARS

As in the case of the tail, all positions of a dog's ears should be gauged relative to the way the dog normally carries its ears when it is relaxed. Dogs with severely cropped or very long ears will be harder to read.

Ears erect or slightly forward: "What's that?" This is a sign of attention in response to a sound or when studying a new situation. Accompanied by a slightly tilted head and a relaxed or slightly open mouth, the meaning changes to "This is really interesting" or "I don't understand that" and is associated with observation of a novel event. When accompanied by bared teeth and wrinkled nose, however, it is an offensive threat by a confident dog.

Ears pulled back flat against the head: "I'm frightened" or "I'm protecting myself against a possible attack." This is usually associated with a challenge of some sort.

Ears pulled slightly back: On a prick-eared dog, such as a German shepherd, the ears take on a slightly splayed, sideways spread in this position and may look like a wide open V or, in the extreme, airplane wings. It means "I don't like this" and "I'm ready to fight or run." This is the look of suspicion and may show both aggression and ambivalence.

EYES

There are two major eye signals, and both have to do with dominance or the lack of it.

Direct eye-to-eye stare: "Who do you think you are?" and "I challenge you for dominance." This is usually part of a social confrontation and is the action of a dominant dog.

Eyes turned away to avoid direct eye contact: "I accept the fact that you're the boss" and "I don't want any trouble." This is the response of a more submissive dog to a challenge.

MOUTH

Dogs cannot produce the range of expressions that humans can with their mouths; however, several basic ones are important.

Mouth relaxed and slightly open, tongue may be slightly visible or even slightly draped over the lower teeth: This is the dog equivalent of the human smile. It means "I'm happy and relaxed."

Yawn: This is probably one of the most misunderstood dog signals. While it is usually interpreted by humans as meaning fatigue or boredom, it is actually a stress-related signal, best interpreted as "I'm tense, anxious, or edgy right now."

Lips curled to expose some teeth, mouth still mostly closed: "You're annoying me!" This is the first sign of menace or threat.

Lips curled up to show major teeth, some wrinkling of the area above the nose, mouth partly open: "If you do something that I might interpret as a threat, I may bite." This is the next stage of threat but may also indicate fearfulness. Pressing a dog at this stage may lead to an aggressive attack.

Lips curled up to expose not only all of the teeth but also the gums above the front teeth, visible wrinkles above the nose: "Back off or else!" This is the full threat display that indicates a dog is ready to release a violent attack. If you are ever confronted with this display, you should not turn and run: The level of arousal is so high that your movement will probably produce a pursuit-and-attack response. Instead, cast your gaze slightly down (a slightly submissive eye position), open your mouth a bit (a bit of a counter-threat), and back off slowly.

In all the threat expressions, the nature of the lip curl produces some opening of the mouth and the impression that the corner of the mouth has been pulled forward a bit so that the mouth opening is roughly C-shaped. The expressions are modified somewhat if the lower corner of the mouth is pulled back or slightly down, which indicates an element of fear in the dog's aggressive display. The dog may still choose to attack, but it also may run if it is strongly attacked. Thus the pulled-back elongated mouth opening turns the dominant threat into something like "You frighten me, but I'll fight if I'm forced to."

BODY AND PAWS

Dogs use their bodies and paws to express a variety of different things. Again, the major concerns are social.

Dog crouches with front legs extended, rear up, and head near the ground: This is the classic play-bow and means simply "Let's play!"

Stiff-legged, upright posture or slow, stiff-legged movement forward: "I'm in charge around here!" and "I challenge you." A dominant dog will use this posture to indicate assertion of authority and a willingness to fight for it.

Body slightly sloped forward, feet braced: "I accept your challenge and am ready to fight!"

Dog rolls on side or exposes underside: "Let's not argue" or "I'm not a threat to you" or "I accept that you're in charge here." This is a submissive response to avert conflict. Many dogs adopt this posture in a fairly relaxed and contented manner when they are around their pack leader. When your dog rolls on its back for a belly rub, it is actually accepting you as leader of the pack.

Dog places head on another dog's shoulder or *places paw on the back of another dog:* "I want you to know who's boss around here." These gestures are commonly used by dominant dogs, pack leaders, and dogs that have aspirations of becoming a pack leader.

Mouthing: This shows up in dog-human interactions as the dog taking the handler's hand in his mouth or, while walking, taking the leash in the mouth (dogs view the leash as part of their handler's hand). Mouthing can be a serious sign of dominance challenging and shows that the dog does not accept the human as pack leader.

Dog places paw on master's knee: "Look, I'm here" or "Pay attention to me." This attention-seeking signal has many variations. They include pawing the air in front of their master or sliding the head under the master's hand.

Hair bristles on back and shoulders: This is a sign of anticipated aggression. A ridge of hair bristling down the back is a sign that says "Don't push me, I'm angry!" When the bristling extends to the shoulders it means "I've had it with you" and is a sign of imminent attack. In some wolves, there is a noticeable line of dark hair down the back, and occasionally darkening at the shoulders, presumably designed to attract the eye to these signals.

Dog sits with one front paw slightly raised: This is another sign of stress but is combined with insecurity. It means "I'm anxious, uneasy, and concerned."

Dog rolls on its back and rubs it on the ground: This is sometimes preceded by *nose rubbing,* where the dog pushes its face, and possibly its chest, against the ground in a rubbing motion or rubs the face with a forepaw, from eyes to nose. I like to look at these signs as part of a contentment ceremony. They often follow feeding or occur as the dog's master begins to prepare food. However they also can occur following or in anticipation of other pleasant activities.

Scraping the ground and ripping the turf with the paws: This is usually after the dog has defecated but may occur at other times. Dogs have glands on the bottom of their feet that provide each with a unique scent. What a dog is saying here is "Everybody should note that I was here. I'm leaving my calling card!"

Urinating: This means "This territory is mine," "This object is mine," "I'm in the neighbourhood now." Scent marking is usually done on vertical objects to place the scent at nose level for the next dog and to allow it to diffuse more widely in the air. Dogs will urinate over the marks of other dogs. If a dog urinates on another dog or a person, the message changes to an assertion of dominance as well as possession.

Urination is sometimes used as a direct signal rather than as the equivalent of a written message. A fearful dog may produce a small puddle of urine when it feels threatened. This is most commonly seen when the dog is approached by a person or dog that makes him anxious. This is a sign of submission and is meant to indicate that the dog is not going to challenge the oncoming individual.

Many of the signals dogs use are quite obvious when you see them but somewhat difficult to describe in words. To make things clearer, I've provided Figures 6.1 through 6.7, which are meant to serve as a sort of pictorial dictionary of dog-productive language.

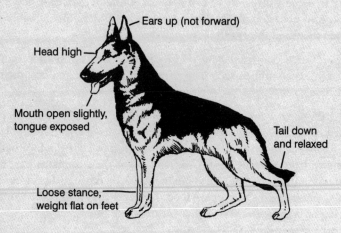

Ears up (not forward)

Head high

Mouth open slightly,
tongue exposed

Tail down
and relaxed

Loose stance,
weight flat on feet

Figure 6.1
A relaxed, reasonably content dog, unconcerned and unthreatened by any activities going on in its immediate environment.

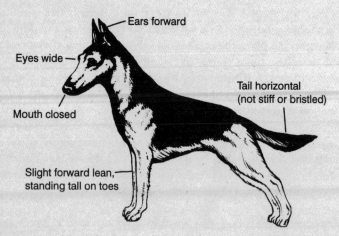

Ears forward

Eyes wide

Tail horizontal
(not stiff or bristled)

Mouth closed

Slight forward lean,
standing tall on toes

Figure 6.2
An alert dog responding to the arrival of something of interest in the environment.

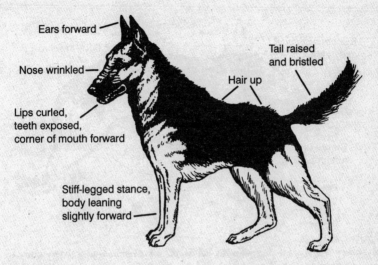

Figure 6.3
A very dominant animal both communicating dominance and threatening aggression if challenged.

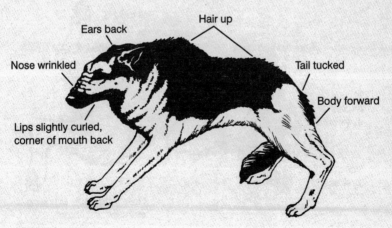

Figure 6.4
A frightened dog that might attack if pressed.

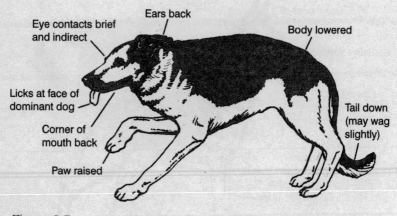

Ears back

Eye contacts brief
and indirect

Body lowered

Licks at face of
dominant dog

Corner of
mouth back

Tail down
(may wag
slightly)

Paw raised

Figure 6.5
A somewhat fearful dog offering signs of submission and subservience to
avoid any further challenges or threats.

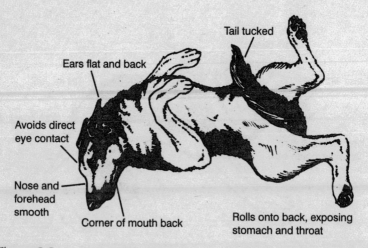

Tail tucked

Ears flat and back

Avoids direct
eye contact

Nose and
forehead
smooth

Corner of mouth back

Rolls onto back, exposing
stomach and throat

Figure 6.6
A dog communicating complete surrender, fear, and submission.

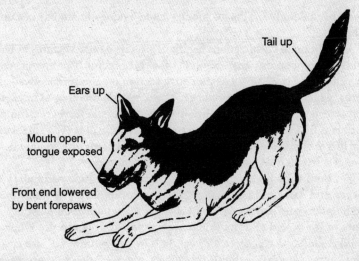

Tail up

Ears up

Mouth open,
tongue exposed

Front end lowered
by bent forepaws

Figure 6.7
A simple invitation to play—it could be accompanied by excited barking or
playful attacks and retreats.

ARE THESE SIGNALS ACTUALLY LANGUAGE?

From the time a child first responds to its name by turning and looking at the person who uttered it, psychologists attribute infants with
rudimentary linguistic ability. At the earliest stages of development,
receptive language—that is, the child's ability to understand the spoken and gestural language of others—is used as the major indication of
the child's language ability. Furthermore, while the child's first word
might not come until twelve months of age, some psychologists assert
that crying, cooing, and babbling have linguistic and communication
content, since they convey pleasure, displeasure, and some information about the child's needs. The first words themselves are often only
approximations of real language. In my own home, they were the "na
na" my daughter used to mean her grandmother or the "mik" that my
son used to indicate he was thirsty. Other sounds that children make
also serve communication functions; whether an anticipation whimper
or an excitement pant, they convey information about the child's state

and are strikingly similar to sounds made by dogs in similar circumstances.

In addition to vocalizations, psychologists recognize gestures as language components. For example, the MacArthur Communicative Development Inventory has an entire section on communicative gestures, which it counts as language. These include pointing to interesting objects or events, waving bye-bye when a person leaves, extending the arms upward to signal a wish to be picked up, and even smacking the lips to show that something tastes good. Certainly, the communicative gestures of dogs are equal in complexity to these.

For both dogs and young human children, receptive vocabulary is larger and more reliable than productive vocabulary. The items they both understand are also more likely to contain information about the state of the world and the things we would like them to do. When a child responds correctly to the request "Give me your hand", we grant him some linguistic ability; obviously, then, a dog's appropriate response to "Give me a paw" represents equivalent language ability. The emitted language for both young infants and dogs (that is, the sounds and gestures they make) is almost exclusively social in nature, attempting to elicit responses from other individuals. In dogs, the emitted language is actually a bit more complex than that of infants, as it emphasizes dominance and status relationships as well as the emotional state and desires of the communicator. Infants will not begin to attempt to communicate statements about dominance and subservience until they are several years old.

Traditionally scientists have suggested that comparisons between infant speech and dog communication begin to break down when it comes to grammar or syntax. Simply put, grammar is a set of rules that controls how we put language elements together to form meaningful communications. Certain combinations are permitted while others are not. Thus, expressions like "these cat" or "an ball" are not sensible phrases in English. We can call this aspect of grammar the *Rules of Combination*. Syntax deals with the fact that the specific order of the words can also determine the meaning of what is said. For example, the phrase "man-eating shark" refers to something quite different from the phrase "shark-eating man". Similarly, "The boy hit the girl" means something quite different than "The girl hit the boy". We can call this aspect of grammar *Rules of Sequence*. Until recently, most scientists seemed to think that dog communication differed from the communication in young children because it did not observe these two rules. However, based upon some recent observations, there are some tantalizing suggestions that dogs may show at least some evidence of having grammar.

Consider the Rules of Combination, which allow some things to go together in language and bar other possible combinations. When we consider the sounds that dogs make, we find that some combinations never occur together. Howls and whimpers are never combined. Nor will you ever hear howls and growls together. On the other hand, howls are happily combined with yips, and occasionally with some types of barks. Barks can be combined with other barks, with growls and with whimpers, but growls and whimpers are never combined with each other.

For many scientists, the most exciting recent observations suggest that dogs may also have grammar in the form of the Rules of Sequence. Let us consider two simple sounds that dogs make. The first is the breath growl mentioned earlier, which sounds something like "harrr." Taken by itself, this growl is a confident warning to another dog or a person to stay away. Dogs use it in situations where they have a prized object, like a nice bone, or a bowl of food, where this growl is used to mean "Back off—this is mine!"

The second simple sound is a single bark, which starts low, rises in pitch, and ends with something like an "F" sound. It can crudely be described as "rrruff." This is the common alerting bark that dogs give to get the attention of other members of the pack with something like "You might want to come over and look at this." It is normally responded to by other dogs moving in that direction to stand near the one who barked.

When we combine these sounds, however, we get different meanings from the interpretations of the single elements, and the specific meaning depends upon the order in which they are combined. The combination "harr-rrruff" is actually an invitation to play, and is usually combined with the typical play bow. Reversing the combination, to produce "rrruff-harrrr", results in quite a different message. It is a threat uttered by an insecure dog, perhaps trying to protect an item like a bone, but sometimes just to ward off another dog who may appear to be dominant and threatening. In this form, the sound means something like "You are making me nervous and if you come any closer I may be forced to fight." The fact that this signals a threat based upon insecurity makes it different from the simple "harrr", sounded by a secure, dominant animal. Taken together this seems to indicate that dogs also have the "missing pieces" which make their signalling system truly language—namely, grammar and syntax.

How does the language of dogs compare with that of humans? Well, if we count the number of sounds and signals that an average dog can interpret, then add the signs, sounds, and signals that it can produce, and finally the evidence that there are a few places where items are combined grammatically, we find that a dog's language abilities are roughly equivalent to that of a two-year-old child. A "super dog", such as the border collie, Rico, might be equivalent to a human a half year older than that. Savage-Rumbaugh's bonobo chimps would be the equivalent of, or a bit better than, a three-year-old child.

With all of this evidence, the idea that dogs have no substantial linguistic intelligence seems unsupportable. If we credit children of two years of age with language and if dogs show a parallel and equivalent ability, then, Descartes notwithstanding, we should credit dogs with some linguistic intelligence. They may not be ready to vie for the Pulitzer Prize, and I would certainly agree with the statement by the philosopher, Ludwig Wittgenstein, who said that "However eloquently [your dog] may bark, he cannot tell you that his parents were honest though poor." Yet it does seem reasonable to accept that dogs have enough language ability to allow them to communicate with each other and with us at about the same level as our own human offspring can, at least up to the age of two or so.

Chapter Seven

Varieties of
Dog Intelligence

> You can say any fool thing to a dog, and the dog will give
> you this look that says, "My God, you're RIGHT! I NEVER
> would of thought of that!"
>
> —DAVE BARRY

The association between dogs and humans stems from the fact that dogs perform functions that are useful to us. Some of these functions are quite utilitarian; others are more personal and psychological in nature. Some of the more common utilitarian functions include guarding and protecting property and people (e.g., police work and war dog work), helping during hunting (finding game, pulling it down, digging it up, and retrieving it), shepherding (tending sheep, cattle, reindeer, and even geese or ducks), hauling (pulling carts or sleds, carrying packs), seeking and finding objects, people, or substances (tracking dogs, drug-sniffing dogs, gas-detecting dogs, truffle-seeking dogs), performing rescue work (retrieving people from water or people buried in snow or wreckage), and assisting the disabled (seeing eye dogs, hearing ear dogs, handicap assistance dogs). At a more psychological level, the most common function of dogs is to serve as companions. In recent years, this has been extended to a more formal use as part of preventive and remedial therapy for the elderly, socially isolated, or psychologically disturbed. Even this relatively short list shows the many different skills we demand from dogs. Some (such as hunting, tracking, and searching skills) reflect aspects of behaviour normal in all wild dogs and their relatives and so probably are hereditary or instinctive in nature. Other skills (such as guiding the blind) involve extensive training.

Perhaps the best way to assess the degree and nature of dog intelligence is to observe how it shows up in the various tasks dogs perform, either for themselves or for humans. There are three different dimensions of *manifest intelligence* (a dog's total measurable intelligence), namely adaptive, working, and instinctive intelligence.

ADAPTIVE INTELLIGENCE

In everyday terms, when we speak of intelligence, we are usually referring to learning and problem-solving abilities. Thus when Paulette can solve complex mathematical problems, we say, "What a clever girl she is!" If Paul can learn to recite any piece of poetry from memory, after only one or two practice readings, we say, "He must be a very intelligent little boy!" *Learning ability* is usually defined as the number of experiences needed for an individual to code something as a relatively permanent memory. Individuals with good learning ability need very few exposures to a particular situation to form usable memories and associations. *Problem solving* is defined as the ability to overcome obstacles mentally, piece together bits of information into a correct answer or response, or to discover new ways to apply previously learned information to novel situations in the environment. Better problem-solvers require less time to reach solutions and have fewer false starts or dead-end solutions. Learning and problem-solving are the dimensions of intelligence that were traditionally measured on a child's report card from school.

In humans and animals, these abilities make up *adaptive intelligence*, since they allow individuals to adapt to their environments or provide them with skills to modify their environments to suit their needs. Everyday examples of the use of adaptive intelligence might be, for a human being, learning how better to sell a product or to cook a specific item of food or, for a wild animal, how to track down prey for dinner or care for its young. If problems occur frequently, their solutions are stored in memory (learned) so that the individual can come up with the best response more quickly on subsequent encounters with similar situations. Thus learning and problem solving interact to make behaviour more efficient.

Robert Sternberg, a psychologist from Yale University who has contributed significantly to our understanding of human intelligence, has analyzed adaptive intelligence in people and found that it can be subdivided into several parts, or components. For this reason, he decided to use the general label *componential intelligence* instead of the label *adaptive intelligence* used here. According to Sternberg's analysis, *metacomponents* make up one important set of components found in adaptive intelligence, with the prefix *meta*, from the Greek root meaning "higher level" or "transcending," indicating that these components serve to control or organize a large number of more specific behaviours. Metacomponents are those mechanisms that individuals use to plan and execute tasks and to select strategies of behaviour or problem solving. When facing problems and new situations, people strong in this area of intelligence quickly develop useful plans to guide their future behaviour. Adaptive intelligence also contains *performance components*, which include the ability to select the specific actions and methods needed actually to perform a task. Performance components involve the ability to carry out the plans or implement the decisions made by the metacomponents.

Next are the *acquisition components*, which are processes involved in learning new information. These include the processes that allow the individual to gain new knowledge and sort out relevant from irrelevant information. Simply put, individuals with good acquisition components learn quickly. There are also the *retention components*, which allow the individual to retrieve information from memory efficiently. Finally, Sternberg notes that adaptive intelligence also contains *transfer components*, which allow information learned in one situation to be transferred or applied to a new situation.

One advantage of looking at adaptive intelligence in this way is that it shows more clearly the actual mental abilities involved: planning the behaviour, selecting specific actions, learning or retrieving information, and applying that information to the situation at hand. In a dog, adaptive intelligence would represent what the dog can do for itself and would be reflected in how efficiently it learns and solves problems. Let me give you a simple example.

A visitor to my house was somewhat amazed to see my cairn terrier

Flint pushing his empty water dish across the kitchen floor toward me. Flint pushed it about a foot and then looked expectantly at me. When I didn't respond, he pushed it another few inches toward me and then looked up at me again. He repeated this action several times until I asked, "Do you want some water, Flint?" At this he gave an expectant bark and wagged his tail as he watched me fill the bowl. The moment I placed the bowl back in its usual place, Flint had a long drink and then pranced happily out of the room.

Despite the fact that my visitor felt this activity had to involve a lot of thought, planning, and understanding on the part of the dog, it was actually a fairly basic example of adaptive intelligence at work. The sequence of learning was quite simple and involved unplanned events in the dog's environment. The adaptive modification of Flint's behavior probably began one day when he found his water dish nearly empty, and, while trying to lick up the last drops, he pushed the bowl a few inches across the floor. Because it is metal, it makes a distinctive scraping sound on the hard floor. It is likely that when I heard the sounds, I went over to fill the bowl, and Flint was rewarded with a much-wanted drink. After a few instances of this sequence of events, the acquisition components of his intelligence allowed him to form an association between the scraping sound the bowl makes when it is empty and the ensuing opportunity to slake his thirst. The retention components allowed him to remember the association and perhaps to remember that louder, more active scraping sounds usually cause me to react more quickly and reliably. Now, whenever his bowl is empty, the performance components allow him to select an activity that will produce the scraping sound—namely, pushing the bowl across the floor with his nose. If Flint performed the same action for a different person or if he tried to elicit an extra meal by pushing his empty food dish across the floor, then he would be demonstrating the transfer components of his adaptive intelligence.

WORKING OR OBEDIENCE INTELLIGENCE

When we think of dog intelligence, we often think of a dog working its way through complex obedience exercises in a dog obedience ring or on a stage. We might also think of highly trained animals, such as police dogs, guide dogs, herding dogs, or search and rescue dogs, performing their intricate tasks in an intelligent and sophisticated manner. The sight of a dog attending to its master's commands and signals, while at the same time responding in a quick assured manner to the task at hand, gives us the impression that we are viewing the peak of dog intelligence. When a dog demonstrates that it understands what particular commands mean by responding appropriately, it is demonstrating one of the most important aspects of its manifest or measurable intelligence—important because, if dogs did not respond to human control and command, they would not be useful to us and would not be capable of performing the utilitarian tasks that we value them for. Since these qualities of intelligence are also demonstrated in dog obedience competitions, where dogs must execute learned exercises according to human directions, we could easily call this dimension of intelligence *obedience intelligence*. However, since it is also the intelligence needed to accomplish tasks in the real world under the guidance of a leader, we could just as well call it *working intelligence*.

It might seem logical to assume that dogs with the highest levels of learning and problem-solving ability will also have the best working and obedience intelligence, but this turns out not to be the case. Many dogs with very high adaptive intelligence seem to be relatively unresponsive to humans' attempts at teaching them obedience exercises; the simplest obedience commands may leave them completely at a loss. On the other hand, some dogs with only moderate levels of adaptive intelligence can, with the right form of training, execute obedience work quite well and even perform apparently quite complex tricks and exercises.

To work effectively under human direction obviously requires that a dog have at least enough adaptive intelligence to figure out which behaviours are expected of it when it receives a particular command. Deciphering what a particular word or signal means is, from the dog's viewpoint, just another problem that has to be solved. Experienced dog trainers often say that the hardest part of training dogs for competition in the higher obedience classes is simply trying to get them to understand what is expected. For example, one of the dog obedience exercises a dog must be able to complete in order to earn the American Kennel Club title "Utility Dog" requires that, on a single command, the animal should go directly to a pile of scattered articles on the ground and then, by scent alone, find the article that its master has most recently handled, pick the article up, and then bring it to its handler. The task itself is not very difficult once the dog understands what is required. Unfortunately, in the absence of the higher-level language abilities that would allow direct instructions to be passed from trainer to dog, the human can only give clues as to what is wanted, leaving the dog with the problem of figuring out what is actually meant by the command *"Find it!"* Many times the communication process is much like a game of charades, with the handler giving different clues and the dog trying a variety of different solutions. A clever trainer can provide better clues, but the dog must still figure them out and recognize the solution for itself and then learn the answer well enough to retrieve it on later occasions.

Yet good adaptive intelligence is not enough to guarantee that a dog will respond to obedience or working commands reliably. The single, most important, additional quality the dog must have is the desire or willingness to perform learned activities or to solve immediate problems at the pleasure and direction of its human master. This is a personality factor, rather than an intelligence factor. (I will return to the importance of personality in determining dog behaviour in Chapter 11.) Then, within the realm of intelligence variables, the dog must have a long attention span (meaning that the dog must be capable of concentrating on a task for a reasonable amount of time). This is important in obedience work because sometimes working out the meaning of a new command doesn't go well at first; several tries must be made, and several practice runs may be needed to stamp the association into the dog's memory. Thus, not only must attention be focused on the task, but the dog must be persistent and not become bored or frustrated too easily. The dog must also be mentally flexible. If the first responses to a particular command are not rewarded, the dog has to be flexible enough to try another strategy and not simply repeat the previous wrong response. Related to this and equally necessary is the ability to withstand distraction. The dog needs the mental control to suppress other activities and to control its responses to interesting sights, sounds, and smells. Without this control, it will be easily distracted during training or working sessions. Such an ability to withstand distractions is one of the characteristics psychologists find to be a common trait in highly intelligent human beings. Working at the direction of a human handler involves social interactions between dog and human; the dog must also possess reasonable communication skills. It must recognize that its handler is trying to communicate with it and must respond to the signs, sounds, and signals meant to guide its behaviour and tell it if the current action is correct.

While adaptive intelligence measures what a dog can do for itself, working or obedience intelligence should be viewed as a measure of what the dog can do for humans. This would seem to imply that working intelligence is relevant only for domestic dogs, but there is a parallel in wild canids. Working intelligence contains a social component. From the human vantage point, it reflects responses to a human master, but from the dog's viewpoint, it is a response to the leader of the pack. In the wild, most canids hunt in groups, the activities coordinated by the leader of the pack, the dominant or "alpha" individual. Each animal in the pack learns to take direction from the leader and learns its role in the hunt. These are the same learning and social control components that go into obedience intelligence in dogs.

INSTINCTIVE INTELLIGENCE

There is a form of intelligence that we seldom consider. It includes all the skills and behaviours that are part of our genetic programming. For dogs, it can account for a sizable portion of their abilities.

People are remarkably lazy and are also clever enough to find ways to reduce their own workloads. I mentioned earlier that particular breeds of dogs have, for all intents and purposes, been invented by people through selective breeding programs. Early in the history of the domestic dog, people recognized that by interbreeding dogs with specific desirable behavioural traits they could sometimes develop a line of animals that carried those behaviours in their genes. Through such selective breeding, we have deliberately shaped the size, shape, color, and temperament of dogs; we have also selected certain behavioural characteristics.

Consider the Chesapeake Bay retriever, for example. The breed began with two puppies, a red dog and a black bitch, that were rescued from the wreck of an English ship off the coast of Maryland in 1807. The two grew to be good retrievers and were bred together. The best retrievers from the resulting litters were then also bred together, with an occasional outcrossing to particularly good retrievers in the immediate area. The unique qualities of this retriever were bred and developed to fulfill the specific needs of early market hunters who operated mostly on the rugged freezing coast of the Chesapeake Bay and the surrounding marshes. They would shoot two hundred to three hundred birds a day, and then load these waterfowl into wagons to sell in the surrounding settlements. These "Bay Dogs" needed to have the determination and perseverance to retrieve enormous numbers of birds from icy rough waters, under severe weather conditions. In addition, the dogs were expected to guard the wagons and possessions of the hunters, especially when they went to town to sell their birds. After several generations, the Chesapeake Bay retriever had been created as a breed that was uniform and recognizable in its look. More important, the breed contained the behavioural characteristic that the hunters had been trying to capture. Chesapeakes retrieve virtually automatically, and the breed is now prized as one of the best of retrievers for regions where the dog must traverse stretches of cold water. However, they differ from most other retrievers, who are generally placid, friendly, and accept strangers, but were not expected to guard anything. Chesapeakes are dedicated retrievers, but because guarding was part of their expected function they are more wary and protective.

Notice that genetic selection may concentrate on one specific behaviour, such as retrieving, but also include a cluster of additional features, such as guarding. The history of spaniels is an example of this. The word *spanyell* dates from the late 1100s, when it was used to name a dog supposedly imported into the United Kingdom from Spain (the *span-* in *spaniel* is supposed to indicate their country of origin). These dogs were already popular in Ireland because hunters had found that they were useful in retrieving fowl from the water. Records from the mid-1300s report systematic selective breeding for spaniels. One line was selected for its ability to work particularly well in the water, and there was a separate selective breeding for land or field spaniels. Today's American water spaniel and Irish water spaniel derive from the selection for water-retrieving abilities, and the most popular breeds resulting from selective breeding for field or land spaniels are the cocker spaniel (named for the woodcocks that were among the most common birds it was used to hunt) and the springer spaniel (which is used to flush or "spring" game into nets). Other specialists for work on land include the lesser-known field spaniel, Sussex spaniel, and Clumber spaniel. That one can selectively breed for characteristics such as "works well in water" or "works better in the field" obviously means that the genes selected encompass a fairly broad cluster of identifiable behaviours.

Many specific canine behaviours seem to be genetically determined and thus can be controlled by selective breeding. Barking is another example. Whether a dog barks or not, how often, and the circumstances under which it will bark are all under a high degree of genetic control. The geneticist L. F. Whitney noticed that while most bloodhounds barked when tracking a scent, a few rare bloodhounds did not. By selectively breeding the nonbarkers, he produced a strain of silent-tracking bloodhounds.

Perhaps the most specific example of genetic control of dog behaviour that has been monitored scientifically comes to us from Clyde E. Keeler and H. C. Trimble, two Harvard researchers working in the 1930s. Their study dealt with Dalmatians. Members of this breed were sometimes referred to as "coach dogs" because of their affinity for horses and fondness for running under horse-drawn carriages or coaches. They were selectively bred for these traits during the 1800s. According to the fashion of the time, the ideal coaching position was a spot under the front axle of the carriage, with the dog running very close to the hooves of the rear horses. Actually, the closer the dog to the horses' hooves, the better the position was felt to be. Obviously, a dog running under the center of the carriage or under the rear axle was in a poor coaching position, and the worst coaching position was when the dog ran behind the carriage.

The researchers took advantage of the fact that they had contacts with a kennel that had been training Dalmatians to run with coaches for over twenty-five years. They noticed that certain dogs seemed to have a preference for good or poor coaching positions. When records were examined, it was found that offspring from a mating of two dogs that both adopted good coaching positions were more likely to adopt a good coaching position themselves than were dogs resulting from the mating of one good and one bad coaching position dog. The poorest performance was from the mating of two bad position dogs. This last group was the smallest, as might be expected, since the kennel had no interest in developing a line of Dalmatians that automatically assumed a bad coaching position.

The abilities that a dog inherits, whether through the action of people deliberately manipulating the genetic makeup of dogs or through natural selection, become the characteristics that determine the differences among the various breeds. These genetically determined abilities and behavioural predispositions constitute that dog's *instinctive intelligence*—those aspects of a dog's mental makeup that can be transmitted from generation to generation through the biological mechanisms of inheritance. Some aspects of instinctive intelligence may be as specific as tendencies to bark or not or tendencies to retrieve or not; others may be quite general and broad and perhaps may affect the dog's overall performance in problem solving, obedience, or other aspects of behaviour.

MIXING MINDS

If dogs display three different types of intelligence (adaptive, working, and instinctive), which is the most important or which dominates a dog's behaviour? Do these different forms of intelligence affect each other in some ways? I have already mentioned that a dog needs some minimum level of adaptive intelligence to produce any measurable working or obedience intelligence; still, a dog's having poor obedience intelligence does not necessarily mean that it has poor adaptive intelligence as well. However, the issue of how instinctive intelligence interacts with the other dimensions of intelligence is a bit more complex. Certainly, most dog breeds have some form of instinctive intelligence that makes them special. This will be reflected in a particular pattern of skills, abilities, behavioural predispositions, and so forth. But some dogs seems to be more dominated by their instinctive intelligence than do others, and for some breeds, instinctive intelligence does not produce a single prominent skill.

The Doberman pinscher and the poodle, for example, do not show very pronounced instinctive abilities to set them off from other breeds. Both do have very high adaptive and working intelligence, but, despite this, professionals who have trained Doberman pinschers to herd sheep and poodles to hunt for rats and vermin report that the dogs found learning the tasks very difficult and demanding. Furthermore, even if such training is completed, it is very likely that the final performance of these breeds will not be very exemplary. The dogs will be able to do the jobs and probably will do them reasonably well, but their performance will never be outstanding.

The collie and the Manchester terrier, on the other hand, not only have known and definable dimensions of instinctive intelligence, but their behaviour is dominated by these genetically determined response patterns. The collie not only can herd almost automatically but wants to herd and will look for opportunities to do so, even if this means inappropriately circling all the members of a family to keep them in a group, as though they were a flock of sheep, when all the humans want to do is move from the front door to the car parked at the kerb. Similarly, Manchester terriers do not need to be taught to hunt mice, rats, and other vermin. They will instinctively chase and try to attack anything that is small and moves erratically. This behaviour is so strong that they will stop in the middle of eating to chase a cloth mouse jerked across the floor in front of them. For the specific tasks for which they were bred, both dogs require very little training to bring out their fullest potential. But training a Manchester terrier to herd sheep and a collie to hunt rats is virtually impossible. The Manchester terrier is much more likely to chase the sheep or their shadows than to circle the flock to bunch the animals together. The collie is more apt to try to herd a group of three rats together than to try to kill them.

There seems to be some systematic pattern in the way adaptive and instinctive intelligence are distributed through the various breeds of dogs. Generally speaking, animals that have less clearly defined dimensions of instinctive intelligence seem to have compensated with higher levels of adaptive intelligence. Conversely, dogs with strongly defined dimensions of instinctive intelligence often seem to be less flexible in their range of possible behaviours, which is also typical of an animal with lower adaptive intelligence. This seems to be a choice that people have made in creating the various breeds. Humans seem content to sacrifice some of the adaptive intelligence in certain breeds in order to obtain dogs that need little training to perform certain functions well. This means that a dog that is a real behavioural specialist in any area, with clear, strong instinctive intelligence for those skills, is probably best suited predominantly for that specific realm of activity and may not adapt well to different environments where those behaviours are not possible or not valued. Thus the beagle is specialized to use his nose and follow a scent. This makes it incredibly easy to teach a beagle not only to track rabbits, but to inspect airport baggage for possible agricultural products being smuggled in, or even to check for the odour that termites emit in order to detect a possible infestation which could damage a home. That very instinctive ability which makes the beagle such a wonderful scent detector and tracker, however, reduces his working and obedience intelligence, since this little hound is easily distracted from the task set for him by his human trainer and responds to any interesting scent that might be present. When he encounters such a scent, it is as if the rest of his brain turns off, and he instinctively goes into his tracking mode. On the other hand, a dog that has no outstanding instinctive skills may have somewhat better adaptive intelligence and, depending on its personality and some other factors, may well be the choice for situations where the tasks it will be called upon to do, and the environments to which it will need to adapt, are complex and varied.

Chapter Eight

Instinctive Intelligence

> Every human child must learn the universe fresh. Every stockdog pup carries the universe within him. Humans have externalized their wisdom—stored it in museums, libraries, the expertise of the learned. Dog wisdom is inside the blood and bones.
>
> —DONALD MCCAIG

Probably we'll never know for sure how dogs and humans first formed their personal and working relationship with each other. It is likely, however, that people did not initially choose dogs—rather, dogs chose to be with humans. As mentioned earlier, the fellowship between humans and dogs began well before formal agriculture had developed. Given humanity's limited attention to sanitation at the time, bones, bits of skin, and other scraps of offal from the victims of recent hunts were likely to have been scattered around human campsites. Doubtless the progenitors of dogs (being ever food-conscious) learned that by hanging around human habitations, they could grab a quick bite to eat now and then without the exertion of actual hunting. And, while primitive people may not have been very concerned with cleanliness, health issues, or sanitation, rotting food does smell and attract insects that make humans uncomfortable. Thus it is likely that people tolerated dogs around the perimeter of the camps because they disposed of the garbage as pariah dogs still do in many less-developed regions of the world.

Food was as much of a constant concern for primitive humans as it was for dogs. Presumably it occurred to our human progenitors that having dogs around the campsite might do more than aid in cleanup and garbage removal. Dogs were, after all, living creatures, composed mostly of protein and quite edible. Undoubtedly our hunter ancestors figured that, if times got hard and larger game became scarce, they could easily find, kill, and eat the canines that had placed themselves so conveniently close by. Dog bones found in some Stone Age campsites show cut marks from tools and even marks suggestive of human teeth, indicating that sometimes the dog that came to supper was the supper.

As repugnant as a contemporary person raised in Western society may find the idea of eating dogs, the practice continued long after prehistoric times and remains to this day. Many early Greek and Roman epicures were extremely fond of dog flesh and wrote extensively on the best ways to prepare it. In Mexico, small dogs such as the Chihuahua and the Mexican hairless dog were popular food items and raised specifically for that purpose. Native peoples in North America often ate dogs, as a treat in some cases and out of necessity in others. The Samoyed people (whose name is now attached to the beautiful white dogs so popular on this continent) used their dogs not only to pull sleds in the Russian arctic but also to serve as food when their pulling days were finished.

Necessity has often driven people to eat dogs. When Paris was under siege during the Franco-Prussian War in 1870, the residents, short of food, resorted to eating dogs (among other things). The radical English journalist and politician Henry Du Pré Labouchère visited the city and stayed with wealthy individuals who could still afford to purchase meat, even if it was only dog flesh. He claimed that the taste of dog was agreeable and ranked them: "Spaniel, like lamb; Poodle far the best; Bulldog coarse and tasteless."

In Hawaii and throughout Polynesia and Micronesia, not only was dog flesh highly prized, but dog teeth, hair, and skin were used as items of clothing and ornament. Dogs raised for food were fed on vegetables and hence were often referred to as "poi dogs" (poi is mostly mashed taro root). Young dogs were the most valued and were cooked much the same way that pigs were—either by placing hot rocks in the cleaned abdominal cavity and then wrapping the package in leaves or by barbecuing the flesh over coals. In 1880, some Hawaiians formed a dog-eating association at Lahaina. First, they captured any dogs they could find roaming around without licence tags. Next, they cleaned them up and fattened them a bit. Finally, on June 11, Hawaii's national holiday, they had a feast. A newspaper account quoted one of the organizers as saying, "Only dogs and sweet potatoes will be served on that day."

The Chinese still treat meat from chow chows as a culinary delicacy. According to popular folk belief, dogs with black coats are considered to be more nutritious and to have better fat for frying. It is not difficult to find dog farms, dog butchers, and restaurants that specialize in dog meat throughout modern China and its neighbouring countries. When the Summer Olympic Games were held in Seoul, South Korea, in 1988, the government passed a temporary law forbidding restaurants in the city limits to serve dishes made with dog meat, fearing that such menu items would offend their Western visitors. Because of public pressure, however, shortly after the Olympics had concluded, dog dishes again became available, and dogs could again be seen hanging in local butcher shops.

If you're interested in dogs only as a food source, then the question of their intelligence is moot. Who wants smart food? What you want is a slow-moving dog (who won't burn off much fat or become tough through exercise or vigorous activity) that is not clever enough to make itself hard to capture. Thus it is not surprising that the dogs primarily used for food may well have been the retardates of dogdom. It seems that virtually every visitor to Polynesia and Micronesia who wrote about the local poi dogs also commented on their absence of intelligence. In *A Voyage Around the World* (written in 1777), for instance, Johann Georg Adam Förster, one of the naturalists accompanying Captain Cook, described the dogs of Polynesia and the South Sea Islands as "lazy" and "unintelligent". Specifically, he commented:

> This day we dined for the first time on a leg of it [dog] roasted, which tasted so exactly like mutton, that it was absolutely indistinguishable. . . . In New Zealand, and in the tropical isles of the South Sea, the dogs are the most stupid, dull animals imaginable, and do not seem to have the least advantage in point of sagacity over our sheep.

In 1967, the director of the Honolulu Zoo, Jack L. Throp, undertook a project to re-create the Polynesian dog, which had completely disappeared, not only through culinary pressure but because of inbreeding with dogs introduced by Europeans. The project was purely of historical interest: In view of the descriptions of early explorers such as Förster, it is probably not surprising that the revived breed failed to achieve much popularity. Somehow, a sluggish, stupid, dull dog just didn't catch on, however tasty it perhaps would have been when it was still on the menu.

WATCHDOGS AND GUARD DOGS

A watchdog's function is to sound the alarm. A dog's bark carries quite well and makes the perfect warning signal. Indeed, the original function of barking was to rally the pack to respond to a problem or a possible intruder, and it comes naturally to most dogs regardless of size—if you want a watchdog, you want any alert dog that will bark, not one that is lethargic and placid. Scottish author and poet Sir Walter Scott once received some advice on the matter of watchdogs from a very credible source. Scott began his career as a lawyer working in his father's law office. His debut at the bar involved the successful defence of a burglar. The burglar, who was in fact guilty of both the crime for which he was charged and several others as well, shared with Scott the following bit of wisdom: "Always keep a small dog that barks, rather than a large dog, which you think may serve as a more formidable guard, but may spend most of its time sleeping. Size doesn't matter, just the sound." Scott took his advice and always kept terriers, which are vigilant little dogs, always ready to give voice at any sound or at anyone's approach.

The first conscious use of dogs for their behavioural characteristics was most likely as watchdogs and guard dogs. For prehistoric people, the world was quite a hostile place. Various animals stalked humans as prey, and campsites were easy targets. A stealthy predator, especially one that attacked at night when the camp slept, could be quite dangerous. Equally dangerous were attacks from other bands of humans, either because of intertribal warfare or to capture food, goods, women, or children. But the dogs hanging around the campsites on the lookout for food scraps quite naturally caused a commotion whenever a predator or band of strange humans approached. Aside from alerting the residents of the camp in time for them to respond, the dogs' warning could even cause approaching threats to seek less wary prey elsewhere. As it became obvious that they made the camps safer, dogs came to serve not only as scavengers but as guardians as well.

It is highly likely that the first specific behavioural characteristic that humans selected in dogs was the tendency to bark. In the wild, adult wolves do not bark very much, although wolf pups may be quite vocal. The first domestication of dogs probably involved the adoption of wolf cubs, and those that proved themselves to be good watchdogs by barking and making noise at any disturbance were more likely to be kept and bred by their owners. This is a primitive form of applied behaviour genetics, which eventually led to domestic dogs that bark loudly at unusual or threatening occurrences and thus warned their owners of any potentially dangerous event. Those dogs that did not serve this function well could still be served as dinner.

There are countless examples of watchdogs serving people well. For instance, in 1572, during the Dutch war of independence against Spain, the Spanish launched a surprise night attack intended to capture the Dutch leader, Prince William of Orange. The attack was extremely well planned, involving six hundred chosen men led by one Julien Romero. The surprise was complete. The sentinels were cut down, and the Spaniards slew hundreds of the Dutch. A small group, led by Julien himself, made straight for the prince's tent. The prince and his guards were asleep, but a small dog who always slept on the bed with the prince turned out to be all the sentinel necessary. Responding as a watchdog should, the dog began to bark furiously at the approaching footsteps. Once aroused, William had just enough time to mount a horse that was always kept saddled for him, and he barely escaped. His guards, servants, his master of the horse, and two of his secretaries (who had actually managed to make it to their horses a few moments after the prince) were all slain. John Lathrop Motley, who recorded this incident in *Rise of the Dutch Republic*, wrote: "But for the little dog's watchfulness, William of Orange, upon whose shoulders the whole weight of his country's fortunes depended, would have been led within a week to an ignominious death. To his dying day the Prince ever afterwards kept a dog of the same race in his bed-chamber. In statues of the Prince a little dog is frequently sculpted at his feet."

Any event can serve to trigger the watchdog function in most dogs. There are so many stories of dogs' alerting individuals to the presence of wild animals, prowlers, and burglars that such tales have lost their novelty value. There are also numerous stories of individuals who have been saved from fires, gas leaks, floods, or other catastrophes by alarms sounded by alert watchdogs. Here's an unusual one:

Stephen Marks was attempting to cross the Pacific Ocean in a small, wooden-hulled sailboat, his only companion a miniature schnauzer named Major. The hours were long, and the weather was not helpful. He had already encountered two nasty storm systems that required standing long hours at the helm. As soon as relative calm returned, the exhausted sailor fell into a sound sleep. Suddenly, he found himself jolted to wakefulness by Major's frantic barking. Completely disoriented, Stephen did not know what was wrong but noticed that Major was looking down at the hold. When he investigated, he found that the stresses generated by the bad weather had caused a bad leak in the hull and water was pouring in. Working frantically, Stephen made a temporary patch, and, with the pumps working at maximum, things were momentarily stabilized. Returning to the deck, he set a course for the Philippine Islands, which was the nearest reasonable landfall. However, the excitement of finding the leak and the effort of the repair work added to his already debilitated state, and he was soon asleep again. It is not clear how long he slept, but he was again awakened by Major's insistent barking. Reentering the hold, he found that his temporary patch had failed and the water was pouring in again. This time, he set the patch more securely, and the next morning he made it safely to land. "I'm sure that Major saved my life," he said. "If he hadn't awakened me after he first sensed the leak and that second time when the patch failed, I'm sure that I would have slept until the entire deck was under water."

While most dogs will bark when something unusual occurs, some breeds are much more alert than others. To gather some information on this issue, I contacted fourteen experts, eleven of them experts in training dogs for property and personal protection and the remaining three dog trainers and dog masters associated with police forces. As a group, they named fifteen breeds best at watchdog barking; these are ranked in roughly descending order of alertness in the following list:

Top Dogs for Watchdog Barking

1. Rottweiler
2. German shepherd
3. Scottish terrier
4. West Highland white terrier
5. Miniature schnauzer
6. Yorkshire terrier

7. Cairn terrier
8. Chihuahua
9. Airedale terrier
10. Poodle (standard or miniature)
11. Boston terrier
12. Shih Tzu
13. Dachshund
14. Silky terrier
15. Fox terrier

All these breeds are excitable and will bark vigorously at the presence of an intruder or in most situations that they think are out of the ordinary. My consultants noted that most dogs are fairly alert and will sound the alarm at least most of the time, but did consider a few breeds somewhat less likely to be good watchdogs. They did not agree as strongly on this question, but at least half of the experts named the following twelve breeds as being the least likely to sound the alarm and judged these dogs to be unsuitable for watchdog tasks. The following list ranks the dogs from least to most alert.

Dogs Least Likely to Succeed as Watchdogs

1. Bloodhound
2. Newfoundland
3. Saint Bernard
4. Basset hound
5. English bulldog
6. Old English sheepdog
7. Clumber spaniel
8. Irish wolfhound
9. Scottish deerhound
10. Pug
11. Siberian husky
12. Alaskan malamute

Of course, if you are looking for a dog that will remain quiet and not disturb you no matter what is going on in the vicinity, these may well be good choices.

While sounding the alarm is a vital protective function, the obvious next step is from watchdog to guard dog. The function of a guard dog is to intervene physically if an intruder disturbs property, enters premises, or attacks a person. The good guard dog is naturally aggressive to any strangers entering its territory and may seem generally suspicious toward strangers at all times. It may attack if threatened or provoked. It may also simply hold intruders at bay by barking and growling and adopting an obviously aggressive stance.

An effective guard dog's aggressive responses are triggered by the same things that trigger aggression in wolves and other wild canids. Territoriality is the most common motive. Most guard dogs will physically threaten anyone they feel is invading their territory. This territorial instinct is what people rely on when they use dogs to guard stores, factories, or warehouses from theft or vandalism. The usual procedure is simply to release the guard dogs after normal business hours so that they can roam free through the buildings or areas to be guarded. The dogs come to view such areas as their territory and will act instinctively to protect it, systematically patrolling the area several times during the night. They will also respond to any sound or other disturbance, and they will physically defend the area against any intruder.

Dogs have been used as guards throughout history. Ancient Romans often kept some fairly aggressive dogs chained near their doors. (Keeping a dog chained or tethered to a small area tends to increase its aggressiveness markedly.) It should come as no surprise that many Roman homes sported warning signs in the form of mosaics showing a chained snarling dog along with the words *cave canem*, "beware of dog" (Plate 8).

In addition to the basic territorial defence response, wolves and other wild canids will also rally to the defence of the pack or to the summons of a pack leader who perceives an intruder as a threat. These are the instincts prized in the so-called attack dogs, guard dogs that will respond spontaneously or on command by pursuing and attacking any person entering their territory or indicated by a handler. A police dog, for example, is trained to attack under two conditions: when it perceives its master being threatened or when it sees or hears a learned signal. According to protection dog trainers, natural guard dogs need very little training to trigger the aggressive response; rather, they require training to ensure that they can be called off reliably. In addition, they also require training to direct their aggression to appropriate targets. Thus, while the abilities associated with guarding are part of the dog's instinctive intelligence, controlling the abilities requires some working and obedience intelligence as well.

The effectiveness of guard dogs cannot be disputed. There are literally thousands of stories of how a dog protected the life or property of its master. Let me just give one rather poignant example, dating from A.D. 79 and discovered by archaeologists digging through the volcanic ash in the ruins of Pompeii.

During their excavations, the scientists uncovered a dog's body lying across that of a child. The major part of the tale was told by the dog's collar. The dog, whose name was Delta, had saved the life of his owner, the child Severinus, three times. The first time he had served as a rescue dog, pulling Severinus out of the sea and saving him from drowning. Later, Delta had fought off four men who were attempting to rob his master. Then Delta saved Severinus when he was attacked by a wolf when he was in Herculaneum to visit the sacred grove of Diana. Apparently Delta was again acting as a guard dog when the catastrophe occurred. The heroic dog was trying, once more, to protect his young master by using his own body to shield the boy from the hot ash of the erupting volcano when they were both overcome by the poisonous gases that also spewed forth. Almost two thousand years ago, Delta sacrificed everything in a desperate attempt to fulfill the role of guard dog once more.

Guard dogs are not infallible, and the major problem is to teach them to differentiate between innocuous strangers and hostile intruders. There are many stories each year of children who are bitten by guard dogs misinterpreting their approach as a threat. An interesting story suggests that the founding of the Anglican church may have been accelerated by a dog's misinterpretation of a situation, which resulted in an aggressive guarding response against an inappropriate person. The event took place around 1530, when Cardinal Thomas Wolsey was sent to see Pope Clement VII with a petition requesting the annulment of Henry VIII's marriage to Catherine of Aragon so that the king could marry his newest interest, Anne Boleyn. The cardinal had brought his dog, Urian, with him when he went for his audience. Unfortunately when the pope extended his leg so that the cardinal could kiss his toe, the dog mistook the foot hurtling toward his master's face as an assault. With the immediate response of a guard dog, it attacked the offending holy toes. The results of this encounter were described by one historian of the time as "riotous", and the pope's displeasure was apparently much more than mere annoyance or indignation—indeed, bordering on "wrath". Obviously, we cannot know with certainty what effect this encounter had on the final decision, given that political considerations were also important, but we do know that Cardinal Wolsey returned home without the desired annulment. We also know that Henry's response involved termination of his association with the

Catholic church and formation of the Anglican church with the king as its head to guarantee a willingness to grant his wishes. One cannot help wondering if this would have come about if the cardinal's dog had not chosen to sink its teeth into his holiness's toe in a misguided attempt to protect its master.

The Dogs of War

The ultimate use of dogs for their aggressive qualities has been as war dogs. The ancient Egyptians, Romans, Gauls, and Celts favored mastiffs for this role. Our contemporary mastiffs are quite large dogs. I know of one who weighs about 220 pounds (110 kilograms) and plays with twenty-five-pound (twelve-kilogram) rocks the way other dogs play with tennis balls. An earlier version of the mastiff, however, known as the Molossian dog, weighed in at around 280 pounds (140 kilograms) and was known for its aggressive tendencies. These great beasts were fitted out in spiked armor to tear at horses or infantry that came too near. Some, trained to run at men or horses, carried lances hooked on their backs. Others, trained to run under horses, carried pots of burning resin on their backs. In other words, these dogs were the ancient equivalent of our modern surface-to-surface missiles (Figure 8.1).

Before the era of firearms, war dogs were a major force in war. They terrorized infantry and could often be extremely effective against

Figure 8.1
Two varieties of armored war dogs, one with a lance and pot of burning resin for use against cavalry and the other with sharpened spikes on its collar for use against infantry.

cavalry. The Celts had their dogs trained so that they would bite the noses of cavalry horses, causing them to throw their riders. This tactic was extremely important in neutralizing the Roman cavalry during the invasion of Britain. The Germanic tribes also made very effective use of war dogs. Attila the Hun used giant Molossians and also Talbots, the precursor to our modern bloodhound. Later, war dogs played a vital role in the battles between the Spanish and the indigenous populations of South and Central America.

The power of the war dog was, perhaps, best illustrated by their use by the Cimbri, a Germanic tribe that allied itself with the Teutoni and other tribes to make major incursions into Roman territory. Supported by their great war dogs, the Cimbri defeated the Romans in 113, 109, 107, and 105 B.C. Ultimately, the Romans teamed two of their most effective commanders, Gaius Marius and Quintus Lutatius Catulus, who met the combined Cimbri army near Vercelli in northwestern Italy in 101 B.C. The Cimbri were badly routed in this battle; however, Roman pursuit and even ultimate possession of the field were delayed for nearly half a day by the Cimbri's war dogs, who effectively continued the battle despite the defeat of their human masters.

Dogs were a vital part of the conquest of the Americas. Starting with the second voyage of Christopher Columbus, war dogs were vital weapons. He brought twenty war dogs with him. The very first military conflict between Indians and Europeans would also mark the first incident where a dog served a military purpose in the New World. In May 1494, Columbus approached the shore of Jamaica at what would become Puerto Bueno. He could see a gathering of natives, painted black and in various colours, and carrying weapons, and felt that a demonstration of Spanish military strength might just frighten the natives enough to cause them to avoid any further hostilities. Three ships approached the shore. Soldiers fired their crossbows and then waded ashore, slashing at the natives with their swords, while others continued to fire bolts. The Indians were surprised at the ferocity of the onslaught; however, when one of the massive war dogs was released, their response was absolute terror. They fled from the raging animal that bit at their naked skin and did them great harm. The admiral then came ashore and claimed the island in the name of the Spanish throne. Columbus would write in his journal that this incident proved that one dog was worth ten soldiers when fighting the Indians.

Sometime later he would revise that estimate to say that one dog was worth fifty men in such combat. The pattern for conquest had now been set. Weapons would be used to take and hold territory, while dogs would be used to worry and terrify the natives. These same tactics would be used by Cortez, Balboa, and Ponce de León in their campaigns of conquest and subjugation of the natives of the Americas.

Dogs returned to the battlefield during World War I. The Germans used them very effectively in guard and sentry service, and by the time World War I was over, more than seventy-five thousand dogs had been pressed into service by both sides. The French took particular advantage of dogs' acute hearing and would place sentry dogs at various points along the front, usually in pairs separated by a hundred feet or so. If the dogs sounded an alert or growled to indicate an intruder or some human activity outside the trenches, the handler would mark the directions of the dogs' lines of sight and then use the two sight lines to triangulate the location for targeting by the artillery. A number of German artillery emplacements, bunkers, and machine gun posts were located and shelled in this way.

Estimates place the number of dogs used in World War II at more than two hundred thousand. In addition to sentry and guard duty, messenger service, and search and rescue work, dogs were used to warn ships of approaching aircraft before the introduction of radar. Dogs nicknamed "parapups" were often sent with airborne troops to serve guard and sentry duties after troops had established camps (although they had to be thrown out of the planes, since they refused to jump voluntarily). Canine kamikaze or suicide troops were used by both sides. Twice during the abortive German invasion of Russia, attacks by Nazi armoured columns were stopped by dogs. After training the dogs to enter tanks and armoured vehicles for food, the Russians would strap electromagnetic mines to the backs of the half-starved animals and release them at the sight of approaching enemy tanks. The same general idea was used by the Japanese, who had dogs pull carts containing fifty-pound bombs into Allied camps.

More recently, dogs were used in the Korean conflict, during the Vietnam war, and during both incursions against Iraq by the United States. In Vietnam, dogs were introduced to stop sabotage and theft from U.S. installations. Within six months after the introduction of these sentry and guard dogs, the number of incidents causing damage or property loss had dropped by 50 percent. It is a sad commentary on men to report that these dogs, who had valiantly served as the soldiers' comrades in arms, were declared "surplus equipment" by the U.S. Army and simply abandoned during the American withdrawal. Most of these intelligent and well-trained guard dogs ended up in the cooking pots of the Vietnamese.

To be a good guard dog, an animal needs more than a territorial sense and a willingness to engage in physical aggression. A Chihuahua makes an effective watchdog by noisily sounding the alarm, but however great its courage and loyalty, a three-pound Chihuahua simply cannot stop an intruder. Miniature schnauzers, fox terriers, Scottish terriers, West Highland white terriers, and cairn terriers all have the will to defend their territory or pack, and all have the courage to attack an intruder physically. Yet none are effective guard dogs because one swift kick can end the assault. Bulk and physical strength are just as important as temperament in determining the value of a guard dog.

The same experts who rated dogs on their watchdog ability also rated the guard dog ability of the various breeds, basing their assessment on the aggressiveness of the dogs' temperament, physical strength, courage, and resistance to counterattack. Thirteen breeds of dog were selected by at least half the experts, in the order given below.

The Most Effective Guard Dogs

1. Bullmastiff
2. Doberman pinscher
3. Rottweiler
4. Komondor
5. Puli
6. Giant schnauzer
7. German shepherd
8. Rhodesian ridgeback
9. Kuvasz
10. Staffordshire terrier
11. Chow chow
12. Mastiff
13. Belgian sheepdog/Malinois/Tervuren*

* The experts did not distinguish among these breeds.

One interesting aside came from three of my experts independently. All said that the standard poodle could be an extremely effective guard dog; according to them, it lacks only a little in its bulk. The major problem appears to be the public perception that a poodle is a "fancy dog" with no substance, kept for its looks. One of my experts wrote:

A major function of a guard dog is deterrence. It has to be able to ward off an attack by looking tough. Poodles can be quite tough and aggressive as guards, but they simply don't look the part and that reduces their effectiveness in this job. A wimpy German Shepherd would be a more effective deterrent since people think of the breed as police dogs and guard dogs and are less apt to test it by attacking.

In recent years guard dog breeds that were virtually unknown in North America have begun to be imported. These are usually big powerful dogs with a reputation for a willingness to attack humans. Sometimes the people who use such dogs for protection are merely worried about their safety or that of their families and their property in certain high-crime areas. In other instances these dogs have been imported by those who wish to intimidate others or protect the sites where they conduct illegal activities. These dogs are often called "fighting breeds" and the ones that you are most likely to encounter are Dogo Argentino, Fila Brasileiro, Cane Corso, Ca de Bou, Presa Canario, Alano Español, Japanese Tosa, and Neapolitan mastiff. Whether any individual dog will be particularly aggressive depends upon a number of factors, but the Web sites of many breeders of these dogs emphasize that they are "fearless", "will not back down in a fight", "will not hesitate if threatened", "are the ultimate protectors", and one even boasts "having one next to you is better than carrying a gun—and it doesn't require a government permit and record check!" Personally, I worry about what specific instinctive intelligence these breeders are trying to produce in their lines of dogs.

HUNTING DOGS

Dogs' association with humans began when we were predominantly subsisting as hunters. It was in the hunt that dogs began to display many of their unique abilities. It was for the hunt that people began to select particular breeds for many new useful characteristics and thereby learned that it was possible to modify the instinctive intelligence of the animal systematically. Dogs have been used for every phase of hunting. Their tasks include finding animals, flushing them, pursuing them, pulling them down, and bringing their quarry back to their masters.

There is a remarkable similarity between the techniques used by wolves in the hunt and the techniques used by primitive humans. The components are the same: Seek the game, indicate its location to the others in the group, encircle the game, and perhaps drive it toward a member of the group waiting in ambush. All these activities are coordinated in the wild by the pack leader. In the process of domesticating dogs, the human dog handler assumed the position of pack leader in directing the hunt. To the extent that dogs have accepted human leadership, they cooperatively hunt with people. As early as Palaeolithic times, dogs were used to help drive game into traps, over precipices, or into positions where humans with bows and spears lay waiting. They flushed birds after human hunters were in position, bows ready. Alternatively, the birds might be flushed into strategically placed nets. These same techniques are still used by many primitive tribes in Africa today. Wild animals (particularly wild pigs) are systematically driven by men and dogs until they hit a line of nets or reach a blind where men are waiting to dispatch them with spears.

Gun Dogs

Today, the best known of the hunting dogs are the so-called gun dogs: pointers, spaniels, setters, and retrievers. Each of these dog types was actually carefully shaped for specific tasks through selective breeding. The term *gun dog* is appropriate, since the skills of these modern hunting dogs have been selected to assist in the style of hunting where game is brought down with firearms. For instance, pointers were developed to complement the invention of the muzzle-loading fowling gun. To use that weapon effectively, the hunter needed a dog that would silently lead its master to where game was hiding and indicate its position. Pointers have well-developed hearing and smell. They also can move very slowly, precisely, and silently. They creep through undergrowth without causing the least disturbance, their heads held high so that their noses can explore the scents carried on the breeze. Once the pointer has discovered game, it freezes, standing immobile with its head and often its whole body pointing directly at the quarry often with one front leg raised from the ground (see Plate 9).

Sometimes hunters use two dogs as a team. One dog can indicate the direction in which the quarry can be found, but not its distance. Two dogs can be used to triangulate, and, just like the French artillery's spotting dogs, the position where the lines of sight from the two dogs cross will mark the exact location of the target. It has been documented that good pointers will hold a point for up to an hour if need be. This was particularly useful in the days of the muzzle-loading gun, as it gave the human hunter time to creep up and flush the game in a manner that would ensure a good chance of hitting the birds with a single-shot weapon. It was important that the hunter not miss, because reloading such a gun could take half a minute or more.

Scientists suggest that pointing behaviour may actually be a sort of neural short circuit or overload that freezes the dog in position the moment before it would otherwise spring at the prey. Similar behaviour has been observed in wolves; a lead animal may halt and hold its position, thus marking the location of game, holding the pose until the rest of the pack assembles and identifies the critical location. A wolf, however, will hold such a position only for a few seconds up to a minute.

Although training can make a pointer's behaviour more precise and controllable, the tendency to point is inborn. This can easily be proved by taking a bird wing and dangling it in front of a pointer puppy. I have seen a five-week-old puppy assume the classical pointing position when exposed to such a stimulus, even though it had had no training to hunt.

The improvement of hunting weapons called for a modification of the dog. Breech-loading firearms allowed a higher rate of fire, and technology made longer-range shooting more accurate. Faster and more intelligent dogs were called for, and breeders responded by developing the setter. The term *setter* comes from the word *sitter*, the dogs' task being to stop and sit, or stand motionless, looking directly at the location of the game. When released from their position, these dogs approach the game with a sinuous weaving or twisting motion, their tails beating from side to side with increasing rapidity as the dogs believe they are getting closer to their quarry. This tail swing pattern allows the experienced hunter to anticipate quite accurately when the bird will break cover and take flight.

Hunting with spaniels is less disciplined but more exciting. Spaniels are especially well suited for working through undergrowth or over marshy terrain. They quarter the ground just a short distance ahead of the hunter, but, though they search for game, they give no warning when they find it. Modern firearms make this faster-moving, but less predictable, form of hunting possible; however, when the aim is to take home a lot of game, birds are usually flushed into nets rather than in front of shooters. Spaniels can also be used as *crouchers* or *springers;* in an older era, they were used to spring birds for pursuit by tamed falcons and to flush hares or rabbits to be pursued by greyhounds (see Plate 10).

Toward the end of the eighteenth century, hunting styles changed. The population had become more dense, and the accessible countryside was now mostly cleared land. This led to the development of a hunting style known as "walking up the birds", in which a line of hunters strolls across a field shooting birds such as partridges or pheasants as they fly away. Hunting this way required dogs that could spot birds as they fell and retrieve them, undamaged, on command. And, while pointers, setters, and spaniels all can be taught to retrieve, a specialist was bred for the job: the retriever.

In marshy or lakeside areas, dogs such as the Labrador retriever are particularly useful, since they love water. They can also be used when hunting from blinds, where they will happily wait for hours and then mark and retrieve the birds falling into the water. Indeed, the retriever's ability to mark a trajectory and discern where an object will fall to earth is quite amazing. To believe that such dogs must have the biological equivalent of a radar tracking device, you only need to wander through any city park on a sunny summer day and watch the Labrador or golden retrievers unerringly marking the flight lines of balls or Frisbees and snatching them from the air.

When a dog retrieves game and brings it back uneaten to its human hunting companions, it is exhibiting a variation of a behaviour seen in wild canids. Wolves have been seen carrying food back to the den for nursing bitches, newly weaned puppies, and even for pack members left to guard the den area while the rest of the pack goes off to hunt.

Hounds

Hunting with hounds is quite a different matter from hunting with gun dogs. To begin with, hounds are usually used in packs. Individual hounds generally do not receive the intimate attention and training that a gun dog receives, and they are less likely to be kept as housedogs during the off season. Pointers, setters, spaniels, and retrievers are all accessories to the hunter's weapon, but hounds do not require the hunter at all: They hunt, and they kill, by themselves.

There are really two quite different types of hounds, although they have sometimes been used together. The first comprises the sight, or gaze, hounds, such as the greyhounds, whippets, Afghans, and borzois (formerly known as Russian wolfhounds). As their name suggests, these dogs hunt by sight, running down their prey with incredible speed (then killing it) once they have spotted it. Salukis and Afghan hounds have been used in hunting or, to use the technical term, "coursing" antelope and gazelle, as well as foxes and hares. Some of the tallest and most courageous dogs in dogdom are found among the sight hounds. The giant Irish wolfhound and Scottish deerhound were used to hunt elk, caribou, and even lions. The Romans knew and described the original Irish wolfhounds in the fourth century and prized them for their ferocity and courage, often using them in gladiatorial combat.

The most important task assigned to the sight hounds was ridding populated areas of wolves. In Russia, for instance, a wolf hunt would begin with mounted hunters, each holding the leashes of three borzois perfectly matched not only in color but also in size and build. The noise of the approaching hunters usually caused the wolf to bolt from cover, when the quick-release leashes were slipped and the dogs set in pursuit. In the perfect hunt, the task of the dogs was to hold the wolf at bay until the chief huntsman could arrive to dispatch it with a knife. However, in the ferocity of the chase, the wolf was often killed by the dogs themselves.

The close matching of the dogs was not simply for aesthetic reasons but based on practicality. If one dog was much faster than the others, and the wolf turned to fight, the single dog might easily be killed. A team of three arriving at the same moment gave the dogs a distinct advantage.

These dogs did their job so efficiently that in some places all of the large quarry they were designed to hunt was eliminated. In fact, because of these dogs, predators such as wolves and lynxes became extinct in the British Isles and were severely depleted over much of Europe. The end result was that the dogs no longer had a function. For example, the Irish wolfhound had been used to hunt not only wolf but also the gigantic Irish elk, whose height of six feet at the shoulder inspired little fear in these enormous dogs, which might themselves stand nearly four feet at the shoulder. With the disappearance of the large game their usefulness was gone and the breed became virtually extinct. Only concerted effort by Captain George A. Graham, a Scot in the British Army, allowed the last specimens of Irish wolfhounds to be gathered in 1862. The breed was then restored, though at a new, more petite height—a mere three feet at the shoulder—that still leaves it the tallest of all dogs. Lord Colonsay similarly rescued the Scottish deer-hound from extinction in the 1800s, long after they ceased to be used to hunt the large Scottish deer (see Plate 11).

The second form of hound is the scent hound. These dogs use their noses to track quarry and include foxhounds, beagles, bassets, harriers, coonhounds, and, of course, bloodhounds. For the most part, the quarry they are called upon to hunt can be classified as pests or vermin that farmers want eliminated because they damage crops and kill small livestock. In Europe these animals include fox, badger, rabbit, and hare, and in North America raccoons, bobcats, cougars, and opossums can be added to the list. In Britain, as elsewhere, much pageantry and tradition have come to be associated with hunting behind packs of these hounds.

Scent hounds have been systematically bred for their scenting ability, their desire to track, and their voices. Their wide nostrils point forward and down, allowing them to pick up scents on the air currents rising from the ground. These scents come from spots where the paws of their quarry have touched the earth, places where they have brushed against rocks or undergrowth, and also from the minute flakes of skin and hair the animals continually shed. The scenting ability of hounds is truly remarkable: The little beagle, for example, has 225 million scent receptors in its nose, as compared to only 5 million for humans. The bloodhound, which is the ultimate scenting dog, has 300 million!

Something called *olfactory adaptation*, however, has produced a major limitation on these dogs' scenting ability. When you walk into a room, you might notice a faint smell—the scent of someone's perfume, a bouquet of flowers, coffee brewing, or some such. Within a few minutes, however, you no longer will be aware of these smells because of olfactory adaptation that results from the receptors in your nose tiring. The same thing happens with hounds. Typically, when a hound picks up a scent, it will begin to bay, or "give tongue". For a strong scent, however, olfactory adaptation will set in after only about two minutes or so, causing it to lose the ability to detect the scent. At this point, the dog will go silent and raise its head to breathe fresh, spoor-free air and allow its nasal receptors to become functional again. This is why hounds are run in packs. At any given time, some dogs will be scenting and giving tongue while others will be running mutely with the pack. Various members of the pack take turns tracking the scent, so there should never be a moment when all the dogs are resting at the same time.

The baying sound that hounds make when tracking is extremely important. Its primary function is to let the hunters know exactly where the pack is at any moment. The number of dogs sounding off, and the intensity of the baying, also gives hunters an indication of how strong and fresh the scent is and hence some notion of how near the quarry is. Signals on a hunting horn can then exert some control over the pack's movement.

The sound of a pack baying can be quite melodious, and hunters sometimes deliberately select hounds to produce the most harmonious combinations of tones. For example, in 1615 Gervase Markham described in his book *Country Contentments* how one could "tune" different packs of hounds for different sounds. For a pack with a sweet cry, he recommended including "some large dogs that have deep solemn mouths . . . which must as it were bear the bass in the consort, then a double number of roaring, and loud ringing mouths, which must bear the counter-tenor, then some hollow plain sweet mouths, which must bear the mean or middle part." Finally, he suggests that "amongst these you cast in a couple or two of small singing beagles, which as small trebles may warble amongst them" to provide a balanced symphony.

Scent hounds have been designed and redesigned to fit certain requirements. For instance, foxhounds and beagles were intended to run with horse-mounted hunters, the former for fox, the latter for hares or rabbits (see Plate 12). Their speed led to lively and occasionally dangerous displays of horsemanship as the typical hunt turned into a wild chase across the countryside. Foxhounds were created to think only of foxes; they will ignore other scents and always pursue the freshest trail. They have incredible stamina and vigor. They leap hedges, walls, and fences, press through heavy brush, and drive on as long as there is any vestige of spoor to follow. During the fox hunting seasons in Britain (which used to go from September to April), an active pack might run forty to sixty miles on each hunt, and typically there were two hunts per week.

The British Parliament recently passed a law banning foxhunting with dogs. This leaves me wondering if we might eventually lose these handsome, athletic hunting dogs now that their "job" in the world has been eliminated. This has happened many times before when we have allowed other breeds of dogs to become extinct because their useful purpose was gone. The otterhound is an example of a breed currently hovering on the cusp of extinction. Like the foxhound, otterhounds were used in packs. Their task was to hunt river otters, as a means of keeping them from depleting inland fish stocks. This was viewed simply as vermin control in the same way that foxhunting was initially designed to keep the fox population down to protect farmers whose flocks of poultry were often the foxes' target. Like foxhunting, however, otter hunting soon became a sport. Unfortunately, many rivers in Britain became polluted, decreasing the number of fish and making those that remained undesirable for human consumption. With the disappearance of their food supply there was also a drastic drop in the otter population. For this reason, wildlife advocates started a campaign that finally resulted in the banning of otter hunting in England in 1978 and in Scotland two years later. The purebred otterhounds in the remaining packs were dispersed to private owners, with a few finding a new career in mink-hunting packs. Without a specific function, these rough, shaggy-coated dogs began to decrease in number. Now, in all of the United States and Canada there are fewer than three hundred fifty in existence, and it is estimated that their worldwide population is less than a thousand.

In contrast to the swift-running foxhounds, other scent hounds, such as bassets, were purposely built low and heavy so that in their pursuit of rabbits or badgers they could not outrun the hunters following on foot. The result was a more sedate hunt, less filled with pageantry and wild action—and considerably less dangerous.

Around 1960, I was training with the U.S. Army at Fort Knox, Kentucky. During that time, mostly because of my love of dogs, I got to know a few of the people living in the rural areas not far from the fort. One of my local acquaintances invited me on a fox hunt that was to be held late one wintry Friday afternoon. I envisioned men dressed in red hunting coats and high shiny boots, riding well-groomed horses behind a pack of excited hounds, all guided by the plaintive sounds of the head huntsman's horn. The actuality was quite different. The hunt had been organized by an old man everybody called Uncle Tyler. Several people contributed hounds (mostly in couples) to make up the pack. About four were clearly foxhounds, and there were also a pair of bluetick hounds, a couple of beagles, a bloodhound, something that could have been a black-and-tan coonhound, a kind of hound I had never seen before that I was told was called a "Drever", plus a couple of generic hounds of mixed parentage. The star of the group was a redbone hound named Hamilton, who had become famous locally for his ability to find and tree wildcats. All together, there were well over a dozen dogs.

The hunt began on foot, with the men leading the dogs to an area on a mountainside where foxes were supposed to be a problem. At some point, the dogs picked up the scent and began yelping and straining at their leashes. In the dimming light, they were slipped from their leads, and the pack shot off together in full cry. Some twenty minutes later, the men and I were seated high on the mountainside around a roaring fire in an area cleared of snow. The dogs continued the hunt without human guidance, while the six men and I sat and watched Uncle Tyler fill some metal mugs with bourbon. We slowly sipped the whisky, smoked, and listened to the "hound music" that floated through the night. Now and then, someone would tell a brief story that began with "I remember when. . . ." Mostly, though, the evening was filled with baying songs sung by the distant hounds, accompanied only by the sounds of the crackling wood in the fire.

Terriers

The last of the specialized hunting dogs is the terrier. The root *terra* in *terrier* means "earth" or "ground" and suggests the special ability of this type of dog, which is to follow game into its burrow or some natural crevice and there either to flush it or kill it (Plate 13). A Scottish breeder of terriers described the desirable qualities of the terrier as being "coat and courage". The heavy hard or wiry coat protects the dog from abrasion as it plunges through rocky areas and down into the lair of a fox or badger. It also protects it against the savage bites that would be meted out by the cornered animal. And the dog needs courage in order to work completely alone, often in darkness underground, in situations where retreat is difficult, if not impossible, and where its life might depend on its fighting ability. Many terriers have perished burying themselves alive in their eagerness to enlarge the passage in which they were digging or locked in a final struggle with their quarry.

The Scottish breeder forgot to mention one other vital feature bred into terriers: their barks. A functional terrier must bark when the least bit excited or aroused. It is this furious barking that alerts the hunters to the location of the burrow. It is the sound of the barking underground that tells hunters where to dig to uncover the quarry and also to retrieve their dogs.

Earlier terriers did not readily bark and had to wear collars with bells on them to guide the hunters in their chase and digging. Unfortunately, many dogs choked to death when their collars caught on some obstruction underground. Others died because the hunters could not hear the tinkle of bells when fox and terrier were lost under the ground, locked in their final confrontation.

Terriers distinguish themselves in another way, by eliminating rats and other vermin. People who have no experience with terriers tend to think that the most efficient rat killers are cats. Yet, while cats are certainly efficient at killing mice, where stealth and patience are the most important qualities for the hunt, rats are often too large and vicious for them to handle. Several breeds of terrier were developed specifically to handle rats. Since terriers generally dispatch their prey by grasping the neck of the rat or other small mammal and giving one or two swift shakes to break it, these dogs were bred with incredibly strong jaws for their size. Even today, many farmers use terriers for rat control, especially in grain- or corn-growing regions. First they suffuse the lairs with smoke or gas or send in ferrets to bolt the rats; then they drive them into the open, where the terriers can dispatch them. Manchester terriers, Scottish terriers, cairn and West Highland white terriers, fox terriers, and bull terriers are all first-class ratters. Even the tiny Yorkshire terrier is quite good at this task, at least for small rats.

To appreciate just how efficient terriers can be at rat killing, we must turn to the Victorian era, when rat fighting was a sport especially popular in lower-class neighbourhoods of the city but drawing a following from adolescents and young adults of the upper classes. Terriers and rats were placed in pits to fight to the death. Side bets were often taken on the survival of dogs or rats and on the amount of time that some of the better dogs might take to finish off a particular group of rodents. A number of records have survived describing particular dogs. For instance, we know that one champion rat fighter was Tiny, a bull terrier that weighed only five and a half pounds. One night Tiny killed fifty rats (some of which were nearly as large as he was) in twenty-eight minutes and five seconds. His owner estimated that Tiny killed more than five thousand rats during his lifetime, which would amount to around a ton and a half of rats!

The propensity to chase vermin and the pattern of attack is part of the instinctive intelligence of terriers. Most terrier owners know that they can arouse one of these dogs to a frenzy of activity by shining a flashlight on the floor and moving it erratically around. A small moving target automatically elicits the pursuit response in terriers. As for the attack mode used by these dogs, again it is part of their genetic makeup. My cairn terrier Flint was nine years old when he was first introduced to country life. We had bought a tiny farm, and the area under the little old house had become the refuge for a number of small animals in the area. One afternoon I watched with some amazement as Flint pursued an opossum, grabbed it by its neck, and swung it in one violent snapping motion, resulting in its instantaneous death. This was an old dog who had lived in the city all his life and never had been exposed to the situations for which terriers had originally been bred! Yet the moment the appropriate stimuli were present, Flint's genetic programming immediately kicked in, causing him to demonstrate this aspect of his instinctive intelligence.

HERDING DOGS

One of the most consistent uses of dogs has been in the management and herding of livestock. Even in countries where dogs are considered unclean for religious reasons, people still recognize that dogs serve an important purpose as shepherds' assistants. While some dogs, like the Great Pyrenees or komondor, are basically guard dogs that stay with the flock to protect it from predators, the most widespread use of herding dogs is to keep flocks of sheep, geese, or cattle together (goats, swine, reindeer, and ducks are also among the beasts herded) and to drive them in specific patterns and to specific locations (see Plate 14).

Dogs have inherited their herding ability from wolves and other

Plate 1. Dandie Dinmont and his terriers as portrayed for Sir Walter Scott's 1815 novel, *Guy Mannering.* This is a breed with courage and pluck but for whom evidence of high intelligence is clearly lacking.

Plate 2. The association between humans and dogs began as a hunting relationship before organized agriculture had been developed. This Paleolithic cave painting dates back to about ten thousand years ago and shows a Stone Age hunter who has successfully killed an eland with the assistance of his dogs.

Plate 3. Many people believe that domestic dogs are basically tamed wolves and that their ability to interact with humans stems from the same behavior patterns that keep the wolf pack together as a coordinated social unit.

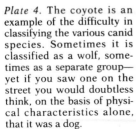

Plate 4. The coyote is an example of the difficulty in classifying the various canid species. Sometimes it is classified as a wolf, sometimes as a separate group—yet if you saw one on the street you would doubtless think, on the basis of physical characteristics alone, that it was a dog.

Plate 5. While there are scientific reasons that make the jackal as likely a candidate for the ancestor of domestic dogs as the wolf, this idea has not caught on with the general public because of the jackal's unwarranted reputation as a scavenger and a coward.

Plate 6. Foxes are descended from the wild canid considered least likely to be the ancestor of domestic dogs—yet they share some common physical and behavioral characteristics, and there is a remote possibility that certain foxes may have been crossed with dogs at some time.

Plate 7. Dingoes, it is believed, arrived in Australia during the Ice Age with the nomads who later became the Australian aborigines. There have been suggestions that dingoes were originally domestic dogs that reverted to the wild.

Plate 8. One of the most ancient functions of dogs was to guard property and persons. *At left,* a Roman mosaic from Pompeii with the warning *cave canem*—"beware of the dog."

Plate 9. A major use of dogs is in hunting. The pointer's instinctive response to the presence of game *(center)* is to freeze in position with its head or whole body pointing in a straight line toward the bird.

Plate 10. Hunting with spaniels *(bottom)* is less disciplined but often more exciting than hunting with pointers or setters. These dogs search the ground ahead of the hunter, giving no warning, simply flushing any birds when they find them.

Plate 11. Many of the great sight hounds, such as the Scottish deerhound shown here, hunted large game so efficiently that wolves, large deer, and related species became extinct in some regions. As a result, these great dogs were also placed in jeopardy of extinction.

Plate 12. Many scent hounds were specifically bred for a particular quarry or a particular form of hunting. Thus beagles were bred to run with horses and to track and hunt rabbits.

Plate 13. All terriers were originally bred with an instinctive ability to hunt vermin and a willingness to go down into the burrows of animals such as the fox and the badger. Hunters, locating the dogs by following the sound of their barking, then used large forks and shovels to dig up the trapped quarry.

Plate 14. Many types of herding dogs have been selected for special qualities. One of the strangest qualities was the absence of the English sheepdog's tail—a desirable trait because of a tax structure that defined as taxable livestock anything born with a tail.

Plate 15. Teams of so-called husky dogs are still used to pull sleds over snow-covered terrain. The dog teams are organized much like a wolf pack, with a leader, or king, whose movements coordinate the activities of the other animals. Most members of the team attend only to the leader and pay little attention to the human driver.

Plate 16. Dogs were often used to haul small carts, especially by the poor. This 1867 scene of New York City shows a group of ragpickers along with their dog-drawn carts, used for carrying salable rags collected from the city's garbage.

Plate 17. Many dogs have never served any function other than as companion dogs and pets. The pug, presumed to be originally from China and first popularized in the West in Holland, is an example of a dog bred solely for its qualities of companionship.

Plate 18. Various breeds of dogs have been specifically bred to emphasize certain behavioral characteristics. The Cavalier King Charles spaniel has been bred to emphasize its loving and gentle personality.

Plate 19. The mother dog, licking and nuzzling her young puppies, establishes an emotional bond and demonstrates social dominance—and we can achieve similar effects by touching a dog systematically and running our hands over its entire body.

wild canids that hunt in packs. The coordinated activity of the pack involves keeping a group of potential prey animals together, driving them to a specific location, and then cutting out the single animal that will be the target for the kill. These hunting behaviours are themselves based on five genetically programmed instructions. The first two have to do with positioning around the designated prey: Number one says that once the quarry is sighted, each wolf will approach the prey to approximately the same distance. Number two says that each wolf will remain equidistant from the hunting mates on its right and left. The implementation of these instructions results in the elegant and complex pattern of encirclement, with the pack forming an almost perfect circle that closes steadily during the hunt.

How does a single sheepdog carry out the genetic instructions intended to guide the movements of an entire pack? From puppyhood on, a sheepdog will stalk and try to herd anything that moves. I have been told of such dogs spontaneously herding not only lambs but also chicks and even children. One person told me that her border collie attempted to herd some insects crawling across her driveway. Another told me that her Shetland sheepdog tried to herd the ripples in a puddle of rainwater. All such herding represents the attempt to fulfill the first two genetic instructions concerning encirclement during the hunt. The problem for an animal on its own is that it will try to do the work of a dozen wolves, performing the entire pattern as if it were every member of the pack. First it decides on the proper distance that the pack should be from the flock. Next it dashes around to occupy the stations that normally would be filled by its packmates. As it goes from station to station, playing the role of each of its missing hunting companions in turn, it encircles the flock in a wide casting motion. This curving outrun, with pauses at each outpost where another wolf should be, drives the sheep on the outer fringes to the center of the circle and thus keeps the flock together.

The third genetically programmed hunting instruction involves ambush. When the wolf pack hunts, a single wolf may separate from the rest of the pack and hide from the quarry. Crouched on the ground, it will wait as the rest of the pack drives the herd slowly toward it. This accounts for the sheepdog's tendency to run and then drop to the ground, staring at the flock of sheep. It is, in effect, playing the part of the wolf that waits in ambush. The *eye*, or staring, of the dog seems to mesmerize any sheep that start to move away from the rest of the flock and holds them in position. However, the moment the flock again starts to move as a unit, the dog immediately returns to the actions that mimic the encircling wolf pack.

The fourth genetic program concerns driving the herd. Wolves have been known to manoeuvre a herd of buffalo, antelope, or deer into areas where the herd's movement will be restricted by the features of the terrain, such as cliffs or bodies of water. Once the herd's avenues of escape have been restricted, the wolves can more easily isolate individual members. Wolves carry out this driving by making short, head-on runs at the animals, which then run in the opposite direction. They also alter the path of the driven animals by means of nipping at their heels or flanks. Sheepdogs use this same procedure to control individual members of a flock or herd.

An amusing example of this behaviour in action features a Bouvier des Flandres, a large dog from Belgium that has been specialized to herd cattle. Lucky, the Bouvier in question had been given to Ronald Reagan shortly after he became president of the United States. Lucky continually attempted to herd the president, nipping at his heels and even drawing blood on at least one occasion. She also jumped up on Mrs. Reagan in the sort of sideways bumping manner occasionally used by big herding dogs to nudge their charges so that they move in particular directions. The resulting press photos of the president and his wife being herded by the dog were embarrassing, and, despite the fact that she was well loved, Lucky was ultimately exiled to the ranch in Santa Barbara, California, where there would be animals to herd, rather than politicians.

The last instruction in the programming that guides the herding dog relates to the social organization that wolves naturally adopt. Every wolf pack has a leader, usually called the "alpha" wolf by scientists. The leader initiates and controls the various moves of the pack, and the other wolves watch him carefully and follow his lead. This maintains the coordination of the pack and makes it an efficient hunting organization. Obviously, for the sheepdog, the shepherd is the alpha wolf. The shepherd relies on the obedience and working intelligence of the herding dog to allow him or her to control the dog's instinctive behaviour patterns. Actually, the shepherd needs to teach the dog only about a dozen commands to maintain full control:

Come: The dog comes to the shepherd.

Stop: The dog stops what it is doing.

Go left or *Go right:* The dog moves in the direction indicated, the movements being relative to the position of the flock.

Circle left or *Circle right:* This indicates that the dog should begin the encirclement manoeuvre.

Lie: This triggers the ambush position, in which the dog drops down and stares at the flock.

Close: The dog draws nearer to the flock.

Away: The dog moves a distance from the flock.

Slowly or *Faster:* These commands are used to control the speed or vigor of whatever activities the dog is performing at the time.

Enough: This is the dog's cue to leave the herd and to return to the side of the shepherd.

These commands can be given verbally, with hand signals, with whistle blasts, or by any combination of these. Surprisingly, this short list of commands (combined with the five genetically programmed instructional patterns) is enough to orchestrate the complex behaviours that allow a single human and a dog to control large herds of animals. One human and a dog can control a herd more efficiently than ten humans alone. Thus, without the dog, livestock management, flock tending, and herding might never have been possible, which means that the development of agriculture as the economic base of much of human society might have been delayed or even stopped.

Some breeds have an instinctive intelligence that allows them to excel in particular herding settings or with particular types of livestock. Collies (whose name derives from the mountain sheep with black feet and masks known as "colleys"), border collies, and Shetland sheepdogs are exceptionally bright and efficient sheep-herding dogs. Belgian sheepdogs, Tervurens, Malinois, German shepherds, bearded collies, and briards are efficient herding animals that are also large enough to provide protection against wolves, coyotes, and other predators. The Welsh corgis (both Cardigan and Pembroke) were specifically bred low to the ground so that when they nipped at the legs of cattle to move them and their charges responded with annoyed kicks, the hooves would pass over the dogs' heads and leave them unharmed.

HAULING DOGS

For most people today, a mention of dogs used as transport animals brings to mind the sled dogs, sometimes referred to as "huskies", of the polar regions. The word husky is actually derived from the slang word for Eskimo, *esky;* the Eskimo are popularly credited with introducing the dog-drawn sled. Most people readily recognize the various dogs used for drawing sleds. They are derived from a now-extinct type of dog called the spitz, with prick ears, full rough coats that stand out from the body, and, of course, the characteristic tail—a full brush held curled jauntily over the back. Many dog breeds have been derived from the spitz and these are usually referred to as "Nordic dogs." The dogs used to draw sleds include malamutes, Samoyeds, Siberian huskies, keeshonds, and elkhounds.

Dog teams are organized much like wolf packs in that there is a leader (sometimes referred to as the "king") whose movements serve to coordinate the activities of the other dogs hitched to the sled. The dogs in the team tend to pay attention almost exclusively to the leader, giving virtually no heed to the human driver. This accounts for the many stories of sleds that got away when their drivers fell off or failed to mount quickly enough. The part that sled dogs have played in the lives of arctic-dwelling Native American groups, such as the Inuit, and also in the modern settlement of the high North has been told many times, to the point where it has taken on an almost folkloric quality (see Plate 15).

Less well known today is the fact that dogs were once commonly used as draft animals in other parts of the world, pulling small carts or carrying packs. Animals such as the Newfoundland, rottweiler, Great Pyrenees, Saint Bernard, and Bernese mountain dog were much prized by butchers, vegetable sellers, milkmaids, weavers, tinkers, bakers, and so forth for their strength and endurance in hauling carts. For instance, in eighteenth- and early-nineteenth-century England, fish (which require fairly rapid transport) was carried in dog carts from Southampton to London. A typical cart might be drawn by a team of four Newfoundlands and might carry three to four hundred pounds of fish, in addition to the driver. In the city of Berne, a single Bernese mountain dog could comfortably pull a weaver's cart carrying well over a hundred pounds of textiles (in addition to the weight of the cart itself). Even small dogs, hooked together in teams, were quite efficient haulers. A team of four foxhounds could carry an average-sized man on a light cart at a speed of twelve miles an hour.

For the poor, the dog was the best transport animal they could have. They were easy to obtain, small enough to keep in a family's living quarters, and could survive on scraps of whatever food might be available. In addition to hauling goods, the dogs effectively guarded merchandise when a vendor was away from the cart and also guarded the home when the family slept (see Plate 16).

Today, dogs continue to be used as draft animals in many parts of the world. In England, however, the practice is now banned by law. In 1824 the Society for the Prevention of Cruelty to Animals was founded, and ever since the members have campaigned against cruelty to dogs. Among the cruel behaviours cited by the SPCA was the use of dogs as transport animals. Although it was pointed out that many of these dogs were well cared for and were vital to the livelihood of the poor who could not afford horses or donkeys, the SPCA was easily able to document some blatant instances of cruelty that were then used as part of a press campaign and lobbying effort with parliamentarians. In the mid-1800s the SPCA managed to get a law banning the use of dogs for transport. In conjunction with the passage of a dog tax, the immediate result was disastrous for the dog population. Dreadful massacres of dogs took place all over England when they could no longer legally be used for cartage but were now taxable. In Birmingham, more than a thousand dogs were slaughtered, and similar carnage took place in Liverpool. In Cambridge, the streets were littered with dead dogs. Because these bodies were becoming a health hazard, the high constable of Cambridge arranged a mass burial of four hundred dogs.

OTHER DOG SPECIALISTS

The uses of dogs that capitalize on aspects of their instinctive intelligence have become more varied in today's world. A quick sampling of some of these contemporary dog careers includes:

seeing-eye dogs, which guide their blind masters around obstacles, warn them of approaching vehicles, and allow them to navigate independently, even in the complex urban environment;

hearing-ear dogs, which alert their deaf masters to sounds, such as the ringing of a doorbell or telephone or the whistle of a teakettle;

assistance dogs, trained to help handicapped individuals with many tasks like turning light switches on and off, opening doors, and retrieving dropped or otherwise needed items;

search-and-rescue dogs, which are used to track and find individuals who are lost or buried by debris, such as in earthquakes or under snow in avalanches;

water rescue dogs, which retrieve individuals and objects from the water, swim lines out to stranded boaters, and even drag small boats to waiting rescuers;

drug- and explosive-finding dogs, which use their scenting abilities to find contraband materials. A variation on this are the dogs that find truffles for connoisseurs of this delicacy. They are better than the pigs that have been traditionally used for two reasons: Dogs have keener scenting powers, and they don't like the taste of truffles, so there is less worry that they will eat them before the gatherers get to them;

arson detection dogs, which are trained to detect hydrocarbons that might have been used as a means of deliberately starting a fire;

termite detection dogs, and a variant that is trained to detect mould and mildew in walls and under carpets;

entertainment dogs, which include racing dogs, diving dogs, dancing dogs, and acting dogs;

medical detection dogs, the newest breakthrough in the use of dogs, suggests that they can be used to detect certain cancers, such as melanomas, lung, and prostate cancer by sniffing an individual's skin, breath, or urine, respectively.

When we see dogs fulfilling some of these sophisticated functions, it is difficult to imagine that their complex behaviours are really pieced together out of the same instinctive intelligence components involved in guarding, watching, herding, and hunting. For instance, the specific ability of protecting or alerting other members of the pack is modified through training, so that a hearing-ear dog will alert a deaf person that the doorbell is ringing. Search-and-rescue behaviours, for their part, depend on exactly the same skills involved in hunting and retrieving, only the targets are changed from prey animals to other things; for the more complex tasks, the specific, instinctive abilities must simply be modified and placed under direct human control. This is done through training, and the success of the learning process depends on both the adaptive intelligence and the working or obedience intelligence of the dog.

COMPANION DOGS

Dogs fulfil one other important function for people—that of companion dog, a job that does not seem to require a particular instinctive intelligence but seems to depend more on a dog's personality. There is evidence that as far back as predynastic Egypt there was a demand for small "toy" dogs, which seemed to have had no other function than as pets and companions. Drawings, paintings, and various sculptures of such dogs suggest that the first of the purely companion dogs were Maltese or Pomeranians. Many other breeds, such as the Cavalier King Charles spaniel and English toy spaniel, developed in England, and the Pekingese, developed in China, had no other function than as pets.

At times, companion dogs have suffered from a prejudice against any dogs that did not work. The pug (see Plate 17), for instance, can be traced back to 400 B.C., when it appears to have been bred to serve as a companion dog to Buddhist monks in a monastery in Tibet. This breed was once roundly attacked in a newspaper in Victorian England. The writer argued that such dogs were completely "useless" and claimed that the finest dog trainers had been "completely unable to make a Pug hunt for anything." Apparently, the ability of these little dogs to bring comfort and pleasure to their owners was not considered useful work by this particular pragmatist.

Today, opinions have changed. It is now recognized that, as companions, dogs fill certain needs for play in children. Since dogs also provide needed affection and social interactions to individuals of all ages, they are often prescribed as part of psychological therapy.

Children with communication difficulties, adults with social-interaction or depressive problems, and the elderly suffering from isolation and loneliness have all been helped by companion dogs. Indeed, there is evidence that stress responses are reduced by contact with dogs. The psychiatrist Aaron Katcher and the psychologist Alan Beck have done a number of studies that demonstrated that when a person strokes a familiar and loved dog, the heart rate slows, breathing becomes regularized, and muscle tension is lessened: In other words, the physical signs of stress begin to disappear. Several other studies indicate that older people who live with dogs have fewer medical complaints and require fewer visits to doctors than do others of the same age who live without dogs, and are much less likely to fall into a clinical state of depression.

Children growing up in a household with a dog seem to be more socially mature and have greater empathy for others than children without such pets. Dog-owning couples are much less likely to divorce. Perhaps one of the most striking findings comes from a researcher named Erica Friedman, who looked at survival rates of people who had been hospitalized as a result of a major heart problem. A year after hospital treatment, she found that the percentage of dog owners who were still alive was more than four times higher than the percentage of non-pet owners. Much of the benefit obtained from companion dogs comes from their instinctive intelligence, which causes them to attend to and appropriately respond to the moods and signals of humans. It seems that the presence of a companion dog in your house can save your marriage, help rear better kids, keep you happier, and actually extend your life. That's not a bad trade for giving a dog a bit of food, time, and affection.

Chapter Nine

Adaptive Intelligence

I have known dogs, especially puppies, who were almost
as stupid as humans in their mental reactions.

—ROBERT BENCHLEY

While the instinctive intelligence of a dog reveals which behaviours
and skills are preprogrammed in the animal's genetic code, adaptive
intelligence relates to the knowledge, skills, and general competence a
dog can acquire during its lifetime. In a dog, adaptive intelligence has
two main components. The first is *learning ability,* which involves the
rate at which a dog can learn new relationships. There are many forms
of learning. *Observational learning* is the casual, natural learning that
allows certain associations between conditions and outcomes to form
but does not require direct involvement of the observer. Thus a dog
learns that its master's going to the refrigerator might mean that
something edible is about to happen, and it anticipates this possible
event by coming into the kitchen and making its presence known.
Environmental learning involves acquiring a sort of mental map or
representation of the immediate environment, including the location
of common objects and where certain individuals are habitually found
or certain activities normally occur. *Social learning* is learning to
respond to human or dog emotional and social signals. *Language comprehension* involves a dog's ability to learn human verbal signals.

Finally, *task learning* requires the dog's active involvement, often on a trial-and-error basis, and eventually results in its responding to specific signals that may bring rewards. A simple example is when the dog responds to the command *sit* appropriately and is rewarded by a pat or a tidbit of food.

Hand in hand with the various dimensions of learning is memory ability, and just as individuals differ in learning rates and efficiency, they also differ in their short- and long-term memory abilities. *Short-term memory* is the vital first stage of any information processing. You have, I am sure, at one time asked for a phone number from an operator or friend and then dialled it immediately. This number was stored in your short-term memory; if you got a busy signal and hung up to dial the number again, you might well have found that you'd already forgotten it. The thirty seconds or so from the moment you received the number and first dialled it to the time you tried to redial are enough for it to have faded from short-term memory.

Long-term memory seems to involve an almost unlimited information storage ability that results in virtually permanent memories. Psychologists have shown that information that can be held in memory for about five minutes has a better than 50 percent chance of being recalled accurately a month later and about a 40 percent chance of being recalled a year later.

The other important dimension of adaptive intelligence is *problem-solving ability*, the capacity to find correct solutions that allow the individual to circumvent the physical or conceptual obstacles or barriers blocking access to rewards. There are two aspects to problem-solving ability. The first involves the ability to plan and select the behaviours that can lead to the solution. The second involves the capacity to remember other learned strategies or information, gleaned from former problem-solving situations, and to transfer them to the present situation.

While a dog's breed is generally a good indicator of the nature of its instinctive intelligence, adaptive intelligence is much more individual. Breeding for high adaptive intelligence is more difficult than breeding for one or two specific sets of behavioural predispositions. For this reason, the best way to determine the adaptive intelligence of any one dog requires actual testing of that specific animal. The testing does not need to take place in a laboratory, nor need it be done by a professional; however, accurate results do require care in the testing.

For individuals who wish to test dogs for their adaptive intelligence, I have designed the Canine IQ Test (CIQ), which is composed of twelve individual problems or subtests that cover the broad spectrum of adaptive intelligence in dogs. Five of the subtests cover problem solving, while the other seven deal with learning and memory. Some, like test 1, may seem almost too easy for some dogs (you will have to take my word that some dogs find it quite difficult); others are a bit more difficult for many animals. All the tests are based on formal laboratory and field testing procedures that have been modified so that they will be fairly simple to administer and will not require much in the way of equipment.

THE CANINE IQ TEST

The subparts of the CIQ are quite simple, and most of the tests should be fun to administer. Dogs tend to enjoy the procedures because they don't know they are being tested and merely think that you are playing with them. I have set up the tests to be relatively independent of each other, so that most can be given separately and in any order. This is true for all tests except tests 7 and 8 (short- and long-term memory), which should be done in the same session, with test 7 performed first. All the tests do not have to be done on the same day, and since many involve using bits of food to motivate the dog, it may be best to do them over two or three sessions. This will prevent the dog from getting satiated and also remove the possibility that fatigue will influence the animal's performance. The entire CIQ takes between thirty minutes and an hour, depending on both the examiner and the dog. Some tests require waiting for the dog to respond appropriately, so some dogs will simply take longer.

Advance preparation on the part of the examiner will speed things up quite a bit. Most tests do not require much in the way of equipment beyond the dog's leash and collar. A stopwatch is quite useful for several tests, although you can use a watch with a sweep second hand instead. Test 2 requires an empty tin can, test 4 uses a large bath towel, test 6 a small hand towel. Test 9 requires a large stack of heavy books or a board and a few bricks, and test 12 needs a large piece of cardboard. You also should have on hand some small tidbits of food. Make these special treats that the dog really likes so that it will be really motivated to solve the problems. If your dog does not reliably sit and stay on command, some tests (for example 2, 7, 8, 9, and almost certainly 12) will be easier to do if you have a helper who can keep the dog in position while you initiate the test.

A few conditions must be met for the CIQ to be valid. First, the dog should be at least a year old, although some of the faster-maturing breeds (mostly the larger dogs) can be given the test at about nine or ten months. However, I recommend that you don't rush it. It would be a pity to rate a dog poorly simply because it was too young to work at its best capacity. Next, the dog should have been living with the person doing the testing—whether its current master or another member of the family—for at least three months, otherwise tests 1, 5, and 10 will not be valid. It is also preferable for the dog to have been living in the same place for at least ten weeks, otherwise test 3 will not be valid. Finally, the analysis of the CIQ is based on the first administration. It should

Test	Time	Score
1 Observational learning (going to the door)	____	____
2 Problem solving (food under can)	____	____
3 Attention and environmental learning (room rearrangement)	____	____
4 Problem solving (dog under towel)	____	____
5 Social learning (smile)	____	____
6 Problem solving (food under towel)	____	____
7 Short-term memory (finding food after short delay)	____	____
8 Long-term memory (finding food after longer delay)	____	____
9 Problem solving (retrieving from under barrier)	____	____
10 Language comprehension (name/false name)	____	____
11 Learning process (teaching *front*)	____	____
12 Problem solving (going around barrier)	____	____
Total Score	====	====

Figure 9.1
Canine IQ Test Scoring Form

probably not be given (for scoring purposes) more than twice, although some people have found that it is interesting to observe the changes in their dogs' behaviour in some of the tests and particular tests do seem to be pleasant socializing experiences. Some people have reported to me that they repeat some of the items now and again simply for fun.

No matter what happens during testing (whether your dog is doing better or worse than you expected), you should remain calm. Don't fuss at the dog, raise your voice, act disgusted or overexcited. Think of each test as little game, and try to get the dog to look at each in that way. Some of the tests require you to encourage the dog to do something, others require that you be quiet, while still others require a bit of ham acting as you point things out to the dog.

Administering the Canine IQ Test

Using the scoring form in Figure 9.1 as a model (you might want to photocopy it), list the dog's test scores on the appropriate lines.

TEST 1

The first test is a measure of *observational learning* as it applies to an everyday association that the dog should have learned simply through living in its current home. This test provides an easy starting point for testing your dog's adaptive intelligence.

Select a time of day when you do *not* typically walk your dog. Make sure your dog is awake and in the same general area that you are. When the dog looks at you, *silently* pick up your coat and keys and the dog's leash (if you usually use one) and then stop where you are, without moving toward the door. If the dog runs to the door or comes directly to you indicating some excitement or interest, score 5. If not, move directly to the door and then stop. If the dog comes to you in anticipation of a walk or going out, score 4. If not, place your hand on the doorknob, and turn it back and forth to make a noise. If the dog comes to you, score 3. If the dog pays some attention during the preceding activities but does not come to you or the door, score 2. If the dog pays no attention, score 1.

TEST 2

This is a test of *problem solving*. You need an empty can (about the size of a typical condensed soup can), some desirable tidbit of food, and a stopwatch (or a watch with a sweep second hand). First, show the dog the bit of food and let it sniff it. Next, with a great show, put the tidbit on the ground and invert the empty can over it. Then start the stopwatch and encourage the dog to get the bait by pointing at the can or tapping it. If the dog knocks the can out of the way and gets the tidbit in five seconds or less, score 5; if in five to fifteen seconds, score 4; in fifteen to thirty seconds, score 3; in thirty to sixty seconds, score 2. If the dog tries once or twice, sniffing around the can, but does not get the bait after a minute, score 1. If the dog makes no effort to obtain the bait, score 0.

TEST 3

This is a test of *attention and environmental learning.* While the dog is out of the house, either you or a helper should rearrange the furniture in a room that is familiar to the dog. For example, you could bring a few additional chairs into the room, move a large piece of furniture toward the centre of the room, place a coffee table in an odd corner, move a side table to the centre of the room, or create several other obvious disturbances of the usual pattern of furniture placement. Try to make sure that at least five things are obviously different in the room. Then bring your dog into the room and start your stopwatch going while you stand quietly. If the dog notices something is different within fifteen seconds and starts to explore or sniff any changed aspect of the room, score 5. If it notices the differences and checks out any one in fifteen to thirty seconds, score 4. If it does so in thirty to sixty seconds, score 3. If the dog looks around cautiously, seems to notice something is different, but does not explore any changed aspect of the room, score 2. If a minute passes, and the dog still ignores the changes, score 1.

TEST 4

This is a measure of *problem solving.* You need a large bath towel, a small blanket, or some other heavy cloth of a similar size. First, make sure that the dog is awake and reasonably active, and then let it sniff the towel. Then, with a quick, smooth motion (you may want to practice once or twice without the dog present), throw the towel over the dog's head so that its head and front shoulders are completely covered. Start the stopwatch, and watch silently. If the dog frees itself in fifteen seconds or less, score 5; if in fifteen to thirty seconds, score 4; in thirty to sixty seconds, score 3; in one to two minutes, score 2. If the dog has not removed the towel after two minutes, score 1.

TEST 5

This is a test of *social learning*. Pick a time when your dog is sitting around eight feet (two metres) away from you but has not been explicitly told to sit and stay. Then stare intently at its face. When the dog looks at you, count silently to three and then smile broadly. If the dog comes to you with any tail wagging, score 5. If the dog comes but slowly or only part way with no tail wagging, score 4. If the dog stands or rises from a lying to a sitting position but does not move toward you, score 3. If the dog moves away from you, score 2. If the dog pays no attention, score 1.

TEST 6

This next test of *problem solving* is similar to test 2 but a bit more difficult. The major difference is that this test demands a bit more cleverness at manipulating objects. You need a hand towel or a dish towel (not the large bath towel used in test 4). Show the dog a fairly substantial tidbit—a dog biscuit is perfect. Let the dog sniff the tidbit, and make sure that it looks at it for about five seconds. Then, with great exaggerated acting, place the food on the floor, and, while the dog watches, throw the towel over it. You can point to the towel to orient the dog. Start the stopwatch, and encourage the dog to get the bait. If it retrieves it in fifteen seconds or less, score 5; getting it in fifteen to thirty seconds scores 4; in thirty to sixty seconds scores 3; in one to two minutes scores 2. If the dog tries to retrieve the tidbit but gives up, score 1. If the dog doesn't even try to retrieve it within two minutes, score 0.

TEST 7

This is a test of *short-term memory*, and it should be followed immediately with test 8. Conduct this test in an average-size room that doesn't have a lot of furniture or other material cluttering it. You need a tidbit of food that has no strong odour (otherwise, the dog's scenting ability will bias the results). If your dog will not reliably sit and stay on command, have a helper present to hold the dog. To start, place your dog on a leash and have it sit in the centre of the room. While the dog watches you, show it the bait; the dog may even sniff the tidbit. Then, with a great exaggerated show (but no sound), place the bait in a corner, making sure that the dog sees you put it down. Lead the dog out of the room, walk around in a small circle, and then bring it back to the centre of the room. Leaving the room and returning to it should take no more than about fifteen seconds. Slip the leash off of the dog, and start the stopwatch. If the dog goes directly to the bait, score 5. If the dog systematically sniffs around the edge of the room and finds the tidbit, score 4. If the dog seems to search in a random fashion but nevertheless finds the tidbit within forty-five seconds, score 3. If the dog appears to try to find the tidbit but still hasn't succeeded after forty-five seconds, score 2. If the dog makes no effort to find the bait, score 1.

TEST 8

The companion to test 7, this is a test of *long-term memory* and should be given immediately after the preceding test. The setup is identical to that of test 7. Make sure, however, that you place the tidbit in a corner different from the one you used for the short-term memory test. Take the dog out of the room and keep the dog out of the room for five minutes. Then return the dog to the center of the room, slip off the leash, and start the stopwatch. If the dog goes directly to the bait, score 5. If the dog goes to the corner where the first bait was and then quickly goes to the correct corner, score 4. If the dog systematically sniffs around the edge of the room and finds the tidbit, score 3. If the dog seems to search in a random fashion but still finds the tidbit within forty-five seconds, score 2. If the dog appears to try to find the tidbit but still hasn't succeeded after forty-five seconds, score 1. If the dog makes no effort to find the bait, score 0.

TEST 9

This is a test of *problem-solving and manipulation ability*. You need an apparatus similar to a low table, which you can make out of some large books or a board and a few bricks. Stack two or so volumes some distance apart, set another large book or a board on top of them, and then weight your "table" with some additional books or other objects so the dog can't move it. (Encyclopaedia volumes are perfect for this.) The idea is to make a tablelike structure too near the ground for your dog's head to fit under it but high enough so that the dog can reach under it with its paws (see Figure 9.2). About three inches high (seven or eight centimetres) works well with small to medium dogs. You may find that a low-set upholstered chair or sofa may work just as well.

Making sure your dog is watching you from nearby, first show it the tidbit, even let it have a sniff, and then, overacting, place the treat under the apparatus or furniture. Start the stopwatch, and encourage the dog to get the bait. If the dog uses its paws and manages to retrieve the tidbit in sixty seconds or less, score 5. If the dog retrieves it in one

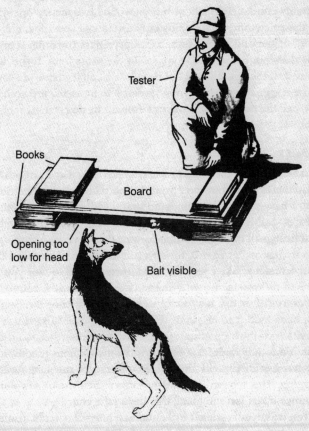

Figure 9.2
The setup for Test 9. Bricks or blocks can be substituted for the books as long as they are heavy enough to keep the dog from moving the apparatus.

to three minutes, score 4. If the dog uses its muzzle only and fails to get the bait or if it uses its paws but still has not retrieved the bait after three minutes, score 3. If the dog doesn't use its paws and simply sniffs or gives one or two tries to retrieve it with its muzzle and then gives up, score 2. If after three minutes the dog has made no effort to retrieve the bait, score 1.

TEST 10

This is a test of *language comprehension*. The dog should be settled comfortably at least eight feet or more (around two metres or so) from you. In the voice tones that you usually use to call your dog, call "refrigerator." If the dog shows some responsiveness to come, score 3. If the dog does not come, call "movies" in the same tone. If the dog comes, score 2. If the dog still has not responded, call its name (do say "come"). If the dog comes or shows any tendency to move toward you, score 5. If not, call the dog's name a second time. If the dog comes, score 4. If not, score 1.

TEST 11

This test looks at the actual *process of learning*. Obviously, the best way to do this is to see how well your dog actually learns something. To this end, I have designed a command that few dogs have ever encountered before—call it the *front* command. The command elicits a behaviour that likely will be as unfamiliar to your dog as is the command itself: It simply instructs the dog to get up from the *heel* position (sitting by your left side), take a step forward, turn around to face you, and then sit with its nose facing your knees. (It is, incidentally, a sometimes useful exercise, so you may want to keep it in the dog's repertoire after you have used it to test your dog's learning rate.) To achieve accurate results, you must conduct the test under standardized and consistent conditions; it is important to follow the instructions exactly, in terms of the number of repetitions and the pattern of movements during the training. This test will take a bit longer than the others—around ten minutes if you have to go all the way to the end.

You will need a pocket full of tidbits, and you should also use lots of praise during this short training/testing session. Start with the dog sitting in the usual *heel* position—that is, next to your left leg. (I am working on the presumption that you have already taught your dog to sit by your side. If you haven't, you should do this as a first step. Every dog obedience program starts with the *sit* command because it is something every civilized dog should know and furthermore is needed for your own sanity.) The dog should have its usual collar on, and a leash should be attached to the collar.

Trials 1 to 3: Begin by giving the command *front* in a clear voice, accompanied by the hand signal, which is one or both of your hands lightly slapping the front of your legs just above your knees. (If you already use the word *front* for some other purpose, choose another command, such as *face me* instead.) Obviously, your dog will not know what you are talking about at this juncture. Therefore, you should guide the dog into the *front* position. To do this, step forward with your right foot, tugging the dog on the lead horizontally in front of its head to cause the dog to stand and move a step or so forward. Then step back with your right leg, tugging on the lead to cause the dog to turn clockwise toward you. For a large dog, you may have to take an additional step back. Then push the dog down into a sitting position in front of you. Immediately praise your dog, and/or give it a tidbit. Place the dog back into the *heel* position beside you, and repeat this practice for trials 2 and 3.

Trials 4 to 5: These are the same as trials 1 to 3, only you should pause about a second after the command *front* and then try to move the dog into the *front* position using only minimal or no movement of your right leg.

Trial 6: This is a test trial. Give the command *front*, but do not attempt to move the dog physically. If the dog moves from your side to the *front* position, no matter how sloppily, score 6, and consider the test over. If there is no movement after about five seconds, treat this as if it were another training trial: guide the dog into place, and reward it.

Subsequent trials and tests: Give an additional ten training trials, just like trials 4 and 5, and then a test trial just like trial 6. If the dog performs the manoeuvre during the test trial, score 5. If not, give ten more trials. At the end of these, repeat the test one last time. If the dog performs the *front* exercise without any assistance on your part (regardless of how out of line, slowly, or messily), score 3. If the dog comes around to the front but doesn't sit, score 2. If the dog stands at the *front* command, but doesn't move around, score 1. If the dog remains sitting, score 0.

TEST 12

This test is a fairly difficult *problem-solving* task, because it requires the dog to move away from the item that it is interested in getting. The setup takes a little advance preparation. You need a large piece of cardboard too high for your dog to want to try to jump over it when it is set on end. Cut out a vertical aperture, starting and ending a couple of inches from the top and bottom, around three inches (eight centimetres) wide. Now prop up the cardboard by taping or tying it to two side "walls" (which can be two additional pieces of cardboard or two boxes or chairs laid on their sides) so that you have an arrangement something like that shown in Figure 9.3. Place the dog in front of the barrier (have someone hold it there if need be), and attract its attention so that it looks at you through the vertical slit. With great exaggeration, show the dog a tidbit through the window, and lay it on the ground a foot or two in from the opening, well out of reach of its paw. As you start the stopwatch, have your helper release the dog while you encourage it to get the food. If the dog goes around the barriers and gets the bait within fifteen seconds, score 5. If the dog gets it in fifteen to thirty seconds, score 4; in thirty to sixty seconds, score 3. If the dog still has not retrieved the bait after sixty seconds, stop actively encouraging it and stand quietly nearby, keeping the stopwatch going. If the dog gets the bait in one to two minutes, score 2. If the dog tries to reach the bait by pawing through the window slit and then gives up, score 1. If the dog doesn't exert any effort to get the bait after two minutes, score 0.

Interpreting the CIQ Results

The interpretation of the CIQ results is fairly straightforward.

Score 54 or higher: This dog could be described as brilliant. A dog with this level of intelligence is quite rare, and fewer than 5 percent of the dogs in our standardization group (averaged across all tested breeds) reached this level.

Score 48 to 53: This is a superior dog with extremely high intelligence.

Score 42 to 47: This dog is in the high average range of intelligence and should be capable of doing virtually any task that a typical dog is called upon to do.

Score 30 to 41: This score represents average intelligence for a dog. A dog in this range may show intermittent flashes of brilliance, but for other tasks its performance may be uninspired.

Score 24 to 29: This dog is low average. Although at times it may appear to act quite cleverly, most of the time it will seem to need to work hard to understand what is required of it.

Score 18 to 23: I would describe this dog's intelligence as borderline. A dog at this level may have difficulty adapting to the demands of everyday life and the expectations of its owner. However, in a structured, low-stress environment, it may function quite reasonably.

Score below 18: Dogs with scores below 18 are clearly deficient in many areas of their adaptive intelligence. Such a dog may be extremely difficult to live with.

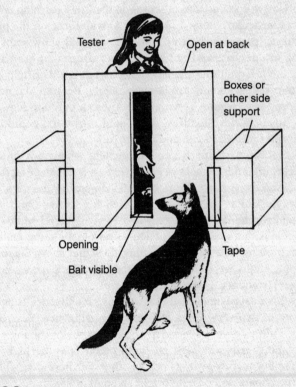

Figure 9.3
The setup for Test 12. Chairs laid on their sides or cardboard pieces can be substituted for the boxes that serve as side supports.

BREED DIFFERENCES IN ADAPTIVE INTELLIGENCE

Within any breed of dogs, there is a wide variability in terms of adaptive intelligence. Unfortunately, not enough dogs have been tested on the CIQ to permit definitive statements about all of the breeds. However, in my experience with the CIQ, some of the more popular breeds have performed extremely well. The highest overall scores have been from (in alphabetical order) Doberman pinschers, German shepherds, Labrador retrievers, poodles (standard, miniature, and toy), golden retrievers, and Shetland sheepdogs. These dogs excel in both the learning and memory areas and in the problem-solving aspect of adaptive intelligence.

Surprisingly, comparisons of scores on the CIQ's learning and memory tests (particularly tests 1, 3, 7, and 8) with those on the problem-solving tests (particularly tests 2, 4, 6, 9, and 12) show some breeds excelling in one area and not in the other. Dogs that are extremely good in the learning and memory aspects but not as bright when it comes to problem solving are (alphabetically) Belgian Malinois, Belgian sheepdogs, Belgian Tervurens, Bernese mountain dogs, border collies, Bouviers des Flandres, flat-coated retrievers, papillons, and Welsh corgis (both Cardigan and Pembroke).

Dogs that are particularly good at problem solving but do less well in the learning and memory areas include a number of terriers and working breeds. Among the good problem-solving terriers are the Airedale, Australian terrier, cairn terrier, fox terrier (both smooth-haired and wirehaired), Kerry blue and West Highland white terriers. Working dogs that are good problem solvers include the malamutes, Siberian huskies, and Samoyeds. Other dogs that showed good problem-solving ability were basenjis, Chihuahuas, schipperkes, and all the schnauzers (standard, giant, and miniature).

What this analysis means is that adaptive intelligence is actually a composite of two very different forms of intelligence. Learning and memory abilities do not necessarily predict problem-solving abilities. While some breeds are high on both, others may be high on one dimension but merely average on the other. Furthermore, within any given breed, there will be both bright and dull individuals.

Chapter Ten

Working or Obedience Intelligence

Trained or not, he'll always be his own dog to a degree.
—CAROL LEA BENJAMIN

Any dog person not only will tell you that the various breeds differ greatly in their intelligence but will harangue you about the merits of some breeds and the limitations of others. Such people are using the word *intelligence* to mean *trainability,* and their assessments have to do with *working* or *obedience intelligence.* A casual sampling of the kinds of comments one can find about specific breeds in the dog literature includes newsman Peter Jennings's comment on the malamute, "Their brain [is] like a piece of river rock"; veterinarian Michael Fox's comment on Irish setters, "They're so dumb that they get lost on the end of their leash"; writer Donald McCaig's, "Border collies are very bright, quick, and more than a little weird." Some people almost gush their praise for certain breeds; here's professional dog trainer Morton Wilson on the Doberman pinscher: "All dobermans should be named 'Einstein'. Well, perhaps that's too lavish praise. They're a bit weak on mathematics, but they certainly could earn a Ph.D. in any other subject." Others are absolutely devastating in their observations; take author E. B. White on the dachshund: "Some day, if I ever get a chance, I shall write a book, or warning, on the character and temperament of the dachshund and why he can't be trained and shouldn't be. I would rather train a striped zebra to balance an Indian club than induce a dachshund to heed my slightest command."

The presumption behind all these comments is that some breeds are easily trained while others are simply hopeless. Most experts are willing to grant that every dog must have some level of instinctive intelligence that makes it useful to man. On the other hand, they presume that some breeds of dogs are too slow or intractable to be capable of learning tasks beyond those for which their heredity programmes them. Is this true? Do breeds really differ so strongly in their working and obedience intelligence?

IS THERE DATA ON BREED DIFFERENCES?

My training is as a researcher in psychology, so when confronted with the question of breed differences in intelligence, I made the assumption that a large number of systematic laboratory studies must have compared the various breeds on this dimension and that I would only need to study the scientific literature in order to determine the relative intelligence of various breeds. Unfortunately, this turned out not to be the case.

I should have realized at the outset that the scale of the task was simply too great for laboratory work under present conditions. Imagine that assessing the relative working intelligence of any breed of dog required a sample of ten dogs to control for variations in individual ability in dogs. But many dog trainers and handlers claim that there are also differences between male and female dogs, so, to be safe, increase that sample to twenty—ten males and ten females. This means that to assess the 154 breeds registered with the American Kennel Club at the time of this writing would require the testing of 3,080 dogs. Even if a researcher purchased all these dogs at bargain basement prices—say, $400 per animal—the bill would amount to $1,232,000. And that's without factoring in the cost of kennels, veterinarians, medication, food, maintenance personnel, and so forth.

Having acquired the dogs, the researcher must systematically train them in order to be able to test their working and obedience intelligence. There's no need to press each dog to its highest limits, which could take hundreds or even thousands of hours, as every dog trainer and handler knows, but each dog should complete a standardized minimal programme of training to bring it to a level where testable differences in performance become visible among the breeds. This might be the equivalent of what a dog is expected to know after an advanced beginner's class in dog obedience. A typical dog obedience class (for either beginners or advanced beginners) will usually run about one hour a week for about ten weeks, for a total of ten hours of classroom instruction. Assuming that during the week between each successive class the average handler trains his or her dog about ten minutes a day (with Sunday off), this would be an additional one hour of instruction a week, bringing the training time up to about twenty hours of actual instruction. If the dogs must complete two class sequences (beginners and advanced beginners) to attain the minimum amount of training that might lead to useful testing, this means that each dog requires about forty hours of training—about one full-time work week per dog. For the 3,080 dogs that need testing, assuming the tester works fifty weeks per year, he or she would be gainfully employed for nearly 62 years. And these calculations don't even take into account the time needed for feeding, exercising, grooming, and cleaning up after the dogs.

The testing could be done more quickly with a large group of trainers and testers. I estimate that, with a staff of twenty-five people and a budget of $4 million a year for a period of three to four years, this project could be done, with the total expenditure reaching around $16 million. And if any members of the executive board of the American, Canadian, British, Australian, or any other kennel club are reading this and happen to have this amount lying around in a budget category designated for research expenses, I'd gladly accept a grant to start the project!

When it became clear to me that data did not exist and that to obtain it would take a research budget that exceeds the annual amount spent by some nations for all their medical research into problems such as cancer, heart disease, or AIDS, I knew that I would have to use a different set of research strategies if I ever hoped to get the information I needed. It occurred to me that one possible source of data on dog obedience and working intelligence might be available in records obtained from dog obedience trials.

WHAT ABOUT OBEDIENCE TRIAL RECORDS?

Both the American Kennel Club (AKC) and the Canadian Kennel Club (CKC) describe the purpose of dog obedience trials in virtually the same words. The AKC regulations state, "The purpose of Obedience Trials is to demonstrate the usefulness of the purebred dog as a companion of man. . . . The basic objective of Obedience Trials is to produce dogs that have been trained and conditioned always to behave in the home, in public places, and in the presence of other dogs, in a manner that will reflect credit on the sport of Obedience." What this means is that the dogs are not simply taught tricks; rather, the specific exercises tested in the obedience ring should serve to indicate the trainability of dogs and their willingness to perform under the control of their human masters. This means that obedience trials test exactly the same behaviours that define working and obedience intelligence.

At the first level of obedience competition, the training requirements are quite simple. For the companion dog (CD) degree, the dog need only be able to walk under control in the *heel* position; sit, lie down, and stand on command; come when called; and stay in one place for a few minutes when ordered to do so. A dog that has earned the CD degree has demonstrated the minimal requirements needed to be a good companion under reasonable control by its master. At the higher levels of competition, the demands are quite a bit more complex. At the second level *(open competition)*, for instance, dogs must retrieve and take a high jump and a broad jump on command. At the highest level *(utility competition)*, dogs must search and find items using their scenting ability, respond to signals rather than to verbal commands, and so forth. Even at this level of competition, however, every breed of dog is physically quite capable of performing the various exercises. Although some breeds have better scenting ability and others have instinctive retrieving tendencies, all dogs can scent well enough and retrieve well enough to accomplish the tasks required for any of these obedience degrees. This means that the performance of any particular dog will depend on how well it has learned the exercises and how willingly it works for humans.

Further on in the obedience trial regulations is another requirement that makes it likely that data from dog obedience competitions might provide data necessary to assess dogs' relative working intelligence.

The regulations state that "all contestants in a class are required to perform the same exercises in substantially the same way so that the relative quality of the various performances may be compared and scored." This means that, regardless of breed, all the dogs perform the same exercises in the same way, except for the adjustment of jump heights and lengths to fit different dogs' sizes. Thus, although the actual degree of control is less than would exist in a laboratory, there should be enough uniformity in the testing to allow valid comparisons across breeds.

The AKC routinely publishes the records of its obedience competitions. I obtained data for a full year of competition, covering nearly two thousand obedience trials in the United States involving approximately 125,000 entries and the awarding of more than eleven thousand obedience degrees. With this magnificent database, I figured I could easily determine the best from the worst breeds by looking at how they fared in competition. Clearly, any breed that did not earn a single obedience degree for the full year would have to be among the worst dogs in terms of working and obedience intelligence. This hypothesis yielded the following list: Dandie Dinmont terriers, American foxhounds, English foxhounds, Lakeland terriers, Australian kelpies, and harriers. Breeds with only one obedience degree for the full year's worth of data that I examined included English toy spaniels, miniature bull terriers, Tibetan spaniels, Sussex spaniels, Tibetan terriers, otterhounds, Petite Basset Griffon Vendeens, Canaan dogs, and komondors. The ten breeds earning the largest number of obedience degrees were golden retrievers, Shetland sheepdogs, German shepherds, Labrador retrievers, rottweilers, poodles, Doberman pinschers, border collies, cocker spaniels, and collies.

As I looked at the breeds in these lists, it became apparent that I had been too simple-minded in my analysis. For example, otterhounds earned just one obedience degree in the test year, while golden retrievers earned 1,284—a noticeable and major difference. But that same year, there were approximately 670,000 golden retrievers living and registered with the AKC but only around three hundred living, AKC-registered otterhounds. Even if otterhounds were the most brilliant of all dogs and every single one of them earned an obedience degree in the test year, they could only garner a total of three hundred obedience degrees. On the other hand, for there to be 1,284 golden retrievers with obedience degrees, only two out of every thousand had to succeed. Relatively rare dogs simply cannot accumulate as many obedience degrees for their breed as can the popular breeds.

Still, there was more to this data than popularity alone. For example, there were approximately 570,000 AKC-registered beagles alive, as opposed to around 200,000 registered Doberman pinschers. Yet 466 Dobermans earned obedience degrees in the test year, as compared to thirty-four obedience degrees for beagles. In other words, even though beagles were nearly three times more common than Dobermans, as a breed they were less than one-tenth as likely to get an obedience degree. This certainly suggests a real difference between these breeds.

With greater care, I tried several alternate means of analysis to get meaningful rankings of the breeds. Unfortunately, each method had its own drawbacks. For instance, people who own truly popular breeds often keep them purely as pets and thus are less likely, on a percentage basis, to show their dogs in either obedience or conformation trials. The reverse holds for owners of relatively rare breeds, who seem to go out of their way to compete with their animals, perhaps in the hopes of increasing the breed's popularity. This means that simple statistics, such as the percentage of dogs registered that get obedience degrees, won't compensate sufficiently for breed popularity to allow ranking of the various breeds.

WHAT DO THE EXPERTS SAY?

At this point, I found myself looking at my desk cluttered with the results of dozens of hours of analysis of the data from obedience competitions. I was beginning to feel really frustrated. Surely, there had to be some way to use the information and comparisons generated by all of those obedience trials to get an answer. There had to be some way to limit the comparisons to dogs actually competing in order to see which breeds perform best. I wondered if I should talk to some dog obedience judges who might have a suggestion. Then it hit me: What I needed to do was to talk to every dog obedience judge that I could get in touch with. These people are trained to observe and evaluate how dogs perform under controlled conditions. It is not unusual for a judge to spend twelve to twenty hours on any given weekend judging and scoring dogs of various breeds. In addition, most judges are also dog trainers, spending many more hours observing and working with dogs. Because of this extensive experience watching and evaluating dogs, if any one group of people had accumulated knowledge of the relative performance of various breeds, it was this one.

I set about getting the lists of obedience judges from the American and Canadian Kennel Clubs and then sent out questionnaires to every dog obedience judge in North America. The questionnaire was fairly long and complicated. First, it asked the judges to rate each of the dog breeds on several aspects of their intelligence. After that, a final set of questions asked the judges to indicate which specific breeds they would rate as the ten most intelligent and the ten least intelligent breeds. Judges were asked to leave blank any breeds if they felt that they did not have enough experience with those particular dogs to confidently provide an intelligence assessment.

To my amazement, 208 experts—approximately half of all the obedience judges listed in North America—responded to my request. Of these, 199 provided complete information in all sections of the questionnaire. In addition, about one-quarter of the judges added letters and notes, many of which contained insights into the way dogs think. Some even added extra statistical data that helped me adjust the placement of particular breeds. Finally, after my preliminary analyses, I telephoned about two dozen of the judges for follow-up interviews that allowed me to clarify some issues and observations and also helped in interpreting some of the rankings.

Ranking the Breeds in Working and Obedience Intelligence

Before I describe what I learned about working or obedience intelligence from these experts, I had best start with the caution that many of them offered. All the judges recognized that there were definite differences in the intelligence and trainability of the various breeds; however, they also noted that there is a lot of individual variation among dogs. They noted that even in the dullest breeds, some dogs work extremely well, while in some of the brightest breeds, certain individuals simply show no capacity to learn or perform. One judge told me, "A lot has to do with the person training the dog. You can start with a dumb breed and make them really quite clever if you are a good enough trainer." What this judge was actually describing was *manifest intelligence*—that is, the sum total of all the dimensions of intelligence that any dog displays. Just like human beings, few dogs ever achieve their full psychological potential. The difference among the various breeds, then, is how easily each can reach a certain level of performance and what the absolute maximum is that a dog of any given breed may be expected to achieve. Good trainers can do a lot with any breed of dog; they just find the job much easier if they start with one that has high working and obedience intelligence.

One of the most striking things about the data was the extent of agreement among the various obedience judges, which suggested that real, observable differences were being reliably detected among the various breeds. For example, 190 of the 199 judges placed the border collie in the top ten! Similarly, 171 judges placed the Shetland sheepdog in the top group, 169 included the poodle, 167 included the German shepherd, and the same number named the golden retriever as among the ten most trainable dogs. There was somewhat less agreement as to which breeds showed the poorest working or obedience intelligence, but, even here, the degree of agreement was still high. Of the 199 judges, 121 ranked the Afghan hound as one of the ten worst breeds for obedience, 99 named the basenji, and 81 singled out the chow chow.

Table 10.1 shows how 140 breeds for which adequate data were obtained ranked in terms of obedience and working intelligence, ranging from a high of 1 to a low of 79. Dogs that share the same number had identical scores. Predictably, in the middle (around average obedience intelligence levels), there are a number of breeds that earned the same ranks since, obviously, many breeds should score near average intelligence. When I initially analysed this data for the first edition of this book, I insisted that I have full rankings from at least a hundred judges for any breed that I included in my list. This left out some breeds that were newly accepted by the kennel clubs, or were being registered only in Canada and not the United States at that time, such as the Nova Scotia duck tolling retriever, the Parson Russell terrier (formerly known as the Jack Russell terrier), and the Havanese, since fewer judges felt that they had adequate information about them. Some of these dogs have achieved popularity since then. I therefore went back to the initial data and found that, although fewer than a hundred judges provided rankings of these dogs, I still had a lot of data on some of these breeds. I conducted a number of statistical analyses which showed that as long as I had rankings from at least seventy judges, the final result was almost as stable and reliable as when I had the full quota, and the existing rankings remained the same. For this reason I eased my restrictions a bit and allowed a breed to be listed if at least seventy judges ranked its intelligence. This allowed me to include seven breeds that were not on the list in the first edition. I have put an asterisk next to the breeds that I added through this process, just so that the reader will recognize that these ranks are based on somewhat fewer data points. Generally speaking, the herding dogs and retrievers tend to score the highest and the hounds the lowest; however, there are brighter and duller breeds within each of the groups of dogs.

What about mixed breed or mongrel dogs? As should be apparent from what we have learned so far, a dog's breed is determined by its genetic makeup. The particular collection of genes that define a breed allow us to predict a dog's behaviour as well as its size, shape, and coat color. When we crossbreed we lose some of that predictability, since which genes will be passed on by each parent and how they will combine is a matter of chance. Fortunately, we can still make some predictions of a mixed breed dog's working and obedience intelligence without even knowing much about its parentage. John Paul Scott and John C. Fuller carried out a series of selective breeding experiments at the Jackson Laboratories in Bar Harbor, Maine. By a happy chance their results revealed a simple rule that seems to work. Their general conclusion was that a mixed breed dog is most likely to act like the breed that it most looks like. Thus if a beagle-poodle cross looks most like a beagle, it will probably act much like a beagle. If it looks most like a poodle, its behaviour will be very poodle-like. In my own experience, this appears to be true. My daughter by marriage, Kari, has a mixed-breed dog, Tessa, who looks much like her German shepherd mother. She also shows the same high working and obedience intelligence that I would expect of a German shepherd. On the other hand, most mixed breed dogs have some predispositions and behaviours that are characteristic of both breeds that contributed to it. The more of a blend that the dog's physical appearance seems to be, the more likely that the dog's behaviour will be a blend of the two parent breeds. Thus if you want an estimate of a mixed breed dog's working and obedience

Table 10.1

Ranking of Dogs for Obedience and Working Intelligence

Rank	Breed	Rank	Breed
1	Border collie		Puli
2	Poodle		Yorkshire terrier
3	German shepherd	28	Giant schnauzer
4	Golden retriever		Portuguese water dog
5	Doberman pinscher	29	Airedale
6	Shetland sheepdog		Bouvier des Flandres
7	Labrador retriever	30	Border terrier
8	Papillon		Briard
9	Rottweiler	31	Welsh springer spaniel
10	Australian cattle dog	32	Manchester terrier
11	Pembroke Welsh corgi	33	Samoyed
12	Miniature schnauzer	34	Field spaniel
13	English springer spaniel		Newfoundland
14	Belgian Tervuren		Australian terrier
15	Schipperke		American Staffordshire
	Belgian sheepdog		terrier
16	Collie		Gordon setter
	Keeshond		Bearded collie
17	German short-haired	35	American Eskimo dog*
	pointer		Cairn terrier
18	Flat-coated retriever		Kerry blue terrier
	English cocker spaniel		Irish setter
	Standard schnauzer	36	Norwegian elkhound
19	Brittany spaniel	37	Affenpinscher
20	Cocker spaniel		Silky terrier
	Nova Scotia duck tolling		Miniature pinscher
	retriever*		English setter
21	Weimaraner		Pharaoh hound
22	Belgian Malinois		Clumber spaniel
	Bernese mountain dog	38	Norwich terrier
23	Pomeranian	39	Dalmatian
24	Irish water spaniel	40	Soft-coated wheaten terrier
25	Vizsla		Bedlington terrier
26	Cardigan Welsh corgi		Smooth-haired fox terrier
27	Chesapeake Bay retriever	41	Curly-coated retriever
			Irish wolfhound
		42	Kuvasz
			Australian shepherd

* Marked breeds represent rankings based upon 70 to 99 dog obedience judges, as opposed to unmarked breeds where the ranking is based upon scores from 100 or more judges.

Rank	Breed	Rank	Breed
43	Saluki	55	Skye terrier
	Finnish spitz	56	Norfolk terrier
	Pointer		Sealyham terrier
44	Cavalier King Charles	57	Pug
	spaniel	58	French bulldog
	German wirehaired pointer	59	Brussels griffon
	Black-and-tan coonhound		Maltese terrier
	American water spaniel	60	Italian greyhound
45	Siberian husky	61	Chinese crested
	Bichon frise	62	Dandie Dinmont terrier
	English toy spaniel		Tibetan terrier
46	Tibetan spaniel		Japanese chin
46	English foxhound		Lakeland terrier
	Otterhound	63	Old English sheepdog
	American foxhound	64	Great Pyrenees
46	Greyhound	65	Scottish terrier
	Harrier*	65	Saint Bernard
	Parson Russell terrier*	66	Bull terrier
	Wirehaired pointing griffon		Petite Basset Griffon
47	West Highland white		Vendeen*
	terrier	67	Chihuahua
	Havanese*	68	Lhasa apso
	Scottish deerhound	69	Bullmastiff
48	Boxer	70	Shih Tzu
	Great Dane	71	Basset hound
49	Dachshund	72	Mastiff
	Staffordshire bull terrier		Beagle
	Shiba Inu*	73	Pekingese
50	Malamute	74	Bloodhound
51	Whippet	75	Borzoi
	Chinese shar-pei	76	Chow chow
	Wirehaired fox terrier	77	Bulldog
52	Rhodesian ridgeback	78	Basenji
53	Ibizan hound	79	Afghan hound
	Welsh terrier		
	Irish terrier		
54	Boston terrier		
	Akita		

intelligence, first decide which pure breed it looks most like and then use that as your prediction. It won't be 100 percent accurate, but it should be close.

Interpreting the Rankings

Even in dealing with purebred dogs, simply having the rankings is not really enough to predict how the various breeds of dogs might perform. Does a rank difference between 30 and 35 really make a noticeable difference in a dog's performance? The following interpretive guide will help clarify what the rankings mean.

Ranks 1 to 10 are the brightest dogs in their obedience and working intelligence. Most dogs of these breeds will begin to show an understanding of simple new commands in less than five exposures and will remember these new habits without noticeable need for practice. They obey the first command given by their handler around 95 percent of the time or better. Furthermore, they respond to commands within seconds after they are given, even when the owner is a distance away. These are clearly the top breeds for intelligence and seem to learn well even with inexperienced or relatively inept trainers.

Ranks 11 to 26 are excellent working dogs. Training of simple commands should take around five to fifteen repetitions. The dogs will remember such commands quite well, although they will show improvement with practice. They will respond to the first command 85 percent of the time or better. For more complex commands, there may sometimes be a slight, but occasionally noticeable, delay before the dog responds. These delays can be eliminated with practice. Dogs with these ranks may also respond a bit more slowly when their handlers are farther away from them. Nevertheless, virtually any trainer can get these breeds to perform well, even if the handler has only minimal patience and not much experience.

Ranks 27 to 39 are above-average working dogs. Although they will begin to show a preliminary understanding of simple new tasks in less than fifteen exposures, on average it will take fifteen to twenty-five repetitions before they demonstrate relatively consistent performance. Dogs in this group benefit enormously from extra practice, especially at the beginning stages of learning. After they learn a given habit, they generally retain it quite well. They will usually respond to the first command 70 percent of the time or better, and their reliability will depend on the amount of training they received. All in all, these dogs act much like the excellent dogs in the group above; they simply respond a bit less consistently, and there is often a perceptible lag between the command and the response. They will not respond reliably beyond a certain distance from their handlers, and at long distances they may not respond at all. Inconsistent or poor training by inexperienced handlers, or harsh and impatient treatment, will result in definitely poorer performance for these breeds.

Ranks 40 to 54 are average dogs in terms of their working and obedience intelligence. During learning, they will begin to show rudimentary understanding of most tasks after fifteen to twenty repetitions; however, reasonable performance will take between twenty-five and forty experiences. Given adequate practice, these dogs will show good retention, and they definitely benefit from additional practice at the time of initial learning. In the absence of extra practice, they may seem to lose the learned habit. These dogs will respond on the first command more than 50 percent of the time, but the actual performance and reliability will depend on the amount of practice and repetition during training. They also may respond noticeably more slowly than do higher-ranked breeds. These dogs are extremely sensitive to the distance of their owners. If the owner is reasonably close, a dog's performance is much more dependable. As the distance between dog and owner increases, the dog's performance becomes obviously less solid and predictable. Beyond a given distance (which may not be very far), several commands may be required, or the voice may have to be raised, in order to get compliance. For these breeds, quality of training is the major factor in determining quality of performance. Better handlers can make these dogs appear as good as any of the best breeds, but poorer handlers, especially those lacking in patience, can make a mess of these dogs.

Ranks 55 to 69 can be rated as only fair in their obedience and working ability. It may sometimes take up to twenty-five repetitions before they begin to show any glimmering of understanding when presented with a new command, and they may require between forty and eighty experiences before achieving reliable performance. Even then, the habits may appear to be weak. They may need extended practice to master the commands and show solid, reliable performance. If they do not get several extra sessions of practice, these breeds often act as if they have forgotten what is expected of them. Occasional refresher sessions are frequently needed to keep performance at an acceptable level. With average levels of training, these dogs will respond to the first command only about 40 percent of the time. Even then, they work best when their trainers are very close. These dogs appear distracted much of the time, and may seem to behave only when they feel like it. Owners of these dogs spend a lot of the time shouting at them, since the dogs seem totally unresponsive if there is much distance between them and their handlers. People who own such dogs usually rationalize their dogs' behaviour with the same arguments that cat owners use to explain their animals' unresponsiveness, claiming that the animals are "independent", "aloof", or "easily bored by the obedience business". These are definitely not breeds for first-time dog owners. An experienced dog trainer, with lots of time and firm but loving attention, can get these dogs to respond well, but even an expert dog trainer will have a hard time getting one of these dogs to perform with more than spotty reliability.

Ranks 70 to 79 are the breeds that have been judged to be the most difficult, with the lowest degree of working and obedience intelligence. During initial training, these breeds may need thirty or forty repetitions before they show the first inkling that they have a clue about what is expected of them. It is not unusual for these dogs to require over a hundred repetitions of the basic practice activities, often spread over several training sessions, before any reliability is obtained. Even then, their performance may seem slow and unsteady. Once they do learn, they still will need numerous, repeated practice sessions. Without such practice the training often seems to "evaporate", and these dogs behave as if they never learned the exercise in the first place. Some judges cited some of these breeds as being virtually untrainable, while others suggested that the difficulties probably lie in the fact that, with average handlers, the initial learning sessions and practice were not being continued long enough for the behaviours to work themselves into becoming permanent habits.

Once these breeds learn a habit, they still show unpredictable failures to respond. They tend to react to the first command less than 30 percent of the time. Sometimes they will turn away from their handlers, as if they were actively ignoring commands or fighting their owners' authority. When they do respond, they often do so quite slowly and seem unsure about, or displeased with, what they are supposed to be doing. Some of these dogs are only reasonable workers on lead and are not trustworthy when free of the leash. Of all the breeds, these most need competent and experienced handlers. Average trainers may soon find themselves frustrated by the apparently unruly and unmanageable performance of these breeds. Even some very competent trainers may find their skills put to the test when working with these dogs.

It is important to note that there is a strong relationship between the handler and a dog's final working and obedience performance, and this shows up much more clearly in the more difficult breeds. For instance, Barbara Baker, one of the trainers in the Vancouver Dog Obedience Training Club, owned a Staffordshire bull terrier named Meg. "Staffies" as a breed rank 49 overall, placing them near the bottom of the average grouping for obedience and working ability. Despite this, Barbara was able to train Meg to the highest level of dog obedience competition, and she obtained both the American and Canadian titles of Utility Dog and Obedience Training Champion. One year she went on to become the third-highest-scoring dog in obedience competition in Canada, far outscoring dozens of brilliant border collies, poodles, German shepherds, and golden retrievers that year.

One might ask if Meg was a fluke of some sort. Perhaps Barbara had simply blundered onto the Einstein of Staffordshire bull terriers. This is clearly not the case: Only a few years before, Barbara had trained another Staffie, named Mori, who rose to become the number five dog in Canada in obedience competition. Neither dog had been specifically selected or pretested to demonstrate any remarkable intellect. They had been chosen as pets by an excellent, patient dog trainer who then proceeded to demonstrate that, with the proper training and handling, even a purportedly difficult breed of dog can show excellent obedience and working performance.

My own dogs, at the moment of this writing, include a Cavalier King Charles spaniel (ranked 44), who is now retired but was a reliable and enthusiastic obedience competition dog, and a beagle (ranked 72) who has just begun to compete in obedience trials and shows all of the inconsistencies that one would expect given his ranking. It took him the better part of his first year of life to learn what my Nova Scotia duck tolling retriever (ranked 20) learned in the first four weeks that I had him. I will continue to keep and train my breeds of dog because of my fondness for their temperaments, looks, size, and behaviour styles. However sometimes, when I am going over a particular exercise for the fifty-fifth time with my beagle, Darby, I wonder whether it is worth the effort. Then Darby suddenly acts as if he has had an epiphany, and he performs the entire exercise perfectly, and thumps his tail and licks my hand happily. It is then that I recognize that all of my dogs have ultimately proven to be trainable given enough time, love, and practice. Despite the fact that I sometimes get quizzical, amused, or even pitying glances when I enter the obedience ring with some of my less-than-bright breeds, they all perform well enough and reliably enough to keep me happy and to allow me to enjoy competing in dog obedience trials with them.

Chapter Eleven

The Personality Factor

Things that upset a terrier may pass virtually unnoticed by a Great Dane.

—SMILEY BLANTON

Like schoolteachers, dog obedience instructors hear it all the time: "My dog really is quite intelligent and can learn whatever you want it to. The reason that it is the worst performer in your class is that it. . . ." Here follow one or more excuses from a list that includes (1) isn't interested in learning these sorts of things, (2) bores too easily, (3) is too independent, (4) has more important things on its mind, (5) doesn't get along well with other dogs (or people, noise, sunlight, walls, or whatever), (6) is too easily distracted, (7) was bred to be a hunter (herder, guard, companion), not an obedience dog, (8) is too timid (or too dominant, too flighty, too laid-back, too happy-go-lucky, too depressed, too manic, too lazy, too dog-oriented, too people-oriented, and so forth), (9) is a leader, not a follower. The reasons are endless, and what they all come down to is that the dog is not unintelligent but rather has certain personality characteristics that interfere with its capacity to learn.

While these claims are often rationalizations covering an owner's fear that his loved pet is really mentally subnormal, there is more than a grain of truth in the notion that a dog's personality is as important as its intelligence in determining whether it will respond to human commands and work for its human masters. This is the reason that I separated the consideration of adaptive intelligence, which reflects learning and problem-solving ability, from the consideration of working or obedience intelligence. Many of the dog obedience judges that I surveyed pointed out the importance of personality, often in relation to sex differences.

In contemporary writing and discussions, it is considered rude, biased, sexist, and politically incorrect to refer to sex differences in behaviour, personality, or intelligence, especially in humans. Yet there are clearly visible differences between male and female dogs (at least for certain breeds) in terms of their problem-solving and obedience performance. Physically, males are often larger, stronger, and more vigorous in their activity than the females. For some breeds, particularly Doberman pinschers and Labrador retrievers, the males perform significantly better in problem-solving tests, such as those presented in Chapter 9. Conversely, females of these breeds tend to do much better in obedience and working tasks. One dog obedience judge, in listing the top ten obedience breeds, noted next to his entry of Doberman pinschers, "females only, males tend to be too hard-headed and are more difficult to control." For some breeds, however, such as the poodle and the English pointer, males are the "softer" sex and females are more obstinate and difficult to train.

Differences in the personality of the sexes are not important for all breeds of dogs. In many terrier breeds (especially the crook-legged terriers such as cairn terriers, West Highland white terriers, Scottish terriers, and Skye terriers) there appears to be no difference in either the adaptive or obedience intelligence of males and females, and the personality differences also are not as marked as those found in some of the working and sporting breeds. For hounds, there are noticeable personality differences, with the females being a bit more sociable, but again no differences in measurable intelligence or performance of the sexes in obedience tasks.

THE IMPORTANCE OF PERSONALITY

Some dog obedience judges placed personality as one of the major factors in the dog's working performance. One wrote, "It is the dog's willingness to work for man that matters, not how smart it is. Terriers don't do well in obedience simply because they have been bred to be independent and loners. Since they don't care about human responses to their behaviours, they don't do well in the [obedience] ring, despite the fact that they are really smart beasts. Herding dogs, like shelties [Shetland sheepdogs] or border collies do well because they want to work for people and seem unhappy unless someone is telling them what to do."

Another dog obedience judge wrote, "The best obedience dog is a dumb golden retriever. Even a dumb golden is bright enough to figure out what you want him to do, and he wants to please so much that he does it. Just as importantly, he doesn't get bored and is not easily distracted. Since he is not trying to figure out what is going on, he doesn't design new ways of responding and ends up doing exactly what you taught him in the first place."

Breeders or trainers seldom use the term *personality* in connection with dogs because it is viewed as a rather mentalistic label that implies too much consciousness and characteristics that are too humanlike. Instead, they tend to use the term *temperament*, which is a bit more objective or neutral. This term was used by Clarence Pfaffenberger, one of the first people to suggest that considerations of a dog's personality are vital for certain working and obedience functions. He was one of the most important figures in the development of training and selection programmes for guide dogs for blind people. In the mid-1940s, when he first became involved in guide dog training and selection, only 9 percent of all dogs that started in training successfully finished the programme. Pfaffenberger was disturbed by this low success rate and developed a series of tests, mostly adaptive intelligence tests of learning and problem-solving ability, to predict which dogs could best learn the complex obedience tasks associated with guiding the blind. He soon found, however, that intelligence was not enough: Dogs with adequate or even excellent learning and problem-solving intelligence were still failing the course. Pfaffenberger quickly recognized that, to be a good guide dog, an animal must have not only adequate intelligence but also an appropriate set of personality characteristics. Apparently, some traits (such as a calmness and focused attention) allow dogs to apply their full adaptive intelligence in such a way that they became excellent working and obedience dogs, while others (such as fearfulness) forever block dogs from achieving useful levels of functioning. With this in mind, he began selecting and breeding for both personality and intelligence, and, by the end of the 1950s, he had raised the percentage of dogs successfully completing the programme from 9 to 90 percent.

GENETICS AND PERSONALITY

Many factors associated with personality are genetically determined, meaning that people can breed for personality characteristics in the same way that they breed for other behavioural characteristics, such as those that make up a dog's instinctive intelligence. Many dogs, primarily those used as companion dogs, have been selected as much for their temperament as for their size. Spaniels, or dogs with spaniel blood in them, have often been selected for their gentleness. An extreme example of this is the Cavalier King Charles spaniel.

As I mentioned earlier, one of my dogs is a Cavalier King Charles spaniel named Banshee. Small toy spaniels, such as the Cavalier, have been known in Europe and Great Britain since the sixteenth century. They are cherished for their friendliness and lack of aggression and hence have been favourite house dogs. Representations of these dogs appear in the works of great artists such as Titian, Van Dyck, Velázquez, Vermeer, and Hogarth (to mention only a few). In most paintings, they appear as family pets or simply as pretty ornaments (see Plate 18). As might be deduced from their name, King Charles II of Britain is partly responsible for these dogs' popularity as companions. He adored the breed and had them bred specifically to be gentle house pets. In return, they were given the freedom to roam the palace throughout his reign (1660 to 1685).

On a visit to England, I was told an interesting story about Cavalier King Charles spaniels. Supposedly, not too long ago, an English gentleman went into a courthouse in London, accompanied by his Cavalier King Charles spaniel. He then proceeded directly into the courtroom where the case relevant to him was being heard. The judge saw the pair enter and stopped the proceedings. With noticeable pique in his voice, he ordered that the dog be removed from the courtroom at once. The gentleman who owned the dog protested, "Excuse me, Your Honour, but it is my understanding that all Cavalier King Charles spaniels have carte blanche in the privy council. I believe that this is interpreted to mean that if he scratches at the gates of Buckingham Palace, he must be granted entry. In addition, under a charter of King Charles II, which has never been revoked, Cavaliers have a royal title. They are thus allowed in court and may not be turned away from any royal palace or any governmental or other function operating under the protection or mandate of the crown. I believe that this would include courts of law." The storyteller assured me that the judge was taken aback by all of this and eventually allowed the Cavalier to remain in the courtroom.

Despite some records suggesting some members of the nobility kept packs of these little spaniels as sporting dogs, I have some difficulty picturing this. My daughter by marriage, Kari, described the breed best when she called mine "a love sponge". Cavaliers seek affection continuously, and show little competitiveness and virtually no aggressive tendencies. Most important, these personality traits breed true and characterize every member of the breed that I have ever encountered.

The case of the Cavalier King Charles spaniel is not unique. Pfaffenberger kept careful records during his systematic breeding programme for guide dogs. Because each dog was tested for both personality and intelligence, this gave a marvellous opportunity to see if these characteristics were genetically based. His records show that many personality characteristics, including the willingness to work for humans, are carried genetically. The personality of a litter was directly predictable from the personality of the sire and dam. Pfaffenberger scored the willingness to work using a scale that ran from a low of 0 to a high of 5 to keep track of the personalities of the various dogs. In one instance he mated a dog named Odin who scored 5 on this dimension with a bitch, Gretchen, who scored 4. If the temperaments of the parents were passed on to the offspring, then all the resultant puppies would have temperaments falling between these values. Sure enough, when Pfaffenberger administered tests to the six puppies, he found that four of them scored 5 and the remaining two scored 4.

Temperament testing of dogs has been conducted for many years by centers that are involved in the selection of service dogs—specifically police dogs, explosive- and drug-detection dogs, search-and-rescue dogs, guide dogs for the blind, hearing-assistance dogs, and so forth and the records from some of these centres provide a rich source of data about canine personality. Probably the largest data bank was assembled by the Swedish Working Dogs Association, with data from behavioural tests that were given to 15,329 dogs representing 164 breeds. This data was recently statistically analysed by two ethologists, Kenth Svartberg, at Stockholm University, and Bjorn Forkman, at the Royal Veterinary and Agricultural University in Frederiksberg, Denmark, and gives us a useful description of the personality of dogs.

The complete testing procedure included tests of sociability, such as the social contact test, in which the dog's reaction to meeting a stranger was assessed. Playfulness was measured by the dog's willingness to play with a friendly stranger. The dog's chase instinct was tested by noting its reaction to an erratically moving furry object. The dog's response to passive restraint is tested by tying him out on a leash, some distance from his handler, for several minutes. The dog's boldness and self-confidence are measured in a number of tests: In one, a human-shaped dummy suddenly pops up in front of the dog; in another, a chain is drawn across a sheet of metal to make a loud metallic sound in a location near the dog; in another, there are gunshots; and in the "ghosts" test, the dog is approached by two slowly moving people with white sheets over their heads. In each of these tests the dog can show a variety of different reactions, including being momentarily startled, being fearful and avoiding, being aggressive or threatening, or being confident and exploring the strange objects and situations that it is presented with.

Statistical analysis of the results from these tests showed that the personality structure of dogs seemed to be described by five basic personality traits: sociability, curiosity versus fearfulness, playfulness, instinct to chase, and aggressiveness. One quirk in this classification was that in retrievers and spaniels, playfulness and sociability seem to merge into a single trait.

One way to see how genetics plays a role in personality is to look for differences between breeds. These researchers used the breed groups of the Federation Cynologique International (FCI) in their reporting. Companion dogs and the sheep- and cattle-herding dogs (excluding the livestock-guarding dogs) got the highest scores for the playfulness trait. The least playful dogs were the so-called primitive breeds, those dogs that seem to be closest to wolves or other wild canines in both their physical and behavioural characteristics. The most common of these are the spitz breeds, which include the majority of the Nordic sled and hunting dogs. (It is often said that if you take a northern wolf and curl its tail, then you effectively have a grey malamute or a Siberian husky.) The second group of primitive dogs includes the basenji, Carolina dog, and the Canaan dog. Because the primitive dogs are close to the "wild dog type", it is not surprising to find that they are not as playful. These dogs are also quite low in the sociability trait. In addition, this latter group seems to be very high in its chase instinct and in overall aggressiveness. In contrast, the first group (the northern spitz) types are quite sociable in spite of a low playfulness rating.

Carefully looking at the data, and doing some additional statistical analyses, allowed the researchers to demonstrate that you could combine all of the traits, except aggressiveness, to form a broad personality characteristic that they called the "shyness-boldness continuum." Dogs that rank high in this personality trait are bold dogs, who are usually very active, interested in other dogs and people, curious and relatively fearless when faced with novel objects and strange situations. Dogs that score low for this trait are shy dogs that tend to be uninterested in play, who are timid, cautious, and evasive in unfamiliar situations. Other research has shown that this shyness-boldness continuum is also found in wolves, which suggests that our efforts at domesticating dogs have simply moved various breeds up or down along a temperament trait that has remained "evolutionarily stable". This dimension of personality is important, since it appears that the dogs that are most bold make the best working and service dogs.

The genetic component in dog personality also explains certain regional differences in dog breeds. For instance, Doberman pinschers and rottweilers bred in North America tend to be somewhat calmer and less likely to initiate aggressive action than are dogs of the same breeds that have been bred in Europe. This seems to be the result of a deliberate attempt on the part of many North American breeders to tone down the breeds a bit, whereas some European breeders seem to prize and select for what is sometimes called "temperamental fire", which is really a willingness to display aggressive tendencies.

The *Dog Mentality Assessment Test*, used by the Swedish Working Dogs Association, requires lots of equipment, space, several trained judges, and a number of assistants. Other temperament-testing systems have been devised that are less demanding. One of the best was established by Jack and Wendy Volhard, who designed their system to select dogs that matched the lifestyles and needs of prospective owners. In the test I put together for this book, I drew items from a number of existing tests, such as those provided by Pfaffenberger, the Volhards, the U.S. Army Service Dog Assessment protocol, and the Hearing Dog Society. I have modified their scoring procedures specifically to measure several personality factors that influence a dog's working or obedience intelligence and to reflect shyness-boldness. I have only used tests that can be easily conducted at home with the assistance of just one person other than the dog's owner. Completing the Obedience Personality Test (OPT) will yield a score reflecting the likelihood that a dog will work willingly and obey a human master.

THE OBEDIENCE PERSONALITY TEST

Testing for the problem-solving and learning intelligence of dogs using the Canine IQ Test in Chapter 9 required that the dog be around a year old and have lived with the person doing the testing for around three months. Personality testing, however, has different requirements. First, this kind of testing can be done when dogs are quite young. Typically, puppies have their personalities assessed at around seven weeks of age—just at the age when they can leave their litters and go to their new owners. Recent data show that the test is more reliable, and has better predictive ability, when the dog is tested at six months, and even better at eighteen months, which would be ages when dogs are being considered for entry into service programmes or training for various working careers; however, the early testing of puppies is still useful.

Another important difference between personality testing and testing for adaptive intelligence is that, for the intelligence test, it was important that the person testing the dog be a person the dog knew well, preferably its master. Some of the tests also required very familiar surroundings. For personality testing, exactly the opposite holds. The person administering the test should be a stranger to the dog, and familiar people should stay well in the background, virtually out of sight or serving only as assistants. In addition, the dog should not be familiar with the testing location, which should be free of distractions. You don't necessarily have to leave your house; just have the test administered in a room the dog has seldom seen.

A final difference between personality and adaptive intelligence testing is that the personality test must be given exactly as it is presented here and it should be completed in one session, which will probably take about twenty minutes. For this reason, you should assemble all the materials you will need in advance. Specifically, you will need a stopwatch or a clock with a sweep second hand; a crumpled ball of paper a bit smaller than a tennis ball; a soda pop or beer can into which five or six large coins have been dropped and then the drinking hole taped shut; a dishtowel or washcloth to which about ten feet (three metres) of string have been attached, somewhat like a leash; an umbrella, preferably one that opens using a spring-release mechanism; a bit of smelly food (cheese, salami, pepperoni, liver, or some such) and two bits of not-so-smelly food (pieces of dog biscuit or kibble, pieces of bread crust, and so forth); a pencil and a copy of the scoring form reproduced in Figure 11.1. You will also need a person to assist you. If the dog knows you, select an assistant who is unfamiliar with the dog and have this person administer the tests. Remember, it is important that the test be given by a stranger.

Testing should be done at a time of day when the puppy is usually active. It should be before a meal, since puppies tend to become lethargic after they've eaten and will be less likely to respond appropriately to the food attraction test. You should also make sure that nothing unusual has happened on the day of the test, such as a visit to the veterinarian for shots, a worming, or simply too much excitement. You want the puppy's responses to be as typical as possible.

ADMINISTERING THE OBEDIENCE PERSONALITY TEST

Remember to give the tests one right after the other in a single session. Enter all scores on a copy of the model scoring form (see Figure 11.1).

TEST 1

The first two tests are measures of *social attraction*. Both measure how much attention the puppy gives to people and how well it is attracted to them. A dog that is not attracted to humans will train poorly and not respond reliably to commands because the minimum requirement for any training is that the dog pay attention to what the trainer is doing.

This first test measures the dog's *willingness to approach an unfamiliar person*. The tester (whom the puppy does not know) kneels on the floor, sitting on his or her heels (this lowers the silhouette of the person and makes him or her less threatening). The assistant carries the puppy into the room (not by the scruff of the neck, please, since this would intimidate the dog) and places it about four feet (a bit over a metre) from the tester, facing him or her. As soon as the dog is on the floor, the tester calls it. It is important that the calling not involve the dog's name and not incorporate the word *come*. Instead, the tester should attract the dog by using a singsong or playful "puppy, puppy, puppy" and lightly clapping the hands. For an older dog, it is especially important to use only variations on a word such as *puppy* and to avoid any name, command, or word that the dog may have already learned.

If the dog comes immediately, score 3; if it comes hesitantly, score 2; if it comes readily but then jumps up on the tester or mouths or nips the hands, or if it doesn't come at all, score 1. Jumping, mouthing, or

Test		Score	A	S
1	Social attraction (approaching)	———	———	———
2	Social attraction (following)	———	———	———
3	Social dominance (restraint)	———	———	———
4	Social dominance (forgiveness)	———	———	———
5	Social dominance (loss of control)	———	———	———
6	Willingness to work (retrieving, trial 1)	———	———	———
7	Willingness to work (retrieving, trial 2)	———	———	———
8	Touch sensitivity	———	———	———
9	Sound reaction	———	———	———
10	Reaction to novel stimuli	———	———	———
11	Response to food incentive	———	———	———
12	Stability (reaction to threatening stimuli)	———	———	———
	Totals	═══	═══	═══

Figure 11.1
Obedience Personality Test Scoring Form

nipping are aggressive signs suggesting that the dog may later refuse to conform to commands, and if these appear, put a check mark in Column A. Not coming indicates low social responsiveness, which will make training difficult; however, it also can indicate fearfulness. To interpret this response further, watch the dog's tail during the test. If the tail is low, or the dog is otherwise obviously anxious, put the check mark in Column S of the score sheet. If the dog was very timid during the test, the tester should slowly reach toward the dog to let it sniff his or her hand, and the puppy should receive a quick pat or scratch and a kind word from the tester before the next test.

TEST 2

This second test of *social attraction* monitors the dog's *attention and willingness to follow or stay with a person*, which really means accepting human leadership in a non-threatening situation. The tester should slowly stand up next to the puppy. Verbally encouraging the dog with "puppy, puppy, puppy" (not the dog's name) and with encouraging pats on his or her own leg, the tester should walk away. Again, especially if working with an older dog, the tester should be sure to use only the word *puppy*, not *heel, come, let's go*, or any other word(s) that the dog may already have learned. If the dog follows readily, score 3; if the dog follows hesitantly, score 2; if it does not follow at all or if it follows immediately but gets underfoot and mouths or nips the tester's feet, score 1. Nipping or mouthing with a tail held high gets a check mark in Column A, and a low tail and/or anxiety gets a check mark in Column S.

TEST 3

Tests 3, 4, and 5 are measures of *social dominance*. The first is a direct measure of the dog's *dominance or submissiveness*, which ultimately will determine its willingness to accept human leadership in less voluntary situations than that of Test 2. This is actually a measure of how the dog responds when it is socially or physically forced to submit or comply. Such physical force is often a part of the early stages of obedience training, as when the dog is physically manipulated into a sitting or lying position. It is unwise, and perhaps unsafe, to use these tests on a mature dog that has a history of aggression. If you are testing an older dog, these tests should be done carefully, and you should immediately terminate any test in which the dog growls or snarls (although you can still enter the scores, including checking the appropriate Column A or S, as if it had run the full duration).

To begin, the tester should kneel on the floor and gently roll the dog onto its back. (It is important that the dog be on its back with its spine against the floor and its legs pointing up rather than on its side.) At this point, the assistant should start the stopwatch. With his or her hand exerting just enough pressure on the dog's chest to keep it on its back, the tester should look directly at the dog. If the dog looks away, eye contact should not be forced. The tester's expression should be bland, not harsh or threatening, and the tester should be silent until the end of the test. When the assistant indicates that thirty seconds have passed, the test is over, and the puppy should be released immediately.

The dog's score is based on its behaviour during the thirty seconds of restraint. If the dog initially struggles but then settles down or gives up, score 3. If the dog doesn't struggle but allows some eye contact, score 2. If the dog doesn't struggle but tries to avoid eye contact, or if the dog struggles fiercely throughout the thirty seconds, or if the dog tries to bite or growls at any point, score 1. Growling or continuous struggling also gets a check mark in column A, while failure to struggle at all, or whimpering during the thirty seconds, gets a check mark in column S.

TEST 4

This portion of the *social dominance* test is really a test of the dog's *forgiveness*, another important personality trait for obedience or working training. A dog that bears a grudge or acts aggrieved and sulks after being corrected or forced to do something it did not want to do will be difficult to train.

Test 4 begins with the tester kneeling down and placing the puppy in a sitting position in front of him or her. The dog should face the tester, not directly but at an angle of about forty-five degrees. When the dog is in position, the tester should begin to stroke it slowly and gently with one hand. The stroking should start at the top of the head and continue smoothly down to the tail. At the same time, the tester should talk quietly to the dog, leaning forward so that his or her face is close enough for the puppy to lick it if it wants to. If the dog snuggles closer to the tester and tries to lick his or her face or squirms a bit and licks the tester's hands, score 3. If the dog rolls over and then licks the tester's hands or jumps up and paws the tester, score 2. If the dog growls, mouths, or nips, or leaves, or tries to get away from the tester, score 1. Jumping, pawing, mouthing, or growling gets a check mark in Column A, while rolling over or moving away gets a check mark in Column S.

TEST 5

This *social dominance* test measures the dog's *response to loss of control*. The difference here is that the dog is placed in a position in which it has no control at all. During training and everyday activities, the dog will often be placed in positions in which its control is limited. This will include visits to the veterinarian or to the dog groomer or times when it is being examined by a judge in a show ring.

The test involves lifting the dog (this is another reason why it is easier to test puppies). The tester bends over the puppy, which is facing in the opposite direction, and then using his or her hands to form a cradle (keeping palms up and fingers intertwined works well here), lifts the dog so that its legs are just off of the ground. The assistant then starts timing. At the end of thirty seconds, the tester returns the dog to the ground.

If the dog was relaxed and did not struggle or if it struggled briefly and then settled down, score 3. If the dog did not struggle but whimpers, growls, or runs away when placed back on the ground, score 2. If, while being held, the dog whimpered or struggled fiercely, or, especially, if it growled or nipped, score 1. Fierce struggling or growling gets a check mark in Column A, while whimpering or running away after having been returned to the floor gets a check mark in Column S. Before continuing with the next test, the tester should speak calmly to the dog and stroke or scratch it gently.

Obviously, if you are dealing with an older, large dog, you may have to modify this test. Slipping a bath towel under the dog's belly and then, with the help of the assistant, using the towel to raise the dog slightly is one possibility. If the dog is simply too large to be lifted, skip this test and enter a score of 2 to keep the numbers balanced.

TESTS 6 AND 7

Test 6 involves retrieving and shows the dog's *willingness to work with people*. Some dog trainers claim that retrieving is the best single test for guide dogs, obedience dogs, field trial dogs, and other working dogs. Test 7 is simply a repetition of Test 6.

The tester kneels and the puppy is placed with its back to the tester just in front of the tester's knees. Dangling a crumpled-up ball of paper (a little smaller than a tennis ball) in front of the dog, the tester teases the puppy a bit, using some verbal encouragement, such as saying "Do you want it? Can you get it?" in a playful voice. The idea is to get the dog interested in the object. As soon as the puppy shows any interest, the tester tosses the paper ball about three feet (around one metre) in front of it. When the puppy starts to move toward the paper, the tester should back up about two feet (about a half metre). If the puppy picks up the paper, the tester should encourage it to bring the ball back. If it does return with the paper, the tester should give the puppy a lot of praise. If not, the tester should catch the dog's attention and then move away and pick up the paper (or retrieve the dog if it has run away with the paper). Whatever the dog's response, the tester should immediately set up in exactly the same way and repeat the procedure (this is Test 7).

Scoring for both tests is the same. If the dog chases the paper and then returns to the tester with or without it, score 3. If the dog chases the paper ball and then stands over it and does not return, or if it starts to chase the paper and then loses interest, score 2. If the dog chases the paper, picks it up, and then runs away, score 1, and check column A. If it fails to chase the paper, score 1, and enter a check mark in Column S.

TEST 8

This next test is a measure of *touch sensitivity*. All obedience training involves touching the dog in some way. Traditional trainers often physically correct a dog, for instance by snapping the leash to produce a momentary discomfort through the tightening of a slip collar. More positively oriented trainers might gently manipulate a dog into a desired position, or use their hands to guide the dog's response in some situations. A dog that is relatively insensitive to the discomfort of snap corrections, or the gentle feel of hands guiding it, may be considerably more difficult to control. A dog that is too sensitive to mild physical discomfort of correction or the touch of the trainer's hands moving it into a position may become frightened or distressed and so have difficulties during training.

This test requires a gradual increase in finger pressure. The tester should practice beforehand on himself, not the dog, by squeezing the forefinger of one hand between the thumb and forefinger of the other, slowly increasing the pressure while counting to twelve, until he or she is squeezing as hard as he or she can. Make sure that the pressure does not involve gouging with your fingernails. When the tester can do this in a uniform, regular manner, it's time for the test.

The tester should grasp a bit of the dog's ear between his or her thumb and forefinger and, as during the practice, count to twelve while gradually increasing the pressure on the ear. As soon as the puppy gives any noticeable sign of pain, such as turning or pulling away or trying to bite, the tester should immediately release the pressure and praise and stroke the dog playfully. If the count was five to eight when the first reaction occurred, score 3. Counts of three or four score 2 with a check mark in Column S, while counts of nine or ten score 2 with a check mark in Column A. Counts of one or two score 1 with a check mark in Column S, while a count of eleven or twelve scores 1 with a check mark in Column A.

TEST 9

This next test is for *sound reaction*. A dog that is overaroused by sounds will be too easily distracted and will readily lose concentration during training. A fearful reaction to sounds is highly predictive of a shy dog. No reaction may indicate inattention or distraction, but it may also be an indication of deafness.

Deafness is more common in dogs than the casual pet owner might recognize. Congenital hearing loss is mostly due to genetic factors. A study by George Strain of Louisiana State University in Baton Rouge involving nearly seventeen thousand dogs confirmed that coat colour is associated with congenital deafness. The genetic defect that produces deafness is closely linked with the genes that produce white coats, roan (a dark colour coat that has been liberally sprinkled with white), merle (desaturated colours, especially where blacks become grays or blues), and piebald (spotty, especially black and white) colours in dogs. The classic example of a piebald dog is the Dalmatian. In this breed, 22 percent are deaf in one ear and an additional 8 percent are deaf in both ears, amounting to an amazing 30 percent born with some form of hearing deficit. While all Dalmatians are more or less piebald, in other breeds the white, roan, merle, or piebald genes are found in some individuals but not others. In the bull terrier, for example, individuals can be either white or can have prominent colour patches. Among those bull terriers who are white, the rate of congenital deafness is 20 percent, while for those with colour patches it is only around 1 percent.

Deafness in a dog may go undetected, especially if you have a reasonably bright dog that is attending to visual and other cues. If a dog does not show any response in this sound reaction test, you might do well to have its hearing checked.

To administer this test, the tester places the dog so that it faces away from the direction the sound is going to come from and then does not touch the dog again until the test is over. The assistant should be standing out of the dog's line of sight with a beer or pop can with a few coins sealed inside of it. When the dog is in position, the assistant should give the can three fast, vigorous shakes in order to make a loud noise and then freeze in position, not making any eye contact with the dog. If the dog acts interested and moves toward the sound or obviously listens and orients its head curiously in the direction of the sound, even if it seemed startled at first, score 3. If the dog locates the sound but stays in place and barks, score 2, and enter a check mark in Column A. If the dog ignores the sound, score 1. If the dog goes directly to the sound and barks, score 1, and check Column A. If the dog cringes, or backs off, or tries to hide, score 1 and check Column S.

TEST 10

Test 10 measures the dog's reaction to *novel stimuli*—in this case, a nonthreatening but strange object. Since a dog must work and respond to its master's commands in a variety of situations where apparently strange and novel events may be going on (at least from the dog's point of view), a better obedience and working dog will likely result from a confident and curious puppy rather than one that reacts fearfully or aggressively.

For this test, the assistant stands off to the side, holding on to the end of a string that has been tied to the end of a towel. The assistant then jerks the towel toward him- or herself (the towel should not move directly toward the puppy but sideways in front of it). The assistant should tug the towel five or six times and then stop. This test occasionally evokes fairly extreme responses, ranging from attempts to kill the towel to running in panic from it, and I was even told of one attempt to mate with the towel. If the dog looks at the test object and displays some curiosity by approaching and trying to investigate it, score 3. If the dog ignores the test object, score 3, and enter a check mark in Column S. If the dog barks, score 2; if the tail was up when it barked, put a check mark in Column A, and if the tail was down or tucked under when it barked, put a check mark in Column S. If the dog attacks, growls, bites, or threatens the test object, score 1, and put a check mark in Column A. If the dog shies away or hides from the test object, score 1, and put a check mark in Column S.

TEST 11

This next test is a measure of the dog's *response to a food incentive*. While it is possible to train dogs using praise alone, several scientific studies have shown that dogs learn faster and are happier and more reliable in their work when trained using food treats, especially during the early stages of learning. Such treats are generally gradually removed in the later phases of learning, once the desired behaviours are established. Even people who dislike using food in training often resort to it when dealing with complex exercises. If a dog lacks an interest in treats, then it may be considerably more difficult to train.

Holding a small bit of some smelly food, such as pepperoni, cooked liver, or an aromatic cheese, the tester should allow the dog to smell the bait, keeping the hand closed enough so that the dog can't get at the food. After a moment, the tester should release the treat and allow the dog to have it. Next, with the dog watching, the trainer should place a treat in a hand that is partially cupped closed and offer the hand to the dog. If the dog nuzzles or digs at the hand to get the treat, it is allowed to eat it. Finally, the tester should show the dog another treat. Holding the treat visibly between his or her fingers, the tester should lower the hand toward the dog and turn slowly in place in a 360-degree rotation, all the while gently waving the hand with the treat at the dog but giving no verbal encouragement. If the dog nuzzles and/or digs at the hand in the previous part of the test and now moves to follow the tester as he or she rotates, score 3. If the dog shows interest in the food but does not try to get it out of the hand in the second part of the test or does not follow in the last part, score 2. If the dog shows no interest in the food, score 1. If the dog growls, barks, or nips at the hand or fingers at any point during the test, put a check mark in Column A.

TEST 12

The final test is a test of *stability*. Somewhat like test 10, it measures a dog's response to a novel stimulus. However, in this case the novel stimulus suddenly appears, is large, and may be interpreted as being threatening. Thus the test permits a measure of the dog's confidence and reaction style.

While the dog is busy with Test 11, the assistant should position him- or herself around six feet (two metres) away from the tester and dog, standing motionless and being very quiet and unobtrusive, holding a closed umbrella (preferably one with a spring release). When Test 11 is finished, the tester should calm the dog down a bit, speaking softly, and then should turn so that the dog is between the assistant and the tester. The assistant should watch the dog carefully. When the dog is looking forward or toward the assistant (that is, not looking hopefully at the tester for more food), the assistant should hit the spring release or pop open the umbrella in one quick motion and then set it on the floor. The assistant should then stand quite still, not making any eye contact with the dog. If the dog reacts but regains its composure within a moment and then approaches to investigate the umbrella, score 3. If the dog stands and barks but does not approach the umbrella, score 2, and place a check mark in Column A. If the dog tries to run or hide but can be verbally encouraged to approach the umbrella, score 2, and place a check mark in Column S. If the dog does not react at all, score 1. If the dog acts aggressively, barking, growling, and/or feinting at the umbrella, score 1, and place a check mark in Column A. If the dog tries to run, hide, or escape and cannot be verbally encouraged back toward the umbrella, score 1, and enter a check mark in Column S.

INTERPRETING THE RESULTS

The interpretation of a dog's scores on the OPT depends on both the score totals and the number of check marks in the A and S columns. Column A indicates signs that a dog may be aggressive, while Column S indicates that the dog may be overly submissive and fearful. Recent studies suggest that aggression and fearfulness are enduring characteristics that persist throughout a dog's lifetime. Aggression is often the result of genetic factors (although defensive aggression can result from harsh or abusive treatment as well). Fearfulness can be genetic in nature, but most often arises in dogs that have not been adequately handled and socialized when they are puppies.

Score 34 to 36: Dogs that score in this range are the best dogs for obedience work. If a dog has this score and has more checks in Column A (aggressive) than in Column S (submissive), you are looking at a bouncy and active dog that will accept human leadership well and should adapt well to new situations. The dog is stable and will have a confident and commonsense approach to most situations. It is a fine prospect for learning obedience or working skills. If the dog has eight or more checks in Column A, it may also be a bit of a handful and may need the obedience training to keep it happy, well adapted, and to stop it from being a nuisance.

If the dog has a few more checks in Column S than in Column A, then you have the dream dog for obedience work—a dog that will seem to understand every word you say and will turn itself inside out to please you. This type of dog will be a bit quieter and not quite as self-assured as a dog with more A checks, but it has all the characteristics that will make it a fine working or obedience dog as well as a good household pet and companion. A dog with eight or more checks in this column, however, may become anxious when stressed, which can interfere with training and working performance.

Score 29 to 33: Dogs that score in this range still have the potential to be excellent obedience and working dogs. Success in working with these dogs will depend on how they are handled. A dog with this score and checks mostly in Column A is highly self-confident and tends toward dominance. It will have to be treated with a firm hand and should never be allowed to assume that it is leader of the pack, or it will begin to take charge and start to ignore its handler. It may be a bit too strong-willed for the first-time dog owner, but trained with steady and consistent control, this is a dog that will attract everybody's eye in the obedience ring. A dog with these scores but with the majority of checks in Column S will be somewhat lacking in self-confidence. This is a dog that will need to be trained with a more gentle hand and lots of reassurance and rewards. If you don't push too hard, especially during the early stages of training, and if you don't overcorrect, you can still produce a fine working and obedience dog. Although this dog will benefit from a quiet and predictable environment, it will gradually gain confidence in new areas if you are consistent and reassuring during training. This will make a really fine family dog.

Score 19 to 28: Dogs in this range of scores do best with experienced handlers. With the right type of training, they can turn into fine working and obedience dogs. Trained in the wrong way (or left untrained), they can be disasters. If you have a dog with a score in this range that has checks mostly in Column A, you are looking at a dominant dog that will use aggression or threats of aggression if provoked. This kind of dog does, however, respond to very firm and very consistent handling. With such handling and when placed in an adult household, it can turn into a good working dog and a loyal pet that respects its human leaders. Dogs in this category may have bouncy and outgoing personalities, but they also have strong tendencies toward leadership and dominance, so they may be too active for elderly handlers and are definitely too dominant for homes with small children. Their major problems will be their sense of independence and a take-charge attitude, which often result in these dogs ignoring their human handlers and doing whatever they want, apparently indifferent to protests and corrections. In a noisy, changing environment, this type of dog will be easily distracted. It may also bite when it feels threatened or frustrated.

If a dog with this same set of scores has a predominance of checks in Column S, it may adapt somewhat better. Such a dog will be extremely submissive. It will require special handling to build its confidence and to allow it to function well outside of the home. Although it will learn to respond to most of its master's commands, it will do so best in a structured environment. Because it will not adapt well to change and confusion, it may be quite inconsistent when it is away from its familiar surroundings or when asked to perform under noisy or busy conditions. This dog will become frightened easily and will take a long time to get used to new surroundings and new people. It is usually safe around children, but it might bite when severely stressed or threatened. This dog is better suited to a quiet, settled life than to the hustle and excitement of competition, change, or travel.

Score 12 to 18: Dogs in this range are definitely problematic. They will require experienced handlers and a lot of work. A dog in this range with checks mostly in Column A is extremely dominant with strong aggressive tendencies. It will not readily accept a human leader. It will continually battle for dominance and will bite when challenged. It is definitely not for a household with children. It can, however, become a successful guard dog or sentry dog, as it will challenge and attack anyone who has not proven leadership and dominance over it. In other settings, this dog may prove to be too aggressive to train and control.

Dogs with this same set of scores but with mostly checks in Column S are a bit harder to describe because they will have one of two possible personality profiles. Some will be extremely independent dogs that show a definite lack of interest in people and may even actively dislike petting and cuddling. It is difficult to establish the kind of relationship with this dog that you will need to train or even to keep it as a reasonable pet. Some working husky-type dogs may benefit from having this personality type, since they need the ability to work fairly independently and would be disastrous if they were always checking back to see if their master was nearby while hitched as part of a team to a dog sled. However, in most situations, these dogs will simply not respond attentively enough to humans to be trained well.

The other personality profile is the spooky, flighty, or shy dog. These are dogs that are easily frightened and may take hours or even days to calm down. Once frightened by a particular person or situation, they may remember it for the rest of their lives and will always show fear and discomfort when faced with the same person or setting. With eight or more checks in Column S, you are looking at a dog that may panic and become a fear biter. These dogs do not train well, since they are so easily swamped by their own terror and insecurity. While they may prove adequate pets in a very quiet home where few demands are made on them, they will go through life in a fearful and timid manner.

It is the combination of personality and intelligence that makes a good working and obedience dog. A dog that scores well in adaptive intelligence and also scores in one of the two highest groups for its personality has a definite chance of becoming an excellent obedience dog that works well under human direction. If you have a breed of dog that judges normally classify as poor in working and obedience intelligence but has a good personality profile and a reasonable adaptive intelligence, you probably have one of those rare members of the breed that will work and perform well. And if your dog does not have the optimal personality or intelligence profile, do not despair: There are things you can do to help the situation.

Chapter Twelve

Increasing a Dog's Intelligence

> The dog has seldom been successful in pulling man up to its level of sagacity, but man has frequently dragged the dog down to his.
>
> —JAMES THURBER

As in the case of humans, the intelligence of dogs is not fixed but can be influenced by rearing and life history. Each of the four principal dimensions that affect manifest intelligence—i.e., instinctive intelligence, adaptive intelligence, obedience and working intelligence, and the personality factor—can be improved. Most of the techniques that I will mention in this chapter work best with young dogs (although even adolescent and young adult dogs will respond to a number of them), and many should be started as soon as the dog moves in.

IMPROVING PERSONALITY

Three aspects of personality play an important role in a dog's obedience and working intelligence. The first is the dog's orientation to humans, which includes paying attention to what a person is doing and seeking social affiliation with people. The second is confidence and fearlessness in new situations. The third is the willingness to accept human leadership, rather than fighting for dominance and control.

To shape your dog's personality, it is best to begin with a young puppy. By exposing your new puppy to appropriate experiences at various critical periods in its life, you can actually mould its character into one that will support later working and obedience ability. For the average dog owner, the most critical period is between seven and twelve weeks of age, although the process (often referred to as *socialization*) should continue until the dog is six months to a year old.

A puppy should remain with its litter mates for around seven or eight weeks. During this period, it develops its identity as a dog, learns to recognize dogs as social objects, and it masters the basic behaviours needed to interact with other dogs. During these first weeks one must rely on the breeder or caretakers doing the right things.

Research has now shown that human handling of puppies, virtually from birth until they are given to their new owners, is extremely beneficial in building a good personality. For small pups, a simple stimulation routine that works is to take each puppy in the litter in turn, hold it in both hands with its head higher than its tail for about ten seconds. Next, change the pup's position so that its head is lower than the tail for another ten seconds, and then repeat this gentle slow rocking once more with head up for ten seconds and head down again for another ten. Next, hold an ice cube in your closed fist for about ten seconds to cool down your hand, and then slip the cold hand, palm up, under the pup. He may wiggle a bit, but since your hand will quickly warm to body temperature, you are really only providing a mild stress for a short period of time. An alternate way to do the same thing is to place the pup on a cool surface for a few moments each day. Next hold the pup on its back and cradle it for a minute while you gently stroke its belly, head, and ears with your fingers. Finally, take a cotton swab and gently spread the pads of the feet and tickle the pup between the toes. This series of activities should take about three to five minutes at the most, although there is no harm in handling the pup for a longer period of time. Exposure to the human voice is also important, and talking to the dog as you pick it up or stroke it will familiarize it with human sounds. Having the radio or television on to provide additional sounds also helps steady the growing pup.

Over the first few weeks you can gently introduce the pup to new sources of stimulation. Introduce toys or objects that can be manipulated or investigated into the nesting area. Take the pup to different areas of the house, where the floor textures are different, the lighting is different, and there are different things to look at. This kind of stimulation will help make the pup more emotionally stable and a better problem solver later on. Let him explore and sniff around at his own pace during these early trips. Exposing the pups to friendly dogs and other people (including children) is also good.

Since the 1960s, when the U.S. Army started systematic handling and socialization of puppies as part of the Bio-Sensor or "superdog" programme, their records have shown that a simple set of handling activities during early puppyhood (such as those outlined above), is psychologically beneficial and also stimulates physical improvements. Puppies that are handled and mildly stressed actually show faster maturing of the electrical pattern of their brain activity, often grow more quickly, and show earlier coordinated movement activities. Increasing the amount of time with people makes puppies more confident around humans and less fearful of strangers, and forges a stronger emotional bond with the people who will be its caretakers and family later in life. Such dogs learn faster and make better working, obedience competition, and working dogs.

The optimal time to remove a dog from its litter and place it in its home is at the end of the seventh or sometime during the eighth week. Over the next five weeks, if the dog is given a lot of additional exposure and interaction with humans, it will come to accept human beings as members of its pack. It is this acceptance that allows dogs to interact well with people. A number of studies have confirmed that puppies that do not receive enough human contact and interaction before they are twelve weeks of age grow up to be difficult dogs. They do not attend to their masters' commands; they are often fearful and may use aggression to cope with their discomfort around people. Such dogs usually turn out to be unsuccessful as working and obedience dogs and later attempts at changing their personalities into something more acceptable requires time, work, consistency, and patience. In some instances, even with all of that effort, your success may be limited.

TAMING THE WOLF

Even after puppyhood, there are still practical ways to improve dogs' personality characteristics, and even the well-socialized dog can benefit from these. If you have a dog who was not well socialized, or a dog that has begun to act dominant and aggressive, or one that is anxious and fearful, or just one that you want to be more responsive to you, you can restructure its personality by focusing on the relationship between the dog and you, its owner and guardian. You can then extend this same process to other people in the dog's life. The basic ideas behind this programme derive from experience gained by taming wolves, which are naturally fearful of humans, strangers, and new places, and respond to captivity with aggression and physical attempts to seize control of the situation. The principles that will alter the temperament of a wild wolf so that it becomes a more manageable and sociable animal that is less fearful and less likely to be spontaneously aggressive will also work for the wolf's close relative, your dog.

We can call this the *Work for a Living Programme,* and it will become clear why this label is appropriate. The prerequisite for the programme is that the dog knows and obeys one or two commands. The dog doesn't have to respond reliably and the behaviours don't have to be complex. If the dog responds to the word "come" when you are a foot or two in front of him by taking a couple of steps toward you, that's OK. If the dog knows the words "sit" and "down" even if he responds slowly and after a delay, that's fine for now. We'll worry about training issues a bit later in this chapter, but for now let's work on the personality.

This is designed to be a nonconfrontational programme. This is important because confronting the dog or using force will cause the dog to respond with confrontation and force, and this will ratchet up the level of aggression in the relationship. Nicholas Dodman, who runs the Tufts University Veterinary Center, put it best when he noted that "You *can* get the better of a dog by fighting with it, but you must be prepared to fight to the death!" The point of this programme is to help your dog become more sociable and agreeable to live with, not to make your relationship more difficult.

Another problem with confrontation or force is that such actions appear aggressive and can result in the dog becoming fearful for its life or safety. This simply makes the dog more anxious and frightened in general. Furthermore, the dog's insecurity will be greatest when you—who is the person threatening it or hurting it—are near.

Given that aggressiveness and fearfulness are the two clusters of behaviours that we want to eliminate or avoid in this new approach to enhancing the dog's personality, we must avoid all confrontation. Thus if the dog tries to guard a bone or a rawhide chew from you, do not chase after it or try to snatch it away from the dog. Simply no longer give such treats to the dog. If the dog has something that is vital, such as your car keys, simply distract the dog either by picking up the leash and going to the door or going to the kitchen and offering the dog a treat. Remember, no force, no confrontation.

Now we start the Work for a Living Programme. This is a process of shaping the dog's mind so that he recognizes you as his pack leader and therefore looks to you for instruction, obeys your commands, and draws reassurance from your presence. In the wild, a wolf pack leader gets first access to any food or resources and effectively controls its distribution. You are going to start to do this by controlling the resource of first importance to the dog, namely his food.

The heart of this programme is hand-feeding the dog. For the next four or five weeks you are going to have to hand-feed the dog. This means that food must no longer appear like manna from heaven, but must be provided only directly from your hand one kibble at a time. The trick is that the dog has to earn each piece of kibble by responding to a command. If all that dog knows is "come", "sit", and "down", that's fine. Just mix them up. The whole process should only take a total of around five to ten minutes (depending on the number and size of the bits of kibble), but don't do this training all at once. If the dog doesn't respond at once, or appears not to be motivated by the food, don't worry. Just take a break and come back later to try again. Sooner or later he will get hungry enough to play the game, and after a while he will become quite happy to do so.

Make the dog work for one half of his ration in the morning and the other half in the evening. Even better is to divide his ration into thirds, doing one part in the morning and one in the evening and the remaining portion spread out at random intervals during the day as you move around the house or take the dog on a walk.

Do not simply reward the dog with the kibble for his response. As you give him the kibble, give a word of praise (I use "Good dog") and reach out with your other hand and touch the dog's collar. If you are living with a spouse, partner, or kids, they can share the distribution of food—but only after the dog has done something to earn it. They must also give the verbal praise and the touch.

Once the dog is responding for kibble, you should extend the Work for a Living philosophy to everything else that the dog wants out of life. That includes petting, toys, play, walks, and so forth. All are rationed out in the same way, with the dog getting what he wants only after he obeys a command. Remember that the dog automatically also earns that touch and the bit of verbal praise for responding to you.

What you are doing by this process is changing the way your dog thinks. First, he comes to understand that you are leader of the pack, since you control and distribute all of the resources upon which his life and happiness depend. This immediately solves both clusters of behaviour problems that we started with. The aggression level immediately begins to drop. In the wild, once pack leadership has been established, there are seldom any aggressive challenges unless the ability of the alpha wolf comes into question because of infirmity. The thought patterns are much the same that might run through your mind if you were introduced to your president or prime minister. You might not like his political programme, but you still speak to him respectfully and of course you don't try to bite him. This is also one reason why all of the family members, including the children, get in on the process. We want the dog to learn that, in his pack (family), all two-footed dogs are higher in status than all four-footed dogs.

Surprisingly, the same acceptance of you as pack leader also helps to control anxiety and fearfulness. This is because canines look to the leader to decide when a situation, visitor, or occurrence is a threat or challenge. If the leader is not showing fear or concern, then there is no reason for the dog to worry. In canine societies not every wolf or dog wants to be leader of the pack, but it is important to know that someone is in charge and making decisions. A dog's anxiety often arises when he gets everything he wants without any responsibility for earning it. Since the leader usually has full access to all of the pack's resources, freely lavishing treats, praise, and social rewards on the dog with "no strings attached" leads him to feel that he must be in charge. With that comes the responsibility to make all of the decisions—even when the dog is uncertain as to what to do or what is actually happening. This uncertainty, combined with the fact that there is no one else in a leadership role to evaluate the situation, is bound to lead to fear and anxiety. This also means that when you try to reassure him because he is acting frightened, he simply doesn't believe you, since you haven't really demonstrated that you are higher in status than he is. That implies that you don't have the prerogative to make such decisions for the rest of the pack—including him. Instituting the hand-feeding programme, where the dog must work for each kibble by obeying a command, clearly establishes you as the pack leader. This relieves the dog of the anxieties associated with making every decision and evaluating every situation.

Once the dog has settled down and is showing the kinds of behaviours that you want, you can phase out the hand-feeding routine for his breakfast and dinner. He still has to come and sit, but now he gets the bowl put down as his reward. At first, the bowl will just contain a part of his meal, so he will have to obey two or three commands before the meal is complete. Later on it can be a single serving. I still prefer to reserve part of my dogs' daily ration, which I dispense much like treats during the rest of the day, but only when each dog responds to my commands.

It is important to remember that we are not simply training the dog; rather, we are trying to restructure his thinking processes. We are trying to change his attitude toward us and people in general. A dog is a creature of habit, and we have succeeded in remoulding his personality when we have established a mind-set where the dog obeys automatically and without question. Responding to you will become part of his life and will give him a sense of control and well-being. You might imagine that your dog is coming to think something like "This is a good life. I can get whatever I want. All that I have to do is to figure out what the word he is using means and I get a treat!" Your very presence will ultimately become a signal that good things are happening and that you are in charge and looking after his safety and security.

Even dogs that are naturally dominant (with lots of checks in Column A of the personality test) can come to accept human leadership and control happily and consistently. Age, however, is still an important factor, and so you want to take action when the dog is as young as possible. You also have to repeat the exercises, at least occasionally, throughout the dog's life. This Work for a Living Programme is the basis of a behaviour modification programme that can give you a dog with the most desirable set of personality characteristics. However, you must do a few additional things to make the dog's new positive attitude toward you and other people more stable and permanent.

Touching: If you follow the programme that I just outlined, you will already be touching the dog more frequently, since you are supposed to touch his collar each time you give him a bit of kibble. The additional touching needed is not the simple stroking or fondling that we do to please the dog or ourselves but rather a systematic touching of the dog's whole body. It mimics the pattern of licking and touching that a mother dog applies to her puppies, which helps to establish an emotional bond but is also an expression of her dominance and control of the litter (see Plate 19). The significance of being touched carries over into adulthood: Among wild dogs and wolves, a dominant member of the pack, such as the leader, can nuzzle, sniff, or touch any of the lower-status pack members at its pleasure. By allowing this treatment, the other pack members signal their acceptance of the dominant dog's leadership. Just as with the mother dog and her puppies, however, the touching also establishes a positive emotional bond between the one touching and the one being touched.

You should be sure to touch your dog systematically on an almost-daily basis, and everyone in the family, especially the children, should be taught the ritual. The procedure to follow is quite straightforward. While talking in a soothing manner, saying the dog's name frequently, have it sit or stand in front of you. Take its head in both of your hands. Stroke or fondle its ears, neck, and muzzle in this two-handed manner, briefly looking into the dog's eyes as you do. Next slide both hands down the dog's neck, back, and sides. Lightly slide your hands over the dog's chest and then all the way down each of the dog's front legs. If the dog is sitting, raise it gently to a standing position, lightly rub its belly and back, and then run your hands down the hind legs all the way to the tip of the paws. Finally, run your fingers quickly and lightly over the dog's tail (or tail region if the dog has a docked tail). Finish by again grasping the dog's head momentarily and saying the dog's name in a happy voice. The entire touching routine takes only about thirty seconds to a minute, and your dog will probably enjoy all the attention.

One additional benefit of this touching procedure is that touching your dog thoroughly on a regular basis will teach you the feel of its body, and you will immediately notice any unusual lumps or tender areas. My Cairn terrier, Flint, had five years added to his life because in my touching him I discovered a malignant lump in time for the veterinarian to remove it before it had time to spread and cause major damage.

An alternative to touching is grooming, which involves the same kind of systematic touching. Grooming is a more vigorous form of touching that makes the dominance of the groomer more obvious. It has the side benefits of making the dog look better and keeping the house freer of hair if you have a breed that sheds. Just remember to talk to the dog throughout the grooming process, using its name frequently.

Enforcing the pack hierarchy: Certain behaviours characterize the leader of the pack and his followers. The leader gets first choice at any food, can sleep anywhere it likes, goes first through any opening or into any new territory, and can demand attention anytime it wants it. If your dog accepts you (and your family) as the pack leader, it will be a happy, albeit lower-ranked, pack member that is much more willing to accept commands and controls. You must reinforce your leadership by exerting the prerogatives of the pack leader.

As the pack leader, you should never let the dog rush out of a door or through a gate ahead of you. When the dog is resting in a favourite spot, you should make it move from time to time. (I simply say, "Excuse me," and shoo the dog a few steps away. After a while, "Excuse me" comes to mean "move" to the dog.) The moment the dog has complied willingly, praise it, and let it return to its original position if it wants. You should also occasionally take an object or some food away from the dog. (It is best to start doing this when the dog is still a puppy, when aggression is less likely and more easily controlled.) The moment you have done so, praise the dog for being nonaggressive, and return the object or give the dog an additional bit of food. Finally, the dog should not be allowed to demand attention capriciously by pawing, barking, or placing its forepaws on you. If the dog does this while you are seated, you should silently restrain it from continuing and then stare momentarily into its eyes. If you are standing, simply turn your back on the dog and take a step away. In both cases you can follow up by giving the dog a command, such as *sit* or *down* and then praising him for responding to it. In that way you change the situation to one in which the dog is gently reminded that you are in control of his behaviour, not vice versa.

Attention and compliance exercises: The preceding exercises are designed to modify a dog's dominance behaviours and increase his security and understanding of where he fits in his family "pack".

Another set seeks to shape the dog's attention to people and its acceptance of human control. The first aspect of gaining control over a dog is to have it learn its name. A dog's name is, perhaps, the single most important word that he will ever learn. Think of it this way: A dog lives in a sea of human sounds and, with only the language ability of a human two-year old, it has to decide which words are directed at it and which are not. Thus if you say to another family member "I am going to sit down and watch some TV," how does the dog know if the words "sit" and "down" were not meant as a command to him? Obviously, if you were looking directly into the dog's eyes and had his full attention, the "sit" or "down" would clearly be directed at him and he should know that you mean for him to respond. In the absence of that sort of body language, however, the dog's name becomes the key to his understanding. In effect, a dog's name becomes a signal which tells it that the next sounds that come out of its master's mouth will have some effect on his life and translates into something like, "This next message is for you."

This means that we should be precise when we are talking to the dog. Each time we want it to do something, we should start off with its name. That means that "Rover, sit" is proper dog talk. On the other hand, "Sit, Rover" is not good grammar for a dog, since the command that you want the dog to respond to will have disappeared into the void before he has been alerted that the noises that you are making with your mouth are addressed to him. That means that when you say "Sit, Rover", since nothing meaningful follows his name, you may well end up with a dog simply staring up at you with that "OK-now-that-you-have-my-attention-what-do-you-want-me-to-do?" look that we all have seen so many times.

All of my dogs have three names, but they know only two. The first is their official name, which is the name registered with the kennel club that appears on their pedigree certificate. These are usually marvelously pompous and meaningless, such as "Remasia Vindebon of Torwood", "Rashdyn's Braveheart Rennick", or "Solar Optics from Creekwood". The American Kennel Club gives you twenty-eight letters (including spaces) to come up with this formal title. If you decide on a name that has already been used by somebody, then you use some of those letter spaces for a number to distinguish your dog's name from all of the others. I sometimes wonder whether there is a collie out there with the name of "Lassie, number 6,654,521".

The dog's second name is its "call name". After all, you really don't want to be standing out in your backyard yelling, "Remasia Vindebon of Torwood, come!" The dog's call name becomes its own unique and solely owned name, which is the one that we actually use when we talk to them. My dogs have call names like Wiz, Dancer, Darby, or Odin. Over the years I have found that two-syllable names seem to roll off of my tongue more easily and tend to produce a better response. Thus Wiz was actually called Wizzer most of the time. Also, hard sounds seem to catch the dog's attention better. Thus, when I adopted my old Cavalier King Charles spaniel, and he came with the name "Banshee", it soon metamorphed into "Bam Bam".

All of my dogs also have a third name, a group name, which is "Puppy" in our house. This is their alternate name, and when I yell, "Puppies, come," I expect all of my dogs within earshot to appear at a run. A friend who only has male dogs uses the word "Gentlemen", while another (a former officer in the Army Tank Corps) uses the group name "Troops". Still another friend uses "Fuzzies" as the call name for her flock of miniature poodles.

If you are systematic about teaching your dog his name, its sound will capture the dog's attention and he will look at you. This attention is vital when you want to teach the dog something or get him to do something. If you are not systematic about teaching a dog its name, then the dog will most likely assume that its name is the sound that it hears most frequently directed at it by its family. There was a cartoon that captured this idea when it depicted two dogs meeting on the street. One introduces himself to the other saying, "My name is 'No, No, Bad Dog.' What's yours?"

Perhaps the most important single command to teach the dog is *sit*. It causes the dog to voluntarily cease any other activities and places it in a position that can conveniently serve as a starting point for other activities. Teaching a puppy this command is also very rewarding, because the dog learns it almost automatically. Simply wave a bit of food once or twice in front of the dog, and then say the dog's name followed by the word *sit*. As you do this, move your hand with the bit of food on a path that goes over his head, between the ears toward the dog's rear end. Most dogs will naturally sit under these conditions because that posture allows them to keep watching the hand. If the puppy does not sit, gently fold its hind legs under its hindquarters to place it into position. Either way, when the dog sits, give it the bit of food and some praise. After a few practice sits, change the pattern a bit. Now, with no food in your hand, repeat the sequence: Say the dog's name and the word *sit* and place your hand above and slightly behind the puppy's head. When the dog sits, again give it a bit of food and some praise. After ten or so repetitions, when the dog is reliably sitting with the verbal command and the gesture, you can probably drop the hand signal, and the dog should begin sitting to the verbal command alone.

Once the *sit* command is established, you can easily use the same form of *lure training* to teach the *down* command. Start with the dog sitting and looking at a treat in your hand. Say the dog's name, then say "down" while you swing your hand in a downward arc from the dog's nose on a path that will place your hand with the treat a short distance in front of his paws. Most dogs will follow the food lure and go into a down position (although you may have to rest your other hand on the dog's rear to keep him from standing to move toward the treat). As soon as your dog lies down, give a word of praise and the treat.

If the dog responds to only three commands ("sit", "down", "come") you have the perfect tools to use in the Work for a Living Programme, described earlier. Each time the dog responds to his name and a command as he is working for the kibbles that make up its dinner, you are also teaching him the habits of attention and compliance. If a dog gets into the habit of watching you and obeying your commands, then it no longer even occurs to him that he can ignore you or disobey. In effect, you have created the perfect personality for an obedient working dog.

The trick is that the dog must feel that you are *always* in control of it. This means that you should never ask the dog to do something unless you are sure that it will actually perform the required action. Obviously, a trained dog will generally comply with your commands, but until you reach that stage, you or someone else should be in a position to enforce the command. For instance, you should not tell the dog *"down"* unless you are close enough physically to lure or place the dog in a lying position. Similarly, until the dog responds reliably, you should not call it unless it is on leash. This allows you to reel it in like a fish if it fails to respond promptly. The idea is to impress on the dog that your commands to it are not requests, or pleas, or the beginning of a negotiation, but rather instructions that must be complied with because they will be enforced if need be. At the same time, whenever the dog does comply (even if you have to assist him in doing so), you must praise or otherwise reward him. This way, the dog comes to associate working for you with pleasant outcomes. The best rule is to avoid confrontation or force by never allowing the dog to get into situations where it is highly likely to misbehave or disobey you.

Once you have taught the dog some basic commands, or even some parlour tricks, practice these on a regular but unpredictable basis, not just at feeding time. While walking the dog, make it come to you and sit down. While watching television, make the dog sit or lie down. This random repetition is important, not simply as practice for the commands but also as reinforcement for the idea that the dog must pay attention to you and follow instructions without question.

An already submissive dog, with many checks in Column S in the personality test, will not need much work to allow you to establish your dominance as leader. Such a dog will, however, benefit from touching and grooming exercises to firm up its bond with its handler. A more submissive dog also will get a lot out of the attention and compliance exercises because focusing its attention on its master will distract it from its own (sometimes frightened) emotional state. With consistent attention and compliance work, the dog will begin to develop some confidence. Systematic training also helps reassure fearful dogs because they learn how to respond and whom to respond to. In the dog's mind, predictable things are safe things, and these dogs seek safety and security.

IMPROVING INSTINCTIVE INTELLIGENCE

This form of intelligence will be the most difficult to influence, since it involves genetic predispositions. Obviously, dog breeders can influence the instinctive intelligence of future generations by paying attention to the abilities and temperaments of the parents-to-be, but most people simply purchase their dogs from a breeder and must live in the present. Nevertheless, although pet owners cannot directly influence instinctive intelligence, they can be aware of its consequences. Obviously, if a dog is bred from parents that have earned obedience degrees, their achievement suggests something about the genetic potential of the pup in the area of working and obedience intelligence.

It also indicates that the breeder cares about temperament, personality, and performance, not just looks. When you are dealing with working and sporting breeds, parents that have earned field and working certificates are a better bet to produce puppies with inborn characteristics to hunt and retrieve.

No matter what behaviour patterns your dog has because of its genetic endowment, there is usually some leeway to modify these behaviours to a degree, although some modifications of instinctive intelligence will be more successful than others. The degree of success depends on the specific breed and the nature of the change that you wish to make. For instance, it is easier to make an active breed more active than it is to make a quiet breed more active. Conversely, making a normally quiet breed even less active is easier than making an active dog more quiet. A highly sociable dog, such as a beagle, cocker spaniel, or golden retriever, is easily made more sociable so that it can tolerate, or even enjoy, crowds of people and a great deal of human contact. To do the same with genetically more solitary breeds, such as Afghan hounds, Chihuahuas, chow chows, or schipperkes, is much more difficult, and many of these dogs will get irritable, fearful, or possibly aggressive when surrounded by many people or when exposed to a lot of social attention from strangers. Simply put, it takes little or no effort to change a breed in a direction that increases its instinctive tendencies, while it may take a very concentrated effort to change a breed in a direction that runs counter to its natural tendencies.

Problems also occur when people forget the instinctive intelligence patterns within their dogs. All dogs, as they mature, develop in the direction of their breed's genetic master plan, unless some set of extreme experiences or very concerted training interferes with these tendencies. Knowledge of a breed's instinctive intelligence and the triggers of particular genetically programmed behaviours can allow you to set up training conditions that will be optimal for your dog. It is better to try to choose a setting where the stimuli that trigger inherited behaviours can be avoided.

Sight hounds, for example, will chase things that move. This means that attempting to work or train your greyhound, whippet, saluki, or Afghan hound in a busy area, such as a park where children and other dogs will be running around, will simply make the task more difficult. If you must train outdoors, use a relatively empty field or yard. A quiet room will work even better, since it offers no horizon for the dogs to scan. Removing the possibility of visual distractions will allow your sight hound to address its full attention to you and whatever training you are attempting. Conversely, you can take advantage of these breeds' responsiveness to visual stimuli by using large and exaggerated hand signals during training rather than simply depending upon voice commands. Of course, it may take saying the dog's name to get him to look at you in the first place.

Scent hounds, such as beagles, bloodhounds, or basset hounds, are relatively unresponsive to visual stimulation but easily distracted by scents, especially the scent of livestock, wild animals, or other dogs. Consequently, training these breeds proceeds more smoothly and learning occurs more quickly when the work takes place indoors or on paved surfaces that are periodically swept or hosed down. Training in a barn or farmyard, or on a playground often crossed by other dogs, or in a field where horses or cattle graze, or where birds and game might roam, may prove to be extremely distracting. For the scent hounds, it takes only a single distraction to render an entire training session useless because the dog will shift its full attention to its nose. Some trainers claim that they can avoid some of these distractions by anointing a dog's nose with a bit of perfume, hair pomade, bath gel, or scented cold cream, the notion being that the scent of the ointment will mask the more distracting natural scents. However, some dogs find this loss of their normal ability to pick up environmental scents very stressful. Hand signals are difficult for scent hounds to learn; with their noses to the ground, they simply may not look at their handlers. For these breeds, the use of voice commands in training is much preferred; however, if you have trained the dog to attend to you and respond to its name, this will bring its eyes in your direction and help a great deal.

Terriers are easily distracted by small animals in their vicinity or by lights and reflections moving on the floor, because these tend to trigger their hunting predispositions. This means that the best training areas for terriers will not have bright areas patterned with moving shadows (such as those cast by a tree on a sunny, breezy day). Training when the sun is low or training indoors is often better for these breeds. An area where flies, bees, or other insects are frequently found can also trigger a terrier's grabbing and snapping responses, which can interfere with its training. Obedience-training systems that reward a dog's correct performance with vigorous play are inappropriate for the terrier. Many breeds of terriers are easily swamped by excitement, making attention to the subsequent training less likely. The best performance in terriers seems to come through very quiet, calm training, with gentle stroking or food rewards rather than exuberant play.

Early in my dog obedience training, my instructor, Emma Jilg, had a marvellous miniature poodle named April. One evening, a student in the class asked about how to improve her dog's attention to commands during training. Emma demonstrated a few techniques and then used April to demonstrate focused attention. She first instructed the dog, "Look at me," and then invited the class to try to call the dog. The twelve class members called seductively, gesticulated, waved bits of food, and acted in various bizarre and clownish ways. The elegant little poodle remained stationary, her eyes and full attention locked on Emma. After the class recognized that their antics were getting nowhere, Emma said, "These attention-focusing exercises should work with any dog." Then she moved next to me and my cairn terrier, Flint, who had been prancing up and down excitedly during all of the activity. She put her arm around my shoulder and said, "Of course, it will be harder for someone who owns a terrier. Terriers are simply too interested in everything to sit still and pay attention to only one person." We both looked down at Flint, who supposedly had been left on command to sit and stay by my side: He was busily trying to attract April's attention with a play invitation bow and a series of frisky short barks.

Most sporting breeds are best trained in areas where birds, rabbits, and deer are not apt to congregate. Once during an indoor obedience match, a pheasant somehow became trapped in the large arena where the competition was being held. As is typical of this species, the bird tried to avoid contact with the people and dogs and simply paced around on some exposed rafters above the show rings. In the middle of its obedience exercise, one German short-haired pointer that had done reasonably well in competition on previous days caught sight or scent of the bird. Its attention was immediately pulled from the handler, who actually tripped over the dog because it had frozen in position to watch the bird right in the middle of a heeling exercise. Feathers, bits of fluff, even crumpled bits of newspaper blown by the wind will sometimes produce the same effect in sporting breeds. Therefore, an unlittered outdoor area or an enclosed or indoor area may be better for training these dogs. When training, avoid wearing fluttery clothing, such as long flowing skirts, scarves, ties, or fringes: During one obedience competition, I saw a novice Irish setter freeze in the classic hunting position in response to a gaily feathered hat worn by a spectator at ringside!

Herding breeds are often distracted by people milling around in crowds and are virtually always distracted by livestock. Areas where children are playing are particularly bad, since something about groups of children seems to trigger herding responses in these dogs. Locations without many people are best for training these breeds, but if you must work in a populated area, choose one where people tend to move more slowly and do not gather in groups. On the plus side, the herding breeds adapt very quickly to background noises, so they can work under relatively noisy conditions that would be difficult for many other types of dogs.

Guarding breeds are exactly the opposite of the herding breeds in that they are most often distracted by noises. Loud or intermittent bursts of sound will tend to elicit responses in these breeds that will compete with any attempted training. Avoid areas where people or children are apt to be running because a retreating person may evoke the pursuit-and-attack response from some of these dogs.

Fluid and Crystallized Intelligence

Albert Einstein is probably the epitome of genius to many people. In fact, we call a person "an Einstein" when we want to say that he or she is clever. We immortalize the man's intellect by putting his image on T-shirts, and we give our stereotyped cartoon scientists Einstein's mane of bushy hair to make them look smart. Yet if Albert Einstein had never gone to school, never learned to write, and never learned the basics of mathematics, he never would have made any of the great discoveries he is known for. Indeed, it is likely that his contemporaries would have judged him to be of quite low intelligence and instantly forgotten him upon his death.

A shift in circumstances and life experiences can be enough to determine whether a man becomes known as a genius or unknown and an ignoramus, because of the nature of intelligence. Each dimension of intelligence discussed in this book can be divided into two parts. Psychologists call the first component *fluid intelligence*. This refers to an individual's native or inborn intelligence potential and is reflected in the speed with which individuals learn, their capacity to store knowledge, and the efficiency with which they attack specific problems. Fluid intelligence is determined by an individual's genetic and neurological makeup—physiological factors such as brain size, brain chemistry, the number of neurons in the cortex, the number of branches that the neurons have, and so on. Fluid intelligence sets the limits for each individual's cognitive ability, establishing a ceiling beyond which intelligence cannot rise. Einstein's fluid intelligence was his potential to learn and solve problems.

The second component of each variety of intelligence is *crystallized intelligence*, which refers to mental processes that require learned components. Crystallized intelligence includes language ability, mathematical ability, the capacity to learn problem-solving strategies, and so forth. It represents the total of what a person learns from formal education and life experiences.

Manifest intelligence is an individual's measurable intelligence, so it is the sum of fluid and crystallized intelligence. To use an analogy from car racing, suppose the average speed of a race car during a race represents a person's manifest intelligence. Obviously, speed is determined in part by the mechanical factors that make up the car—the fluid intelligence. It is also determined by the learned skills of the car's driver and the learned abilities of the pit crew—the crystallized intelligence. The car cannot exceed its mechanical limit for speed, regardless of the skill of its crew. Similarly, it may never come close to its potential if the learned skills of its operator and mechanics are not adequate.

To illustrate in another way, a mentally retarded individual, depending on the degree of mental deficit, might never achieve full use of language no matter how long and intensively he or she was schooled. Here the limit is set by the low capacity of the individual's fluid intelligence. Alternatively, a mind with a genius IQ of 200 might never acquire language if not exposed to an environment in which there are people around him who speak. Here the limitation is set by the restrictions on the experiences that increase crystallized intelligence. Put simply, crystallized intelligence reflects mental achievement; fluid intelligence reflects mental potential.

Some tasks depend more on fluid intelligence, while others rely more on crystallized intelligence. Mathematicians and theoretical physicists are generally individuals with high fluid intelligence, which gives them an edge in creative problem solving, and many of them rise high in their professions at relatively early ages. Historians, economists, and psychologists tend to achieve their most important contributions when they are somewhat older because mastery of these subjects depends more on the accumulation of knowledge and the learning of specific techniques, which is crystallized intelligence.

In a dog, fluid intelligence is reflected in the learning and problem-solving abilities measured in Chapter 9. Crystallized intelligence represents what a dog actually knows, including much of its human language comprehension (and all of its responses to obedience and working commands). Many of the dog obedience judges I surveyed for this book felt that, in dogs, crystallized intelligence carries the most weight and that few dogs ever reach the full potential of their fluid intelligence.

Increasing a Dog's Fluid Intelligence

It may be difficult for nonscientists to believe, but it is possible to alter neurological and physical aspects of a dog's brain and thus directly affect the animal's fluid intelligence. After genetics, it is the environment that most influences the structure of a dog's brain early in the dog's life. The most obvious of these factors is nutrition. For the first year of a dog's life, balanced nutrition is vital. Without it, the nerve cells of the dog's brain will not mature properly; the brain will actually be smaller in volume and weight and will not function as well. Poorly nourished dogs will act less intelligent throughout the rest of their lives.

Chances are, you had no control over the nutrition of the female that bore your dog. However, especially for the first year of your dog's life, you can be extremely careful about your dog's health and diet. Many dogs are reared on table scraps, which may provide an adult dog with adequate nutrition for survival (although not necessarily optimal health), but they probably are not adequate for a young puppy. You should feed your dog some form of balanced diet. Many inexpensive commercial dog foods and kibbles fill this need, as well as many more expensive but better balanced products. A number of books also explain how to provide adequate nutrition from home foods.

While most people will find it easy to accept that nutritional factors can influence brain function, they may have trouble believing that an animal's life experiences also can affect brain growth and efficiency. Experimental psychologists have noticed that animals reared as pets (whether dogs, cats, or rats) seem to learn more quickly and to solve problems more efficiently than laboratory-reared animals. Laboratory animals, of course, eat scientifically balanced, nutritional food, so diet cannot account for the difference. What really seems to matter is the fact that home-reared animals have many more varied experiences during their lives. Most laboratory animals spend the bulk of their lives in a cage or kennel, with at most one or two other animals as company. In comparison, the average pet has been exposed to many different environments simply as it wanders from room to room in a home or as it travels with its master. The pet is exposed to more social interactions as visitors pass through its master's home. The pet is called to solve many everyday problems, to learn from its master's activities cues as to what is happening next, and so forth. In other words, the mind of the pet is kept more active processing information, learning, and searching for solutions to problems than is the mind of the laboratory-reared animal.

Extensive research has been conducted on the effect of experience on brain function and structure. It has shown that experience, especially early experience, can shape the physiology of the brain. Experimentation on this issue has been going on for more than thirty years at the University of California at Berkeley in the laboratories of psychologists Mark Rosenzweig, David Krech, and Edward Bennett. They have shown that animals who are kept in environmentally impoverished conditions, where they are socially isolated, are exposed to low levels of light and sound stimulation, and have limited opportunities to explore and interact with the environment, tend to do poorly on learning and problem-solving tests. Their litter mates, who were reared in an enriched environment that included lots of toys, a complex architecture, other animals to interact with, problems to solve, and constantly changing sources of stimulation, were much better at learning and problem-solving tasks. When the animals from the enriched environment were later examined, it was found that they actually had larger and heavier brains than did the animals that lived in normal laboratory environments. Their cerebral cortexes were thicker, and the concentrations of certain vital brain enzymes associated with the transmission of information to and from various parts of the brain were also higher. Similar increases in brain size and weight are seen for young puppies that have been handled and extensively interacted with people in the manner that I described earlier in this chapter.

Psychologist William Greenough of the University of Illinois looked further at the effects of experience on brain structure and was able to demonstrate that living in an environment where many decisions had to be made and where there were new things to explore actually changes the wiring pattern of the cortex of the brain. Information is carried to and from brain cells by branches that extend away from the cell body. The branches that take information from other neurons are called *dendrites,* and those that send information to other neurons are called *axons.* The larger the total number of branches going to and from a cell, the greater the amount of information that cell can receive, process, and transmit. The increased stimulation and more varied experiences that come from living in a complex environment actually seem to cause the growth of new branches in these nerve cells and new connections *(synapses)* with other nerve cells. Animals with many such branches seem to perform better in a wide variety of different psychological tasks: In other words, they appear to be smarter. One particularly interesting aspect of Greenough's research is that the number of connections seems to increase even in older adult animals that have been taken from an environment with limited stimulation and limited behavioural opportunities and placed in a more enriched environment. This means that some of the opportunities to reshape the brain remain with an animal throughout its life.

In practice, there are many ways to increase the fluid intelligence of a dog. The simplest techniques involve exposing the dog to new environments and new patterns of stimulation under safe, controlled conditions. The greatest increase in brain size and wiring complexity will come about when the enriched experiences occur during the dog's first year, but growth in connections can continue throughout the dog's life and may even slow the normal decline in mental ability that occurs in elderly dogs.

Setting up an enrichment program for a young dog is actually quite simple. As soon as you bring your puppy home (usually at seven weeks of age), you should fit it with a flat buckle-type collar. (Make sure the collar is comfortable but secure enough so that it won't slip over the dog's head on a straight pull.) Then, let the dog wander around the house under supervision. A simple, automatic way to introduce your puppy to new situations is to attach a very light six-foot (two-metre) lead to its collar and then to tie the lead to your belt loop for the hours when you are awake and with the dog. Whenever you get ready to move, announce this to the puppy by saying its name and then get up and do whatever you have to do. At first, you may need to coax the puppy to follow you without any pulling, but after a couple of days, the puppy will follow you without help. Praise and stroke the puppy often during this time to reassure it. After a while, the puppy should follow you without the need of the lead, simply at the sound of its name.

This behaviour programme provides the puppy with a much more varied set of experiences then it would get if it were simply enclosed in a kennel, kitchen, or backyard. It will face continual challenges, such as how to go up stairs or around furniture. It will also experience a constant variety of sensory inputs, as sights, sounds, and smells vary from room to room, and especially when you leave the house and take the puppy to different places.

To ensure enriched experiences, especially during the dog's youth, leave the dog alone as little as possible. Try to take it along on errands, whether on foot or in the car. Whenever possible, expose your puppy to new environments, such as parks, shops, school yards, other homes, and the like. Be sure, however, *never* to let your dog off its lead during these excursions, except when it is safely enclosed, as in the car. You should introduce your puppy to as many different people and dogs as possible. Meeting people is easy, since most like puppies or young dogs. Take some care, though, when introducing your puppy to young children—they may inadvertently be too rough—and always introduce the puppy to other dogs only when under supervision. For the first few months, puppies give off a particular smell, a pheromone that tells other dogs it is still young. Most normal dogs respond to this pheromone by acting solicitously, but don't take this for granted unless you know the other dog very well.

All this social interaction and environmental change provides additional stimulation for the dog. Social interactions, toys and objects to manipulate, new settings are all simply problems that must be solved. Ultimately, all this stimulation should lead to the benefits that laboratory research says results from enriched experience. Your dog's brain size and weight should increase, as should the number of neural connections. This should result in increased brain efficiency and greater fluid intelligence.

Interesting new data suggest that additional stimulation and attention to nutrition can stop the decline in mental ability that is observed in older dogs, and which is also accompanied by a loss of brain size and weight. William Greenough, whose work on the effects of enriched experience on young animals' brains was discussed above, recently extended his research to look at older animals. When old animals that had been housed in the rather barren, solitary normal laboratory settings were moved to an enriched environment, with many animals to interact with and things to do, the surprise was that their brains improved. It had previously been believed that the benefits of environmental stimulation would affect only young brains, but Greenough found that the number of neural connections increased in the range of 25–200 percent, depending upon which types of neural connections they considered. Several findings make this research important. First, it shows that individual nerve cells are capable of growing new connections even when an animal has reached old age. Secondly, it shows that this new growth is triggered by exercising and stimulating the brain with new experiences and problems to solve, which can greatly slow, or even reverse, the effects of aging on the size and weight of the brain.

With age, in addition to loss of neural tissue and a shrinking number of connections between brain cells, chemical changes also occur in the brain that affect behaviour, memory, and learning for the worse. As tissues degenerate, protein deposits called "amyloids" accumulate in the brain. High levels of amyloids, especially when associated with clusters of dead and dying nerve cells, are taken as evidence of Alzheimer's disease. Studies conducted at the University of Toronto by a team of researchers including psychologist Norton Milgram have shown that older dogs develop these amyloids and the dogs with highest levels of amyloids in their brains had the poorest memories and the greatest difficulties learning new material, and also were less able to do more complex thinking and problem solving. The good news is that giving older dogs a diet rich in antioxidants (particularly vitamin C, vitamin E, and carotenoids such as beta-carotene), plus certain minerals (particularly selenium) and fatty acids (such as DHA and

EPA, carnitine and alpha lipoic acid), will also help prevent the formation of these amyloids.

Next Milgram's team combined this change in diet with "cognitive enrichment" to exercise the brain. Specifically this meant that, five to six days a week, groups of old dogs were challenged with learning tasks and puzzles, such as finding hidden food rewards. After a year, dogs were tested on a series of mental problems and learning tasks. Milgram summarized his results this way: "We say that we *can* teach an old dog new tricks because it's possible to slow down, or partially reverse brain decline. Some dogs in our tests definitely became smarter." Whether your dog is young or old, adequate nutrition and mental stimulation will keep his brain functioning at its peak, and allow him to develop and keep a high level of fluid intelligence.

Increasing Crystallized Intelligence

If crystallized intelligence comprises everything an individual has ever learned, it should be obvious that the more a dog learns, the more its crystallized intelligence will increase. The learning need not involve formal instruction; the enriched experiences that you give the dog to improve its fluid intelligence will also contain opportunities to improve crystallized intelligence. However, some systematic activities have proven to be extremely helpful in expanding the mental abilities associated with crystallized intelligence. You can easily work these activities into your everyday life with the dog.

The first thing you must do is talk to your dog. By *talk*, I don't mean the play talk or love talk that most people engage in when casually interacting with their dogs. Rather, you should talk to the dog as you engage in activities that are relevant to its life. Repeat simple phrases that anticipate activities that affect the dog, such as the statement "Let's go for a walk" or the question "Do you want to go for a walk?" before the daily walk. Before snapping on the leash, say "Lead on"; before taking it off, say "Lead off". Before going up or down the stairs with the dog, say "Upstairs" or "Downstairs". When you want the dog to follow you into the kitchen, say "Let's go to the kitchen." The list goes on.

The point of all this is to expand the dog's receptive vocabulary by increasing the number of words and signals that it knows. For this reason, you should always use the same words and phrases. When you give the dog its food, whether you use the word(s) *suppertime, dinner-time, who wants to eat?, mess call,* or *luncheon will be served on the veranda* doesn't matter; what's important is that you select one word or phrase and use it consistently. (Later on in the dog's life, you may introduce synonyms, but they are sometimes confusing.) It is also important that each word or phrase imply only one action. If you use the word *out* when you are going out the door or sending the dog through it, you should not use *out* when you want to remove an object from the dog's mouth. The idea is to get the dog to understand that specific human sounds predict specific events.

In a short time, you will begin to notice that the dog responds to frequently used words. *Let's go for a walk* will cause the dog to move toward the door, *lead on* will cause the dog to raise its head to allow you to reach the collar ring, *let's go* will cause the dog to look at you and begin to get up to follow you, and so forth. Each phrase will begin to elicit a specific action from the dog, both demonstrating that it has been learned and giving you added control over the dog's behaviour. Remember that whenever you talk to the dog, you should begin with its name, so that you are also teaching him to pay attention to you at the same time.

During the early stages of your dog's life you can begin what I call *autotraining* but which is sometimes referred to as *behaviour capture*. This is really the beginning of the dog's obedience training, but it does not involve formal instruction. When dealing with a puppy named Rover, for example, you would watch the puppy's activities carefully as you interacted with him. If he begins to move toward you, you should say *Rover, come;* if he begins to sit, you should say *Rover, sit.* At the end of each action, you should praise the dog, just as if it had performed the action at your command. This serves to attach a label to the activity, and, with a few repetitions, the word will come to signify the action in the dog's mind. (Psychologists refer to this as *contiguity learning.*) From here, it takes very little to turn the word into a command. In some instances, no additional training should be necessary; in others, after the groundwork had been done with contiguity training, a mere one or two repetitions of giving the command (for example, *come*) and demonstrating what you want by encouraging the dog to approach (by clapping your hands and backing up, for instance) should do the trick.

Contiguity learning is particularly useful when you are teaching a dog activities that are difficult or impossible to enforce. For example, when housebreaking one of my dogs, I walk it down a familiar route. As soon as the dog begins to squat to eliminate, I say the words *be quick* and repeat the phrase once or twice during the elimination process. The dog is then praised after the action is finished. After a couple of weeks, using *be quick* as a command begins to cause the dog to sniff around to choose a place to eliminate. In this way, some aspects of the dog's elimination can be placed under control.

My dogs understand the word *settle* to mean that they are to remain quiet, with little activity, in a particular region of the room or house. Unlike *sit* or *down*, the command is not specific to any position, because I don't care if the dogs move around, as long as they remain quiet and in the same general area. This is another command that I teach by autotraining. When the dogs are quiet, I say the phrase *puppies, settle* and then walk over and quietly stroke each one of them while repeating the word *settle*. After a number of such repetitions, on hearing the command *settle*, the dogs will look for a comfortable place to sit or lie and simply watch the activities going on around them.

Autotraining can make other learning easier. If you use a voice command and a hand signal at the same time during training, the dog will learn to associate both with the desired behaviour by contiguity learning. In a short time, you will find that the dog will respond to either the verbal command or the signal when presented on its own.

One of the most important things that a dog learns during these early interactions is that the sounds its human master makes are designed to carry meanings. Sometimes, they tell the dog what is about to happen next. At other times, they pose problems that the dog has to solve in order to receive rewards of praise or tidbits. For many dogs, this conceptual breakthrough comes when formal obedience training begins. When teaching your dog the commands *sit, heel, come, down*, and so forth, you are also teaching it that your sounds and signals are problems for which it can learn the answers. The earlier a dog learns this, the easier it is to train.

Psychologists refer to this process as "learning to learn". When a lab animal is set a particular problem, the initial problem-solving process may take many attempts. After a number of problems, however, the animal seems to work much more efficiently. It begins to learn the answers to new problems more quickly and easily. This pattern also holds true for humans. Learning one foreign language may be quite difficult, but learning a second is easier, and learning a third proceeds even faster and more efficiently. Students in their later years of high school maintain that the courses are somehow easier. In fact, they aren't, but the student has learned to learn, and this makes acquiring additional knowledge less effortful. In the same way, a dog will take some time to learn the simple commands of *sit*, *down*, and *stay*, yet that same dog will learn much more complex commands, such as those to do with retrieving or jumping, at a faster rate later on in its life. In other words, the more you train your dog to do, the faster it will learn to learn, and the more easily you will be able to teach it additional things. The specific things you teach your dog make little difference; its capacity to learn will improve as much from learning parlour tricks, such as how to beg or roll over, as from formal teaching of competition obedience exercises.

Recent evidence shows that dogs can learn by simply observing other dogs or even people behave. Long before this research appeared in the scientific literature, however, the idea that dogs learn by observation had been well-established among people who work with dogs. The standard practice, for instance, in training a herding dog is to put him to work with a dog that already knows the job. The young dog seems to pick up the complexities of keeping a flock of sheep together, and even the meaning of the shepherd's signals, through the simple act of observing another dog who already knows the job. In fact, shepherds claim that this practice works far better than having the shepherd train the dog himself.

Another example of observational learning is the work of Saint Bernard rescue dogs, named for the hospice founded by Saint Bernard and located in the Swiss Alps. These dogs assist the monks in their searches for travellers who have strayed off the main route, or got lost in storms or covered by avalanches. They are credited with saving thousands of lives over the years. These rescue dogs work in three-dog teams. When a lost traveller is found, two of the dogs lie down beside him to keep him warm and lick his face to keep him conscious, while the third returns to the hospice to sound the alarm and bring back help. These dogs are not given any special training, and no one is exactly sure how one could train a dog to do these things in any event. Young dogs are simply allowed to run with the older, experienced dogs when they go on patrol. In this way, the dogs learn what is expected of them. Ultimately, each dog learns his job and also decides for himself whether his professional specialty will eventually be to lie with the victim or go for help. Just as an aside, it is interesting to note that the hospice considered ending the rescue dog programme for financial reasons. Fortunately the public outcry, government intervention, and an infusion of funds has allowed this unique rescue programme to continue.

Recently it was shown in studies conducted at the South Africa Police Dog School in Pretoria that puppies could learn the basics of searching for and retrieving drugs by simply watching their mother perform the task and seeing her rewarded for it. This means that a quick way to train a dog is to have another dog in the house who already knows the basic commands and household routines. Simply observing the other respond to words seems to teach the new puppy its basic vocabulary.

By the way, since dogs also observe people, we can model many actions that we want the dog to learn. Suppose that you want to teach a dog to jump over a hurdle. You simply put the dog on leash, then move toward the hurdle, and as you jump over it, say his name and the word *jump*. Generally the dog will stay with you and go over the hurdle. Usually after only a few trials you can put the dog into a sitting position on one side of the hurdle, then go to the other side and give the command "Rover, jump," and in most cases the dog will respond correctly and jump over it without you.

One of the best ways to increase your dog's experience—and incidentally improve your own outlook on life—is through play. Retrieving games are stimulating and useful. Just remember to use words such as *fetch* or *take it* when throwing and *give* or *out* when removing the object from the dog's mouth. Chase games (let the dog win sometimes) are fun and increase the dog's attention to you. Even games that cause the dog to bark (say *speak* or *protect* to autotrain barking) and games that get the dog very excited (such as wrestling and rolling the dog) are useful because they allow you to teach the words *enough, stop it*, and *no:* Say the word, reinforce it by placing the puppy in a restrained *down* position, and then praise it for stopping.

One should be careful during play never to allow the dog to play attack or use its teeth. Don't wiggle your fingers in front of its face to get it to use its mouth on your hand. Don't play tug-of-war with it. These behaviours foster dominance in the dog and will affect its personality negatively. A good rule of thumb is, Don't play games that encourage any aspect of behaviour that would displease, hurt, frighten, or worry you if it were shown by an adult dog, especially toward a child.

Konrad Lorenz, the Nobel Prize–winning expert in animal psychology, says that playful animals learn to manipulate both inanimate and social objects. He feels that play develops a dog's mind by leading it into novel situations where it has to develop new or innovative behaviours that provide unique new experiences and thus accelerate the dog's mental growth. If you choose the games that you play with your dog properly, you will actually be creating a more intelligent dog.

Chapter Thirteen

The Dog's Mind and the Owner's Happiness

If dogs could talk, perhaps we would find it as hard to get along with them as we do with people.

—KAREL CAPEK

Do you really want an intelligent dog? "Of course," most people would reply. "Do you think I want a dumb dog running around my house?" But the answer really deserves a bit more thought. Some people want an intelligent dog for the same reasons they want the biggest, most powerful computer in their office, or the fastest and flashiest sports car, or the computer, DVD player, or digital camera with the largest number of dials and controls. They want the best, and they reason that an item that allows the greatest amount of flexibility and the maximum range of action must be the top of the line. Yet not only will operating a very sophisticated computer be demanding, possibly requiring some additional training, but its user may well find in the end that its capacity far exceeds his or her needs. Similarly, learning to use a camera equipped with cutting-edge technology may take a great deal of time, and an operator who is not willing to devote enough energy to the project may actually end up with poorer photographs than he or she would have gotten with a simpler, cheaper, less flexible system, which has fewer options but also fewer ways to go wrong.

During the late 1950s and early 1960s, psychologists made a

startling discovery. They found that, for many jobs, high intelligence is actually a handicap, especially where work is quite repetitive, where the same actions or decisions are required many times during the day, where work is interspersed with long periods of relative inactivity, or where the rate of work-related activity is slow. Under these conditions, an individual with higher general intelligence is actually apt to perform worse than one with lower intelligence on a day-to-day basis. Not only will the brighter person perform less well, but he or she will be considerably less satisfied with the work and the job as a whole.

There are many reasons for this. Individuals with high intelligence require more stimulation, more challenges, and more varied activity. In the absence of such changes and challenges, they become bored. Once bored, they become inattentive and may even make up games to amuse themselves while they work. When they notice how many errors they make because their minds drift from the job, or when they recognize that they are not working as well as those others around them, they become frustrated and unhappy (a state that may also contribute to further inefficiency). On the other hand, individuals who are not so brilliant do not bore as easily. They will pay careful attention to the ongoing flow of information and tasks to be done. They notice small challenges and small deviations from the normal flow of activity. Meeting these small challenges provides enough stimulation to keep them attentive and is a source of real satisfaction that allows them to be happier in their jobs. Furthermore, since they lack the internally generated problems resulting from the boredom of the higher-intelligence person, their work is in fact more accurate, and their rate of productivity higher.

Like people, bright dogs may do badly in circumstances where less gifted animals thrive. The most important thing is to match a dog's characteristics to its owner's requirements. Its temperament, activity level, and level of intelligence all should fit its human family's lifestyle. If your aim is to compete at the highest levels of dog obedience competition, you should choose a dog with the best working and obedience intelligence. If you have a specific task that you want the dog to fulfil, such as hunting, tracking, guarding, herding, rat killing, or whatever, you should choose a dog whose instinctive intelligence will make it most likely to behave as you desire. Choosing a house dog, however, is more complicated.

THE PROS AND CONS OF AN INTELLIGENT DOG

A dog with high learning ability will be able to learn things about its environment more easily and will readily form associations between the stimuli that it encounters and the outcomes of particular activities. Dogs with good learning ability absorb household routines quickly. We are all creatures of habit, and a smart dog learns its family's habits and anticipates them. For instance, the intelligent dog quickly learns that when its owner puts on a coat and picks up the leash, the upcoming behavioural sequence will involve the words *"Do you want to go for a walk?"* followed by movement to the door and the great fun of going outside. The less intelligent dog is not as responsive. It may not bestir itself from its comfortable position in the centre of the room or may only look up vaguely, as if to say, "Is something happening now?"

While the more intelligent dog may be a more responsive and hence better companion, however, it also may learn to pick up cues that are only weakly associated with certain events. Thus, since picking up the leash to go for a walk is normally preceded by putting on a coat, the bright dog may begin responding to that weaker association. As its owner dons a coat to go to the grocery store, the excited dog may begin prancing and barking at the door. Some bright dogs anticipate so well that they become pests. Simply moving toward the door may trigger the dog's excited anticipation of a walk. One owner of a standard poodle said she couldn't use the word *walk* even in casual conversation without the dog's rushing to the front door and barking at the prospect of going out. When she began to spell out the word, it took only a few weeks for the dog to learn that the sound sequence *w-a-l-k* meant the same as *walk* and to react to the spelled-out word as well.

The really intelligent dog will also learn other associations quickly, whether you want it to or not. If the sound of an opening refrigerator has been followed by a treat a few times, you may soon find your dog underfoot every time you open the refrigerator—or even every time you go into the kitchen. When the smart dog notices you laying out grooming or bath materials, it may suddenly disappear into some hiding place, and you may find your normally obedient dog refusing to respond to your calls.

I have been told numerous anecdotes about intelligent dogs, such as Doberman pinschers, Labrador retrievers, poodles, and German shepherds, driving their owners crazy because they learned so rapidly and solved problems so efficiently. Dogs like this learn to open doors by using their mouths on doorknobs, may figure out how to get into floor-level cabinets for biscuits or other goodies, or may act in bizarre ways to get attention. Smart dogs are the ones that learn best from simple observation of other dogs or people. Because they are so intelligent, they think their way into a number of problems.

One animal behaviourist who works with problem dogs told me that the dogs most frequently brought to him with problem behaviours are the really intelligent dogs. Part of the reason for this is that bright dogs quickly become sensitive to exactly which behaviours bring them the greatest rewards. For most dogs, especially sociable breeds, any form of human attention is rewarding. The problem is that we tend to focus more of our attention on a dog when it is doing something "bad"—defined as something we don't want it to do—than when it is doing something "good"—defined as something we do want it to do. For example, some owners try to stop their dogs from barking by giving them biscuits to distract them from whatever caused them to bark in the first place. What these people don't realize is that they are actually rewarding their dogs for barking. After a few repetitions of the sequence, truly intelligent dogs will learn—"If I bark, I get a biscuit." They then begin to bark more frequently and vigorously.

Sometimes, owners "train" their dogs to behave even more reprehensibly. Consider the story of Arnold, a miniature poodle. When Arnold's owner was by herself, she paid a good deal of attention to the dog. However, like many of us, she paid more attention to the dog's misbehaviour than to his desirable activities. One particularly undesirable behaviour, which had brought Arnold a lot of attention, had been his habit of urinating on the bed, something his owner was confident she now had under control. When her boyfriend started coming to visit, however, she began to pay considerably less attention to her dog. Arnold remembered the amount of fuss he had caused by urinating on the bed and was smart enough to figure out that this behaviour would lead to similar results in the present circumstances. The end result was obvious: Whenever Arnold's owner hosted a male guest, the dog would head for the bedroom with malice aforethought. It was a guaranteed showstopper.

The consequences of inadvertently teaching a smart dog an unwanted behaviour are not always so innocuous. One German shepherd owner noticed that his dog was mouthing his child's hand. Worried that this might turn into biting or dominance-related behavior, he went over to the child and told it to pet the dog, thinking that this would distract the animal. Instead, the dog learned that one way to get petted was to take someone's hand in its mouth. The tragic outcome was that the dog later took the hand of a young stranger in its mouth and the child panicked, frightening the dog; the child was injured as she tried to pull her hand back and it caught on the dog's teeth, badly tearing the skin.

The basic principle behind dog learning is that any behaviour that is rewarded will be strengthened and the likelihood that that behaviour will appear again will increase, while any behaviour that is not rewarded will be weakened and the likelihood that it will appear will decrease. The big difference between a bright dog and one that is not so bright is that the more intelligent dog looks at life as a problem that must be solved in order to get rewards. Thus he might see a child open a low cabinet or drawer and take something edible from it. Now he has a focus for his problems solving. He will go through a number of behaviours, trying each to see if it opens the cabinet and allows him to reach the food. He might paw at the door, bite at the hinges, nose the handle, and so forth. Each of these behaviours will have to result in no reward before he stops. However, since he is bright he will continue inventing new behaviours to try to get at the food, and may ultimately hit upon grasping the handle in his teeth and pulling, which now results in a reward and a new behaviour problem for his family to solve. A less bright dog will try one or two things, but his lack of inventiveness may not suggest the one behaviour that might be rewarded, and so he will give up and return to the living room for a nap, and his family will not find a new and unwanted behavior in his repertoire.

Increasing the activity level in a household and the number of people present in it also increases the likelihood of chance associations. For the intelligent dog, this means that it will have greater opportunities to learn things that will be useful in adapting to everyday life but also to learn odd or annoying behaviours. Consider the case of Prince, a border collie whose great joy in life was to race around outdoors. Whenever people were about to leave the house, Prince would race after them, trying to get outside. Once, after Prince had started his mad dash for the exit, the screen door swung closed, and the dog ended up crashing through the wire mesh. Rewarded by the chance to romp outside, the dog learned from this one instance that it could create its own door simply by running full tilt at the screen. After several repairs had been attempted, Prince's owners added a protective layer of heavy farm wire that the dog could not break. Frustrated by this new development, Prince began casting around the house and noticed that many of the open windows were covered with the same material that had covered the screen door. It was easy for this intelligent dog to reach the conclusion that it could use these windows as exits. Every open ground-floor window quickly became a target for Prince's headlong rush for the joys of the outdoors, much to the dismay and annoyance of his owners.

Like Prince, many bright dogs—German shepherds, rottweilers, and such—turn their considerable problem-solving skills to figuring out how to get out of the house. Clever dogs are even bright enough to interpret some failures as partial successes, which will cause the behaviours to continue. Thus the bright dog that scratches at the wall near a door and notices that some of the plaster comes away may well recognize that this change may be the precursor to the creation of a hole large enough to exit through. The results may well be torn-up walls and floorboards or moldings and trim torn from windows or doors, leading to large repair bills and great unhappiness with the dog.

A less intelligent dog will be considerably less likely to form these kinds of associations. Furthermore, the less intelligent dog will be far less likely to generalize knowledge in order to apply its problem-solving skills to other challenges. Remember that such dogs typically try a few things, and when these fail or make little progress, they tend to give up. Since the less intelligent dog can envision no solution, it will simply accept the status quo.

For the same reasons they are less likely to form bad habits based on chance associations, less intelligent dogs are also more likely to adapt to being left alone a lot, which is important for families that are typically away from home for eight or ten hours a day at work or school. To begin with, the less bright dogs will not get bored as easily. When a dog is bored, it will start to look for ways to amuse itself—perhaps by digging the stuffing out of the sofa. Intelligent dogs quickly learn that when their owners are not around, certain behaviours that are normally punished or prevented become possible. Owners of intelligent dogs may find that, when they are at home, their dogs never attempt anything out of the ordinary, but that everything becomes fair game after they've gone to work.

It is possible to drive a bright dog completely mad with poor handling. In a large household, many individuals of different ages and degrees of attentiveness may share some responsibility for the dog. Under these conditions, the dog must often deal with a variety of confusing and inconsistent situations and instructions. Children, adolescent teenagers, and unobservant adults often don't know just how badly they communicate with dogs. A dog that is normally intelligent enough to figure out what is going on and seems to be functioning well may become quite stressed when confronted with impossible human demands.

I was once told an interesting story about a golden retriever named Shadow. This dog was enrolled in a beginner's dog obedience class. Normally the wife of the large family that owned the dog brought him to class, and, as could be expected from a breed with very high working intelligence, the dog was making good progress under the woman's reasonably steady and consistent handling. He had learned all the basic commands quite well and was quick and responsive. For some reason, however, the woman could not attend the next-to-the-last class of the course, and her seventeen-year-old son took her place. The dog seemed to be having difficulties during the session, and the instructor went over to see what the problem was. "Let's see how Shadow is doing," she said. She asked the young handler to leave the dog in a standing position and had him step a couple of paces in front of the dog. "Now tell him to sit," she instructed.

"Come on, Shadow, sit down!" the boy commanded. The dog shuffled its feet uncertainly as the boy complained, "See, he just doesn't know what he's supposed to do." Then the dog did a very odd thing: He lowered himself to a sitting position with his chest low and forward, and then, with his rear end still on the ground, he began to drag himself toward the boy, whimpering as he moved. As the boy gave a whine of disgust and began to move toward the dog, it dawned on the instructor what was going on: The boy's communication was so imprecise that he had actually given Shadow three conflicting commands, effectively telling the dog to *come*, to *sit*, and to *lie down*. The hard-working and very intelligent animal had then desperately tried to perform all three actions at once, resulting in his bizarre behaviour. The dog's whimpering indicated the stress and uncertainty he was feeling. The real problem, of course, was that the animal was simply too intelligent for such poor and inconsistent handling. Exposing such an intelligent dog to similar situations on a daily basis could easily cause both its personality and its performance to deteriorate.

This story was of particular interest to me because I had recently had some evidence that a less intelligent dog might not experience this kind of stress under the same circumstances. In one of my beginner's obedience classes, a mother and her teenage son were training a pair of bulldogs together. The mother was quite steady with the dogs, but the boy lacked interest and precision. He typically used multiple-word commands much like the *come on, sit down* sequence that had led to Shadow's creative response. The bulldogs, however, reacted with much less stress. Regardless of the number of words used to instruct them, they always responded to the last word spoken. Thus on hearing the words *come on, sit down*, these dogs would have simply gone into the *down* position. The breed's lower intellectual ability did not permit the dogs to keep the entire string of words in consciousness and so precluded the necessity of trying to integrate the conflicting parts. Instead, the dogs applied what psychologists call the "recency principle," which says that one tends to remember best and process most easily the information that one received most recently. For example, when tired people are listening to a story or a conversation, they often find that, although they may recognize and understand the sentence last spoken, they have already forgotten or can no longer process the earlier part of the discussion. It is as though this earlier information simply didn't exist. Less intelligent dogs operate on this level most of the time, and while this can be very frustrating for someone trying to train a dog to perform a complex sequence of behaviours, it can be a godsend in a busy, noisy, and chaotic environment. The less intelligent dog perceives all of the noise and confusion as it happens but ignores all but the most recent stimulation. With only one item at a time available for processing, life is less confusing, and there are no conflicting demands that must be resolved. Thus the dog is much happier and fits in much better than it would if it were brighter.

LIVING WITH THE NOT-SO-SMART DOG

Some less intelligent dogs cause problems, of course, but their difficulties often arise from the fact that they don't have a clue as to what is expected of them. For these slower breeds, often a basic dog obedience class is enough to give the dog the idea that those funny sounds its master makes have a meaning, and to teach it that responding appropriately to that meaning can lead to rewards. One owner of a bulldog reported that taking a beginner's dog obedience class made a world of difference in his life with the dog. "Before the classes, he acted as if we didn't exist. He wouldn't respond to us at all and would continue what he was doing as if we were invisible. He now looks at me when I'm talking. He comes when I call him and sits or lies down when I tell him to. I really don't need much more from a housedog, you know."

To live and work well with the not-so-smart dog, there are several important things to keep in mind. (For the purposes of this discussion, a dog will be considered not so smart if it was ranked 45 or lower in working intelligence in the table in Chapter 10. However, many of the recommendations given here will work for any dog that seems to be having trouble figuring out what is happening and what is required of it.)

Train young: You should start teaching your less bright dog the basic commands (*come, sit, down, heel, stand,* and *stay*) as early as possible in its life—that is, as soon as you bring it home and certainly before it is six months old. For some breeds, a dog that is a year or more has already lost its flexibility and become set in its ways. However, even breeds that can be quite intractable as adults (such as beagles or boxers) respond well to early training and can be easily civilized as puppies.

Another reason to train young, even for brighter breeds, is that it is easy to correct a puppy without resorting to harsh measures. One can gently mould a puppy into a *sit* or *down* position by physically manipulating its legs and body, whereas the same action can take considerable force when dealing with an adult Akita or bullmastiff that weighs over a hundred pounds (forty-five kilograms or more). Moreover, harsh force is interpreted by many breeds as aggressiveness; some breeds of dog may respond to it with an aggressive response of their own. Early training, with firmness but no harshness, can avoid the problem. The larger the dog will be as an adult, the earlier you should start to train it to obey the basic commands of *come, down,* and *stay.*

Be consistent: You should be as consistent as possible, using exactly the same words and signals all of the time. Even using the same tone of voice is helpful. It also helps to train the dog in the same place at about the same time of day until the commands are well set and reliable.

Dogs love predictability. If you have a household where things occur with regularity, where schedules are relatively fixed, you have an environment where most dogs will thrive. Regularity and consistency are particularly helpful to the dog who is somewhat less bright and also benefit the dog that is a bit more submissive and timid.

Be explicit: Whenever you are talking to the dog, before you give it any command, always start with the dog's name. As I noted earlier, this trains the dog to pay attention to you and lets it know that the information coming next will be of relevance to it. Using a voice command and a hand signal together is especially helpful, because it gives the dog two chances to pick up the command and to respond.

Begin quietly: Start all training in a quiet setting where there are few distractions. This will help to concentrate the dog's attention on you. Later on, when the dog has learned the basics, training can be moved to noisier and busier settings.

Begin close: Always stay close enough to your dog so that you can correct it directly. Even after the dog begins to learn the basics, leave it on the leash during training so that you are still in physical contact and can exert direct control. Later on, you can extend your distance from the dog and eventually remove the leash.

Keep training sessions short: For your sake as well as that of the dog, it is best to keep training sessions short. Your dog will respond much better to several shorter sessions, with breaks in between them, than to one long session. Some of the more active breeds, or even more active individuals of a normally placid breed, will also benefit from a good run or some other exercise before the actual training session.

Be patient: Patience is extremely important in training a slower dog. It takes a lot of patience to keep going in the sixth week of an obedience training course when the lady with the golden retriever is beginning to get bored with her dog's reliable, almost machine-like, performance and you are still waiting for your dog to show its first glimmer of understanding. Just keep in mind that repetition, practice, and patience do pay off and that in the end you can have a dog that is just as reliable and dependable as one of the easier-to-train breeds. Do not get frustrated if your dog does not immediately respond. The easiest way to make a dog tense is to make you, its owner, tense, since he observes your behaviour in order to interpret what is happening. When a trainer gets tense, the dog will start worrying about what is happening to upset its master, and focus on trying to find the threat rather than focusing on what it is supposed to learn.

Practice: Practice in the form of refresher lessons may be needed throughout the life of the not-so-smart dog. These do not need to be formal training sessions but rather reminders when the dog has failed to respond to a command in an everyday situation. Slip the leash back on the dog, give it one or two lessons with lots of praise for good performance and firm but good-tempered corrections if performance is poor, and then slip the leash off, and go about your usual activities. In this way, the basic control commands will become part of the dog's life and, regardless of its native intellectual capacity, it will respond in a predictable, trustworthy fashion. Refresher lessons with plenty of rewards for good performance also reinforce the notion in the dog's mind that it has something to gain from complying with your commands.

Be flexible: Take your dog's conformation into account. A basset hound will never respond as quickly and precisely as a border collie, not because it does not know what it is supposed to do or because it is unwilling to respond, but simply because its particular shape does not allow it to respond more rapidly.

Be insistent: One of the great problems people have in training dogs is that they can look so cute; it is hard to be firm and insistent with pugs and Pekingese when they look so endearing and helpless. Yet every command must be enforced, especially during the early stages of training. If the dog doesn't respond to a command that you know it already understands, you should make it do so. You could go back to luring the dog into a correct position with a treat; however, if you are sure that the dog already understands the command, you should be firm and physical. By physical here, I mean actually touching or manipulating a dog so that it responds correctly—I do not mean that you should be rough with your pet. If the dog is told to sit and doesn't, a light tap on its rump may remind it as to what it is to do, or you may even have to physically place it into a sitting position by gently tugging up on the leash and pushing down on the dog's rear. Remember that this is the way that we correct the dog, not initially teach him. Don't be harsh or aggressive; just be sure that the dog always ends up doing what you have told it to do. These more difficult breeds must learn that each command ends only when they complete a particular action.

Make obedience rewarding: No matter how a command is obeyed—by the dog on its own or with a lot of help from you—once the appropriate action is performed, you should praise the dog. After all, the required command has now been fulfilled. Even after the dog has learned the commands, don't forget to praise it occasionally, just to make sure that the behaviours remain strong. There is a tendency that we all have to take good, obedient behaviour for granted and only to single out misbehaviours for attention. To keep behaviours strong, dogs need some praise or reward, at least intermittently, throughout its life.

When you are praising the dog, be lavish and effusive. You may think you sound insincere and silly when you coo "What a clever dog!" or "What a good girl!" while you rub the dog's chest or head, but your dog will think you sound heavenly. With more difficult breeds of dogs, a food reward often works best. A few pieces of dog kibble tucked in your pocket will provide you with a constant flow of tidbits for training or simply for rewards when the dog responds during normal activities.

LIVING WITH THE SMART DOG

Surprisingly, more intelligent dogs (dogs with a working intelligence rating of 30 or more) need basic training even more than do the less bright breeds. Without training, these dogs are simply too much to handle. Most of the recommendations for the lower-intelligence dogs still make good sense even for the brighter dogs; however, there are some specific requirements for these smarter animals.

Train early and train continuously: As with less bright dogs, early training for smart dogs, at least for the basic commands, is desirable. The brighter the breed, however, the longer the dog will be receptive to training. Thus, while it may require a lot of effort to upgrade a basset hound's training after it is a year or so old, a German shepherd or poodle will show a high degree of trainability throughout its life. And whereas a slower dog will keep the habits it learned early reasonably intact for the rest of its life, a brighter dog may begin to learn new habits and associate them with the earlier ones. This means that if you get sloppy in your handling of your dog and stop insisting that all commands be obeyed, the brighter dog will learn that the conditions have changed and that the old rules no longer apply. You must, therefore, treat every command that you give to the brighter dog as if it were part of a training session. If the dog does not respond adequately, correct the dog, and then praise it. Always remember the sequence *command, correct, praise*. The dog can avoid correction by responding appropriately, but it should always receive praise at the end.

Although you should start training the dog as young as possible, do not rush the training. Always make sure that the dog fully understands what you have been teaching it by reviewing earlier lessons. When the dog knows all of the basic commands, it has *learned to learn*. Take advantage of its ability, and start to teach it new commands. These can be parlour tricks, such as begging, rolling over, playing dead, praying, barking on command, or whatever. The brighter dog must understand that there is always something new to learn and that it will be rewarded by you for doing so. This will keep the dog's attention on you and its mind active.

These dogs should never get *anything* without having to work for it. Even if you just want to pet your dog, make it come and sit on command before it gets stroked or played with. In this way, the dog is continually reminded that responding to human-generated sounds and signals is a much more reliable route to rewards than is operating on the chance associations formed during everyday activities in the environment.

Throughout training, you should be consistent in your commands and requirements. The brighter dog will look at each command as a game or a puzzle to be solved, and he will revel in working out the answer that will gain praise and attention. Just knowing that he came to the right answer will be rewarding to him, in much the same way that figuring out the correct word in a crossword puzzle is rewarding to humans. Don't change the rules, since that will ruin the fun of the game.

Control your emotions: Smarter dogs are more aware of their masters' emotional states than are less bright animals. For this reason, you should be aware of and control your emotions when dealing with a smart dog. Never direct overt anger at the dog. It will recognize the emotion and may react with an aggressive-defensive response. Even if it does not, it will remember your display of anger, and this memory may weaken its attachment to you. For instance, border collie handlers claim that their dogs "never forget a slight". Obviously, it is also important never to hurt the dog physically during a correction. Before you start working with your dog, try to figure out how corrections might hurt the dog and take steps to avoid doing so inadvertently. For instance, when training a dog with long floppy ears, make sure that during corrections the ears do not catch on the leash or collar.

Never show fear to one of these dogs. A Doberman pinscher, German shepherd, rottweiler, poodle, or other bright dog can recognize fear as easily as anger, and it is bright enough and large enough to use it to its own advantage. It will become stubborn and unyielding and may even challenge you for dominance. Even if handling a big dog makes you nervous, you must be consistent and insistent. Firmly but not abusively, enforce every command. One way to avoid problems is to teach the dog the *down* and *down-stay* commands when it is still a puppy. The *down* position signifies submission in a dog's mind, as we noted earlier; once it's down, it has acknowledged you as leader of its pack. If you are having problems with a bright dog who is now becoming dominant and difficult to handle, you need to use the Work for a Living programme that I described in the previous chapter.

One emotion that you never need to control is joy or happiness. When praising your dog, be effusive and giving. This is the best way to control most dogs.

Watch the dog's behaviour carefully: A brighter dog should respond to all commands quickly. Obviously, a Newfoundland will move more slowly than a miniature poodle, but when your dog has learned a task, it should move as promptly as its size and build allow. Brighter dogs should be encouraged to move quickly and they should be corrected for slow responses as if they had not responded at all. Often the slow response is simply the bright dog's attempt to see what it can get away with.

How do you speed the dog's behaviour? Suppose the dog is slow when responding. Do not tug the dog, since most dogs have a counter-reflex that causes them to resist being pulled or pushed, and tugging may ultimately slow the dog's response. Instead we can take a clue from Patricia McConnell, of the Department of Zoology at the Madison campus of the University of Wisconsin, who found that some common human sounds produced consistent responses in dogs. She reasoned that animal trainers derived their knowledge about communicating with dogs based upon what seemed to work and what did not. Thus, unconsciously perhaps, they may have tapped into the basic makeup of dog language. If animal trainers use consistent sound signals, these might give us some insights as to how to best communicate with dogs. To eliminate any biases that might creep in if she studied only one language, Dr. McConnell interviewed and recorded a large number of animal handlers who were native speakers of many different languages.

She was most interested in the kinds of signals that were used to change the dog's activity level, either exciting him to increase activity or causing him to slow down and inhibit his activity. She found that the trainers, regardless of their language and culture, used short sounds that were repeated several times to increase a dog's activity level, while long, drawn-out, single sounds were used to slow activity or get the dog to remain still. Nonword signals could be repeated hand claps, hand slaps against the trainer's thigh, finger snaps, tongue clicks, lip smooches, or kissing sounds to get a dog moving, especially when coming toward the handler. Vocal signals might include "Fetch it up!" or "Quick, quick!" since each involves several short sound signals. Out of more than two thousand signals that McConnell analyzed, these kinds of repeated short signals were never used to stop activity or to get the dog to stay in place. To slow or stop a dog's activity, longer, single signals were used, such as "Down", "Stay", or "Whoa" in English. In telling the dog slow down or stop, each word was pronounced with the vowel sounds drawn out for a longer duration than might be used in normal conversation. In whistle signals used by shepherds, two short, sharp whistles might get a dog to run out toward the herd of sheep and one long whistle gets the dog to stop or lie down. Once the dog is moving toward the herd, the short sharp whistles can also be used to speed up the dog.

Returning to our problem of the slow-moving dog in response to the command *come*, you could speed the dog up then by clapping your hands two or three times along with an encouraging "Quick, quick." It is important that you not simply repeat the command. For instance, if the dog is already coming toward you and you are now repeating the command *come* to speed him up, the dog may actually hesitate or slow down, since he might reason something like "I thought that 'come' meant to approach my master, but since he's still yelling 'come', perhaps I'm wrong." The command to speed up should be separate, and the same "go faster" and "slowly" commands can be combined with any other commands that you give to the dog.

Don't presume too much: One common pitfall is the tendency to assume too much about the brighter dog. Make sure that your dog has fully learned a task before correcting it for not responding well. Pushing a bright dog too far and too fast can cause a great deal of stress and may make it lose its motivation to learn.

Do not overtrain: A dog can learn a great number of tasks and should be taught as many new things as possible, but you should avoid overtraining the dog on any single command. Brighter dogs easily become bored with the repetition necessary to keep the less intelligent breeds active and alert. There should be stretches of days or even weeks when you do not rehearse the dog on any of the commands it has already learned. During this time, you may teach new material, but don't review the old commands and exercises.

Provide adequate stimulation for the dog: A bright working dog is a pleasure to live with, but it needs mental stimulation. Training the dog provides it with some stimulation, but it should also have other diversions. Exercise, walks in unfamiliar places where there is an opportunity to explore, contact with new people, or even just tagging along on chores and shopping expeditions will help to keep the dog mentally sharp and entertained. If you have a bright breed of dog and it shows behavioural problems, ask yourself whether the dog could be bored. It might be digging, chewing, jumping, and trying to escape from the house because these activities are more interesting than lying around all day waiting for you to come home.

On the flip side, some active intelligent dogs, such as the Belgian sheepdog and Belgian Tervuren, are easily overstimulated, and their excitement distracts them from their training. For these dogs quiet familiar surroundings are needed *during* training. However, when training time is finished, novel and more exciting stimulation is necessary to keep the dog mentally happy.

CHANGES IN INTELLIGENCE OVER THE LIFE SPAN

Prior to five weeks of age a puppy's brain is still immature in its electrical responsiveness, as seen on EEG measures. After about seven weeks, however, there is little to distinguish the response pattern of a puppy's brain from that of an adult's. For this reason, one might think that a dog at this age has enough brain circuitry to show its full fluid intelligence and that its ability to learn new material is fully active. This is not quite true, however.

Dogs and humans are actually much the same in the way their intelligence changes over their life spans. In human beings, manifest intelligence increases rapidly between infancy and midadolescence, probably peaking in the later teens. Measures show negligible changes in this ability between fifteen and twenty-five years of age. After that, there is a slow, gradual decline in fluid intelligence. Crystallized intelligence, however, which is based on what an individual has actually learned, doesn't reach its peak in human beings until around forty years of age, and in some people increases throughout life. This same pattern holds for dogs, only the time spans are shorter. Dogs increase their manifest intelligence up to about three to four years of age. After that, fluid intelligence begins to decline, and whether the crystallized intelligence continues to increase depends upon whether you are still giving the dog new experiences and learning opportunities.

There are noticeable changes in the physiology of the older dog. After age four or five, the brain begins to lose weight and bulk at a rate of 2 to 5 percent per year. Thus the brain of a twelve-year-old Labrador retriever may weigh 25 percent less than it did when the dog was four. Much of this decrease in brain mass has to do with the loss of some of the interconnections between brain cells, while some of it may reflect a breakdown and shrinking of brain cells. With the loss of neural interconnections, the speed with which information travels from place to place in the nervous system slows. The four-year-old Labrador retriever sends information from its eyes and ears to its brain at a speed to 225 miles per hour (360 kilometres per hour); in a twelve-year-old Lab, this may slow to around 50 miles per hour (80 kilometres per hour).

There are other changes as well, such as reduced blood flow to the brain, which ideally uses around 20 percent of the blood flow exiting from the heart. The rate of oxygen metabolism also decreases. Brain cells consume oxygen during neural activity; only the muscles use more. In the last chapter we also mentioned the development of the amyloid accumulations in the brain, which reduce thinking efficiency. Taken together, some dogs can show the canine equivalent of Alzheimer's disease, which is called *Canine Cognitive Dysfunction*. Like the human version, this condition causes major losses in memory and the ability to remember new information.

The sensory systems are also affected. Hearing deteriorates, especially in the high-pitched frequencies. Some breeds, such as the retrievers and some of the herding breeds, have a tendency to lose their hearing completely. There is also a loss of vision as the eye's receptor cells deteriorate and the lens and cornea cloud. With the decrease in hearing and visual efficiency, the dog might not notice a person's approach, and it may react irritably when a sudden touch startles it. The sense of taste, particularly the ability to taste sweetness, dulls as well. Smell and touch seem to be most resistant to aging changes, but eventually they too diminish. As the senses dim, the leash becomes more important. Obviously the leash keeps the dog from wandering into danger because he has not seen or heard an approaching vehicle or other imminent danger. However, it also is psychologically important, since the dog can sense your presence by the pressure of the leash and feels more confident and secure.

The age at which these changes begin to take place at a noticeable rate depends somewhat on the genetics of the dog. Generally speaking, small dogs live longer and don't show signs of aging until somewhat later. Thus aging effects usually don't appear in small dogs of around twenty pounds (ten kilograms) until they are eleven-and-a-half years old, while they appear in medium-sized dogs averaging between twenty and fifty pounds (ten to twenty-five kilograms) at around ten years of age. Large dogs weighing fifty to ninety pounds (twenty-five to forty kilograms) begin to show the effects of age at around age nine, and in the giant breeds weighing more than ninety pounds, aging is noticeable at about seven-and-a-half years. On average, dogs live for about two years after the first appearance of these changes. There's a margin for error of about two years in either direction for all these estimates (if we ignore accident or infectious diseases), and genetics can lead to further variations. For example, a cairn terrier with its roughly twenty-pound frame can expect a typical life span of thirteen to fourteen years. A miniature poodle, however, which is much the same size, may well live for fifteen to sixteen years, while a similarly sized Cavalier King Charles spaniel lives only about eleven to twelve years.

All of those sensory and neural changes lead to a decrease in the manifest intelligence of the older dog. The dog becomes less responsive to commands. It reacts more slowly and sometimes seems to have forgotten things altogether. Predictably, it becomes more difficult to teach the dog new material.

Some ageproofing of your dog is possible. The first and simplest technique is to teach the dog all the basic commands using both voice and hand signals. That way, if either sight or hearing fails, you can still use the other signal. This goes a long way toward making old age more comfortable. One instructor from my dog training club, Barbara Merkley, had a marvellous old Shetland sheepdog named Noel. At age thirteen, Noel participated in a veteran's obedience competition, working well and seeming to derive a great deal of pleasure from being back in the obedience ring again. None of the spectators unfamiliar with Noel had the slightest clue that she was completely deaf and had been so for more than a year. Barbara simply used the hand signals that the dog had learned at the same time as the voice commands. Because of this foresight on Barbara's part, Noel got to prance out of the ring with a big pink rosette held daintily in her mouth at the dog equivalent of ninety years of age.

The second way to ageproof the dog has to do with early learning and repetition. Dogs act much like people as they age. Their strongest memories become those of their youth, and their behaviour becomes more puppylike. Thus, a dog who has been taught the basic obedience commands quite early in life may respond a bit more slowly as it ages but will continue to obey. There are occasional changes, though. For instance, I was told about one old German shepherd which, as a puppy, was trained by his first owner to respond to commands in the Czechoslovakian language. When his owner died, the dog was adopted by his son, who retrained the dog to respond to dog commands in English so that the rest of his non–Czech-speaking family members could also control the dog. In his old age the dog stopped responding to verbal commands, although he still responded to signals. Everyone suspected that the dog was simply losing his hearing. One day, the first owner's brother came to visit and began telling the dog what to do in Czech. The dog responded perfectly to *Knoze* (kno-zay), "heel", *Lehni* (leh-nee), "down", *Sedni* (said-nee), "sit", and *Zustan*, "stay". The elderly dog had not lost his hearing, but rather had reverted to his earlier, stronger memories, which included his "first language".

Repetition is also useful for the older dog. Once a dog has established a regular daily pattern of activities, it will hold to that pattern through its older years. The simple repetition and working through of familiar behaviours allow the dog to continue to fit into the normal functioning of the household and gives it security and a feeling of comfort. Dogs can still learn when they are older; it just takes a lot more time and a lot more patience. Recent research shows that the real problem that an older dog has is in changing behaviours that have already been learned. If a dog has already to do something, "unlearning" that behaviour and substituting a new one is more difficult in the older dog. Thus, an older dog that has always jumped up on people who enter the house may take a long time to learn the new behaviour of simply sitting calmly when visitors arrive. Think of this older dog as not so much less able to learn, but rather more set in his ways.

If you have established a good rapport with your dog, training is possible at any age using some of the techniques that I outlined for slower dogs. I recently saw a rescued cairn terrier named Whistler get his first obedience degree at the age of twelve. He had started his training only the year before. Whistler walked out of the ring with his tail beating as quickly as any proud puppy, and if his master had a tail, I'm sure that it would have been wagging just as happily.

Shotgun

An older dog is still that same puppy that you reared. It still cares; it just lacks stamina and is showing some signs of wear. To illustrate this, let me tell you the story of Shotgun.

Shotgun was a big chocolate-coloured Labrador retriever. His owner, Fred, had always liked hunting water birds when he lived on the East Coast. When he moved to the beautiful countryside of British Columbia, in Western Canada, the plan of owning a gun dog and returning to hunting as a fall pastime seemed ideal. It never quite worked out that way. When Shotgun was only seven months old,

Fred's job took him back to the city. Shortly thereafter, Fred married, and when Shotgun was around two, Fred and his wife Clara had their first child, Melissa. Somehow, finding time to train the dog for hunting just never worked out. Shotgun became a city dog and a family dog. He learned the routines of city life and over a period of six years watched the family grow with the addition of two boys, Steven and Daniel. While Shotgun had never been trained to hunt, he had gone through a beginner's dog obedience course taught in a local church and knew all the basic commands. His job was mainly to be a plaything for the children, a companion for Fred and Clara, and the ever-vigilant watchdog who sounded the alarm at the occurrence of any new or suspicious sound or unusual condition around the house.

Time passed, and Shotgun was now eleven years of age, which is old for a Labrador retriever. He moved more slowly and had given up trying to jump on the sofa. He seemed content to sleep more hours than before, although he could still be stirred for short romps with the children, whom he seemed to view as his particular charges. He ran more slowly, though, and no longer jumped very high when chasing a ball or Frisbee, and he tired a bit more easily. His hearing was going, and he responded more slowly and a bit less reliably to the commands that he had learned so many years before. But many things were still the same. He knew when it was time for a walk and stationed himself expectantly at the door each afternoon from around three o'clock on, waiting for the children's return from school. He continued to sleep nights in the middle of the living room floor, and, as he had always done, he would patrol the house every hour or so, sticking his nose into each of the children's bedrooms and then checking on Fred and Clara before returning to his central post in the living room.

One summer night, Shotgun arose with the feeling that something was definitely wrong. There was smoke in the house, and if the windows and inner doors had not been open, the whole place would already have been filled with the noxious fumes of burning materials. The dog began to bark furiously to rouse the household, but nothing happened. Moving as quickly as his arthritic body would allow, he entered Fred and Clara's room. His barking still did not cause them to rise, so with a great deal of effort the dog painfully leapt up on the bed, placing his front paws on Fred's chest and barking loudly. Fred sputtered to a confused state of wakefulness. He immediately became aware of the smoke and wakened Clara. Fred and Clara rushed to the rooms of the two young boys, each grabbing one of them, and raced through the now flame-filled house toward the outside. Both shouted for Melissa, the oldest at nine, assuming that the noise and commotion would get her up and moving from her bedroom in the rear of the house. When the two of them reached the front lawn and looked back, most of the house was covered with flames. Fire trucks were arriving, but Melissa was nowhere in sight. Fred tried to dash back into the house, but the heat and the flames were too much for his bare feet, and he was forced to retreat.

Shotgun was still inside. Perhaps somewhere in that great old head of his, he had remembered to count, the way that mother dogs know how to count to make sure all of their pups are present. Like all of his breed he could easily count to three, and that count told him that one of his charges was missing. He slowly lumbered into Melissa's room, only to find her standing in the midst of the smoke, bewildered and crying. Shotgun barked and moved toward the door, but Melissa didn't understand or was too confused to follow. He then gently grabbed the ruffled sleeve of her nightgown and began to pull her toward the door. The front of the house was completely impassable, so the old dog turned, half dragging and half guiding the frightened girl toward the rear entrance. As the flames leapt around them, they were confronted with the rear screen door, which had been secured with a simple hook and eye latch. Perhaps, had he been younger and more agile, Shotgun could have pushed through the screen mesh, but at that moment it seemed to be an impenetrable barrier. Melissa was too stunned to help and stood in a daze. Shotgun dropped her sleeve for a moment and reared up on his hind legs. He then pushed up on the screen door latch to unhook it, a technique that had brought him a severe reprimand several years before when, as a younger dog, he had used it to open the back door in order to respond to the harassment of a fox terrier that had learned how to enter the backyard and had a fondness for digging in the small vegetable garden.

Shotgun's manipulations were not as deft as they used to be, and as he pushed his nose against the hook, it tore his skin. Still, he persisted, and the latch rose from its eyelet, and the door flew open. Shotgun again grabbed Melissa's sleeve and pulled her to the centre of the yard before letting her go and turning to the task of licking at his singed paws. Moments later, the firefighters arrived to find Melissa with her arms around Shotgun's neck, sobbing quietly and stroking his bleeding muzzle where the screen door hook had cut him.

Shotgun was old, slow, and less reliable than he had been in years past. Yet he was still the self-appointed protector of the house, and his intelligence and problem-solving ability were completely dedicated to his masters' safety and well-being. Old certainly does not mean dumb, useless, or spent. Shotgun had shown great intelligence that night. He had figured out that something was wrong, then had solved the problem of waking his sleeping masters to warn them. He had discerned that one child was missing and had found the answer to the dilemma of how to bring her through the house. When faced with the predicament of the front door blocked by fire, he had found an alternative solution, and when confronted with the latched back door, he had solved the last problem standing in the way of their escape. The five human beings who made up his pack, his family, his masters, his charges and his friends, all owed their lives to that old brain's information processing and problem solving.

Further Reading

This is not a reference list, but rather a jumping-off place for those of you who want more information about the dog's mind, and also some idea of where the information was obtained for this book.

For further general reading on dogs' mental abilities I recommend V. Csányi's *If Dogs Could Talk* (New York: North Point Press, 2005) and one of my own books, S. Coren, *How Dogs Think: Understanding the Canine Mind* (London, Pocket Books, 2005). An older but still useful book is B. Fogle's *The Dog's Mind* (London: Pelham Books, 1990).

For information on the behaviour of dogs in comparison with the other wild canids, R. F. Ewer's *The Carnivores* (Ithaca: Cornell University Press, 1985) and M. W. Fox's *Behaviour of Wolves, Dogs and Related Canids* (London: Cape, 1985) are somewhat technical but valuable sources, while K. Lorenz, *Man Meets Dog* (London: Methuen, 1954), provides an informal but extremely entertaining discussion of this topic.

The landmark book on the genetics of behaviour is E. O. Wilson's *Sociobiology—The New Synthesis* (Cambridge: Harvard University Press, 1975), while the classic discussion of this topic with relationship to dogs is the book by J. P. Scott and J. C. Fuller, *Genetics and the Social Behavior of the Dog* (Chicago: University of Chicago Press, 1965).

A valuable treatment of the domestication of dogs is found R. Coppinger and L. Coppinger, *Dogs: A Startling New Understanding of Canine Origin, Behavior and Evolution.* (New York: Scribner, 2001).

275

Data on the most recent fossil evidence on dog domestication comes from M. V. Sablin and G. A. Khlopachev, "The Earliest Ice Age Dogs: Evidence from Eliseevichi 1" (*Current Anthropology*, [2002] 43, 795–799), while use of DNA information to trace the origins of dogs is found in P. Savolainen et. al., "Genetic Evidence for an East Asian Origin of Domestic Dogs" (*Science*, [2002] 298, 1610–1613).

Discussions of the history of dogs and their relationship to people can be found in my book S. Coren, *The Pawprints of History: Dogs and the Course of Human Events*. (New York: Free Press, 2003), in M. Derr's *A Dog's History of America* (New York: North Point Press, 2004), R. A. Caras's *A Dog Is Listening* (New York: Simon & Schuster, 1993), and C. I. A. Ritchie's *The British Dog* (London: Hale, 1981).

The issue of animal consciousness has been discussed in detail in several books by Donald R. Griffin, such as *Animal Minds* (Chicago: University of Chicago Press, 1992), in M. Bekoff, C. Allen, and G. M. Burghardt, *The Cognitive Animal: Empirical and Theoretical Perspectives on Animal Cognition* (Cambridge, MA: MIT Press, 2002), and D. Radner and M. Radner, *Animal Consciousness* (Buffalo: Prometheus, 1989). A dissenting view can be found in S. Budiansky, *The Truth About Dogs* (New York : Viking, 2000).

Canine communication is dealt with in S. Coren, *How to Speak Dog: Mastering the Art of Dog-Human Communication* (London, Pocket Books, 2005) and in M. M. Milani's book *The Body Language and Emotion of Dogs* (New York: Morrow, 1986). M. W. Fox's *Understanding Your Dog* (New York: Coward-McCann, 1982) also contains an excellent treatment of this topic, with specific reference to the dog. An interesting discussion of the topic in relation to human communication can be found in K. Lorenz, *Studies in Animal and Human Behavior* (Cambridge: Harvard University Press, 1971).

Breed differences in behaviour and personality are discussed in B. Hart and L. Hart, *The Perfect Puppy* (New York: Freeman, 1988), and D. F. Tortora, *The Right Dog for You* (New York: Simon & Schuster, 1980).

The two theories of human intelligence that set the pattern for my analysis of dog intelligence are H. Gardner's *Frames of Mind: Theory of Multiple Intelligences* (New York: Basic, 1983), and R. J. Sternberg's *The Triarchic Mind: A New Theory of Human Intelligence* (New York: Viking, 1988).

The dog intelligence and personality tests were drawn from a number of manuals used by various Guide Dog for the Blind organizations, hearing dog associations, rescue dog associations, and the U.S., Danish, Norwegian, and German militaries. In some instances, members of these organizations kindly provided me with information and manuals; others I obtained from the American Kennel Club Library in New York City. (This library, by the way, is open to the public and is staffed by some marvellously helpful librarians. It is the best source for dog-related publications that I have ever encountered, and I highly recommend it to people seriously interested in studying the dog.) Several items were also modified from W. A. Luszki and M. B. Luszki, *How to Test Your Dog's IQ* (New York: Tab Books, 1980). A history of the initial development of testing programmes to assess dog intelligence and temperament can be found in C. J. Pfaffenberger's *The New Knowledge of Dog Behavior* (New York: Howell, 1963). The rationale behind many of the tests will be found in the Scott and Fuller book mentioned earlier. More popular writings on the topic are scattered through a number of journals. A few of the more helpful ones include G. T. Fisher and W. Volhard, "Puppy Personality Profile" (*AKC Gazette* [March 1985]: 36 42), M. Bartlett, "Puppy Aptitude Testing" (*AKC Gazette* [March 1979]: 31 42), G. R. Johnson, "Temperament Testing Adult Dogs for Service Work" (*Off-Lead* [April 1980]: 27–30), H. G. Martin, "Assessing Temperament" (*Off-Lead* [September 1978]: 14–17), K. Phelps, "Evaluating Litters" (*AKC Gazette* [March 1985]: 43–47), K. L. Justice-March, "Hearing Dog Test" (*Off-Lead* [September 1985]: 34–37), R. Fjellanger, R. Gimre, and T. Owren, "Behaviour Analysis of the Dog," part one (*Off-Lead* [February 1988]: 20–23) and part two (*Off-Lead* [March 1988]: 15–20), and W. Handel, "The Psychological Fundamentals of Character Evaluation" (*Rocky Mountain Schutzhund Tales* [September-October 1981]: 7–12).

There are many good books on dog training available. However, I like M. R. Burch and J. S. Bailey's *How Dogs Learn* (New York: Howell Book House, 1999) because it gives information on the nature of learning in general, and also I. Dunbar's *How to Teach an Old Dog New Tricks* and J. Donaldson's *The Culture Clash* (both New York: James & Kenneth Publishers, 1996) because they emphasize socialization and exercises that build a dog's temperament and manifest intelligence. On the matter of socialization and early rearing, the material about the

U.S. Army's Superdog Program was obtained by application under the Freedom of Information legislation, since it was embedded in documents meant only for internal use by the military.

Finally, if you are interested in the folklore of the dog, there could be no better starting places than M. Leach's *God Had a Dog* (New Brunswick: Rutgers University Press, 1961) or P. Dale-Green's *Lore of the Dog* (Boston: Houghton Mifflin, 1967).

Index

About the Author

STANLEY COREN, Ph.D., F.R.S.C., is a professor of psychology at the University of British Columbia and a recognized expert on dog-human interaction. He has appeared on *Dateline*, the *Oprah Winfrey Show*, *Good Morning, America*, and National Public Radio, and hosts a weekly television show, *Good Dog!*, currently showing nationally in Canada, Australia, and New Zealand. He lives in Vancouver, British Columbia, with his wife and her cat, in addition to a beagle, a Cavalier King Charles spaniel, and a Nova Scotia duck-tolling retriever.